# A
# COLD
# SPELL

# A COLD SPELL

## A HUMAN HISTORY OF ICE

### MAX LEONARD

BLOOMSBURY PUBLISHING
LONDON · OXFORD · NEW YORK · NEW DELHI · SYDNEY

BLOOMSBURY PUBLISHING
Bloomsbury Publishing Plc
50 Bedford Square, London, WC1B 3DP, UK
29 Earlsfort Terrace, Dublin 2, Ireland

BLOOMSBURY, BLOOMSBURY PUBLISHING and the Diana logo are
trademarks of Bloomsbury Publishing Plc

First published in Great Britain 2023

A catalogue record for this book is available from the British Library

ISBN: HB: 978-1-5266-3119-0; TPB: 978-1-5266-3117-6;
EBOOK: 978-1-5266-3118-3; EPDF: 978-1-5266-7585-9

2 4 6 8 10 9 7 5 3 1

Typeset by Newgen KnowledgeWorks Pvt. Ltd., Chennai, India
Printed and bound in Great Britain by CPI Group (UK) Ltd, Croydon CR0 4YY

To find out more about our authors and books visit www.bloomsbury.com
and sign up for our newsletters

*Ice is an interesting subject for contemplation.*
        Henry David Thoreau, *Walden* (1854)

*Our civilisation is like a thin layer of ice upon a deep*
*ocean of chaos and darkness*
        Werner Herzog, *Herzog on Herzog* (2002)

*Some say the world will end in fire,*
*Some say in ice . . .*
        Robert Frost, from 'Fire and Ice' (1920)

# Contents

# Author's note

When dealing with measurements of weight, distance and other things, I've tried to use metric units, except where the context clearly calls for imperial or where quoted text differs. However, many of the sources are themselves not consistent, so there is some jumping between the two.

# On learning how to see (an introduction)

*That's what history is: the story of everything that*
*needn't have been like that.*
                    Clive James, *Cultural Amnesia* (2007)

*As if everything in the world is the history of ice.*
                    Michael Ondaatje, *Coming through*
                                        *Slaughter* (1976)

In June 1741 the Englishman William Windham climbed the
Montanvert valley above Chamonix in the French Alps. His goal
was a close encounter with the glacier whose snout protruded
almost into the village itself, but whose heights the locals
frequented only in the summer, to hunt for ibex or crystals. He
published a pamphlet describing the trip, *An Account of the
Glacières or Ice Alps in Savoy, in two letters, one from an English
gentleman to his friends at Geneva; the other from Peter Martel,
Engineer, to the said English gentleman*, in 1744.

This short work with a lengthy title is notable because it is the
first account in English of a glacier up close, and because Peter
(more often known as 'Pierre') Martel's contribution contains the
début appearance of the name 'Mont Blanc' in print. Previously,
the whole range seems to have been known simply as Les
Glacières: the 'ice mountains'.

It is also notable for a rather wonderful failure: the failure to
convey what a glacier is actually like. 'I own to you, I am extremely

at a loss how to give a right idea of it,' Windham writes. 'The description which travellers give of the seas of Greenland seems to come the nearest to it . . .' And yet: 'perhaps even that would not produce the same appearance.'

Thus Windham is confounded. Confounded because he is trying to describe something singular (the glacier) that his readers have never laid eyes on by comparing it to something else (the Arctic seas) neither he nor they have seen either. He is at the limits of experience, beyond the capacity of words to snare the thing. Off the map. Just like those sailors on those seas of Greenland.

It's around here that the penny drops and – this is the wonderful bit – you realise that Windham has never seen ice before. Or at least *not really*. It is often claimed that Windham gave this glacier its modern name, the Mer de Glace ('Sea of Ice'); if he did it's nowhere in the pamphlet, but during the eighteenth century the marine metaphor slipped into common usage in Europe, both for this particular glacier and for others.[1] By transporting the briny depths thousands of feet up a mountain, the name shows how strange ice is, and calls to mind the catastrophe that stranded Noah on Ararat. It is also interesting because it is imprecise: glaciers, even if ruffled by fearsome frozen forty-foot waves, do not really resemble seas. If anything, they are supercooled rivers. So Windham, grasping for a description, again failed to communicate.

But Windham, the scion of an ancient Norfolk family, must have seen ice before. Thin sheet ice, dirty and congested on the duck ponds of the village on his estate. On the Norfolk Broads, near Felbrigg Hall, his ancestral home, he may have skated upon it. And, like many aristocrats from the seventeenth century onwards, he may have enjoyed ice-cooled drinks. Felbrigg Hall had an ice house, a building specially constructed for storing large amounts of the stuff; perhaps it was even this William (the family contained many) who, inspired by the memory of the strange sights above 'Chamouni', built the ice house. It was probably within his lifetime.

---

[1] A major tributary of the Lower Grindelwald glacier in the Swiss Bernese Oberland is called the Eismeer or Ischmeer, which means the same thing.

It's ironic that Windham travelled a thousand miles on a young gentleman's caprice to climb a mountain, only to discover something he already had at home. Ice has, of course, always been a basic fact of existence for people in many parts of the world, and something that for most of human history has presented mainly hardship and danger. Yet until this moment, when he is confounded, delighted, surprised, he seems not to have noticed it at all.

Windham's pamphlet excited a lot of interest, and was enough to secure his admission into the Royal Society, England's premier club for scientific endeavour. He was at the leading edge of a wave of scientific enquiry that would lead to a better understanding of glaciers: 'Not a *Sea*, but a *River*,' the famous scientist John Tyndall wrote crossly in 1860.[2]

Still, the point remains: glaciers were something that humankind had to *learn how to see*. And perhaps, by extension, that's true about ice in general.

We've all seen glaciers now. Maybe only on TV news and David Attenborough programmes, but glaciers, ice sheets, bergs, floes, the lot. We are generally well versed in these things that are nonetheless very remote geographically and outside most people's direct experience. This book is born from one such moment seeing glaciers on the TV news. One recent hot summer I was at an academic conference in Newcastle, watching a muted TV above a pub bar as I waited for the other attendees to arrive for dinner. On it, a reporter stood in front of a grey torrent of meltwater disgorging into the seas of Greenland, describing the latest effects of the climate crisis. It wasn't only that the subtitles were lagging: the disconnect between the ice in my glass and on the screen seemed almost total. And I thought, how can we be asked to care about this remarkable thing so much in some contexts and not even notice it when we encounter it, every day, in the ordinary business of our lives?

---

[2] Actually the idea of the glacier as a river of ice, whether or not Windham knew it, had been current in English since the previous century. Since he was the first to get up really close, to stand on the ice, we can be charitable and say he was distracted by those waves.

Over the past decade or so I have spent long periods living and working – cycling and walking and writing – in the Alps. There I developed a love for hanging around in out-of-season ski resorts, for tramping over high-altitude snow in August and for skirting glaciers sulking sadly under the sweltering summer sun. This gave me a sense of how the seemingly immutable and eternal world of the high mountains is changing under human pressures. It helped me understand the vulnerability to climate change not only of the landscape but of my friends who live there – the ski-shop owners, refuge wardens, mountain guides and shepherds. The more I saw with my own eyes, the more I sought to read, in local Swiss newspapers and on community forums in French valleys, about the retreating glaciers and the mountain peaks shattering from the inside that are signalling – signalling clearly, but only high up and far away, in the corner of our collective vision – this change.

Paradoxically, I also became fascinated with the nuggets of unexpected beauty that this slow-motion disaster is revealing: the hobnailed boots and pistols and B-17 bombers emerging from the ice. With every revolution of the earth around the sun there is more of the past melting into the light of day. More that ice is giving back to us of ourselves. I also began to research ice in the popular imagination, how it has inspired literature and poetry, and therefore how we might be being diminished as it disappears. It convinced me there was more to discover about ice, to fix in place, just at the point when we are losing so much of it.

Ice is inspirational and yet slippery. Try to secure a meaning on it and it becomes intangible: it grinds mountains to dust and sinks ships, yet it is also ephemeral and delicate. It has pervaded our language and thinking in diverse and wonderful ways. Ice can be greasy or black, thin or slab, frazil, brash, a growler or a bergy bit. In many cultural and religious traditions it has been nothing short of miraculous. According to the Norse creation story, as set down in the thirteenth century by Snorri Sturluson in the *Prose Edda*, the world began when ice met fire in the Ginnungagap, the primal void. Raining down ice storms was a favourite Old Testament punishment, and Job is one of the oldest and also iciest books in the Bible, constituting, perhaps, some kind of trace folk memory of the trauma of the Ice Age. 'From whose womb comes the ice? And the frost of heaven, who gives it birth?' Job writes. 'The waters harden like stone, and the surface of the deep is frozen.' Ice here is nothing short of miraculous, and it retained its uncanny magic even as Christianity migrated to colder climes. Sebaldus, an eighth-century hermit, used icicles to make a fire at a woodsman's cottage, a feat performed en route to becoming the patron saint of Nuremberg.[3] It is present in the folklore of Inuit peoples and those from mountain regions, in Japanese, Scandinavian and Native American legends, not to mention the fairy tales of Hans Christian Andersen. The *Codex Exoniensis*, a tenth-century collection of Anglo-Saxon poetry described by UNESCO as one of the 'world's principal cultural artefacts', echoes Job in a rhyme describing ice's transformative properties:

The wave, over the wave, a weird thing I saw,
through-wrought, and wonderfully ornate:
a wonder on the wave – water become bone.

There is so much that is contrary or contradictory about ice. Metaphorically, it can connote calm and grace under pressure, yet also heartlessness or fear, disdain or resolve, or danger. When we break the ice (a phrase we get from Plutarch, via Shakespeare), we cease being awkward and become closer. You put something on ice if you want to stop it, yet we know that things on ice are liable to slide out of control. Most people are probably familiar with the tragic story of Captain Scott and his men who froze to death after being beaten to the South Pole by Roald Amundsen, yet through cryonics the freezing of bodies holds the tantalising promise of rebirth.[4] When we touch ice, it can freeze or it can burn; it is sensational and yet numbing. Direct the torch of human

---

[3] Interestingly, there was also ice in the *Inferno*: Dante's ninth circle of hell was deathly cold and Satan is portrayed as a giant beast half immersed in ice.
[4] The prefix 'cryo' comes from the Greek κρύος (*krúos*) meaning 'ice', 'cold' or 'frost'.

intelligence upon it to determine its true substance and it is liable to melt into nothingness.

Ice has long confounded and confused. $H_2O$, for all its ubiquity, is a surprisingly complicated molecule, and the physics and metaphysics of ice are as unexpected as the metaphors it has given us. Ask yourself: why does ice float on liquid water, and what would the world be like if it did not? If water froze from the bottom up – which it manifestly doesn't – it would make life very difficult for marine creatures, which, millions of years ago, might have disrupted the chain of creation and we humans might not exist at all. Why, if clouds are just condensed water vapour, often at subzero temperatures, do they not freeze and fall out of the sky? In the nineteenth century John Tyndall's friend Michael Faraday proved that ice was wet, settling a matter of long conjecture, but we did not understand *why* until 2016. Why does it appear that warm water freezes more quickly than cold water – and why can scientists not agree if this is true?

The more I researched, the more it seemed to me that this bizarre, paradoxical substance might be a mirror in which to see ourselves from a new and unexpected angle – and that a history of ice could be an alternative history of us. It has been one of our prime points of contact with the natural world, integral to our cares and wants, and fundamental to shaping who we are today. Ice influenced human development in deep prehistory, it was a companion to the farmers and nomadic herders of protohistorical times, and was beginning to be used as a tool when the first great historical civilisations emerged. It has played so many important roles for us, and our relationship to it only deepened as time passed. Without ice, we would not feed ourselves or heal our sick as we do. Science would not have progressed along the avenues it has. It is something we have thought about, debated and experimented with – and our wrong-headed thinking is sometimes as illuminating as when we were right. Without ice, our towns and cities, countryside and oceans would be very different, and our galleries and libraries would be missing many masterpieces.

We have achieved these things, it seems to me, because, since the earliest times, we have been bewitched by ice, this water become bone. Its appearance, its touch and its startling qualities have enchanted us. Consequently, the pages that follow are filled with fanatics, visionaries and obsessives: people who have succumbed to ice fever, whose fixations have taken them literally and metaphorically to incredible places. Ice dreams that have led to the heights of success, as well as shimmering delusions that have ended in bitter failure.

However, over the past hundred years or so, for millions if not billions around the world, the numinous has become normal. Ice has been brought into the home, domesticated. (The *unheimlich* has become *heimlich*, as Freud might have put it.) No longer a thing of shining and transparent wonder, it is a commodity we quietly grow in a small box in the corner of the kitchen and consume at will. A substance that is now figuratively as well as literally almost invisible to us.

This brings us back to that unheralded ice in my glass, and my question about its kinship to the glaciers on the TV screen. The question, it turns out, is a version of one that is increasingly urgently debated in academia. In a book entitled *Cryopolitics*, Dr Michael Bravo of the Scott Polar Research Institute in Cambridge writes: 'What hasn't yet been adequately explained are the politics of frozen ecologies, and why they matter for the majority of the citizens of the globe living in cities with no special interest in the polar regions.'[5] During these years of unprecedented heating and attempts to reach binding international agreements to address the climate crisis and mobilise a global consensus, it is a critical question. What he is calling for is a sense of connection – and fast.

This book is concerned with making that connection too. The danger with television images of Greenland and Antarctica is that these places are a very long way from western Europe, from

---

[5] 'Cryopolitics' was coined in 2006 by Bravo and his Scott Polar Research Institute colleague Dr Gareth Rees as they sought to articulate the potential impacts that renewed geopolitical interest in the Arctic, driven by the melting ice, would have on the region's peoples and landscapes. Since then the term has been used to examine a wide range of human interventions into the cryosphere, that part of the world that is constituted by frozen water. We will be meeting the concept again.

the contiguous states of the USA and from most of the world's developed urban areas that are recklessly fuelling the changes in the global climate. Which means that these changes risk feeling unreal, or seeming somehow not to be our problem. I wrote some of this book during the Covid-19 lockdowns, when the Alps, once relatively accessible, seemed as far away as an iceberg in the Ross Sea. My hope is that by bringing ice into a more intimate sphere, by trying to understand the richness and complexity of our relationship with it and restoring the sense of wonder, the catastrophe happening in remote places will become more tangible – that we might feel more keenly what is being lost.

***

A few notes on method and some caveats before we begin. Most importantly, this is not really a book that explores extreme latitudes or remote, deserted icy wastelands. These are subjects that have their own long literary traditions, their own Dewey decimal numbers – whole libraries even – and I am not a polar explorer. Instead, the book is about the experience of the multitude who live in temperate climes: how we, who do not have ice as a defining feature of our everyday natural environment, have encountered it and used it, and how it has shaped us in thought and action in return.

This is not to diminish or marginalise the experiences of many different peoples who live near the icebound top of the earth, or close to the 'Third Pole' of the Hindu Kush, Karakoram and Himalaya. They all have important stories to tell of their own, but this book sticks closer to home – my home. Where the poles do come in, their appearance will be tied to political, cultural or other events falling within a European or Western sphere.

Second: this is a human history. It is about our relationship with the non-human, but primarily us first. I'm not going to claim that X or Y happened *because* of ice. Ice didn't do these things: we did.

I should also say that this is really about 'normal' ice (which admittedly encompasses a wide variety of things). Ice – put simply, water in its solid crystalline state – appears in many forms: snow consists of fragile ice crystals that grow from water vapour while suspended in the atmosphere; hail is solid $H_2O$ precipitation, small ice balls falling from the sky; graupel is supercooled water freezing on snowflakes; and there is rime, permafrost and scores of other names for other forms of frozen water. Not to mention freezing, the process of liquid water turning into ice. However, most of what is in these pages will relate to the kind of ice that William Windham failed to describe above Chamonix or which clogs your freezer at home.

When one thinks of ice, these days – as I did in that Newcastle bar – global warming inevitably looms large. And changes in climate do indeed play their part in this narrative, but the current climate crisis is an unspoken presence rather than an explicit subject – at least until the final pages. Ice has been many things during human history: it has been a warning and a promise and a metaphor, but now, most prominently, it is a synecdoche. Melting ice is such a visible constituent of the climate emergency that it has come to stand as a symbol for the whole thing. Against this backdrop, I want to talk about other aspects of ice, and tell its story through facts, dates, actions, art and literature.

The book will move roughly chronologically, alighting at moments in history in which ice has marked us in particular ways. Chapter 1 deals with the Ice Age, a time of great migrations during which humankind first encountered ice, and Chapter 2 continues by looking at how ice connects us to our pre-writing past; but then we'll leave prehistory behind to land in the Little Ice Age, a period generally agreed to have started in the fourteenth century and which lasted for hundreds of years, in which Europe in particular experienced markedly lower temperatures. It is around this time, I think, that our interactions with ice become more numerous, varied and complex, and the historical record far more illuminating. Following chapters will each take another important moment and a new theme, while filling in any gaps left earlier, and so on towards the present day.

Around 650 million years ago (650 Ma),[6] the so-called 'Snowball Earth' was probably completely covered in ice and,

---

[6] 'Ma' for millions of years ago and 'Ka' for thousands of years ago are the current preferred way of talking about the deep past, so I'll use those here and move to BCE and CE when the dates get closer to the present time.

since then, around 85 per cent of the time there has been no ice on 'Greenhouse Earth' at all. Given those odds, I suppose, we are lucky to know natural ice at all. It is something of a miracle that our earth's natural temperature *right now* means that water exists on our planet naturally in all its three states: liquid, solid and gas.

Ice was there at the beginning, but will it be there at the end?

I

# The Cave Painters

## *Our first journey to the cold north and the Ice Age of the mind*

> *So many dreams are crowding upon me now that I can scarcely tell true from false: dreams like light imprisoned in bright mineral caves; hot, heavy dreams; ice-age dreams; dreams like machines in the head.*
>
> Anna Kavan, *Ice* (1967)

> *I like cave painting . . . ancient, preliterate, from a time back when you were speaking to the lightning god, the ice god, and the cold-rainwater god.*
>
> Michael Heizer, in Dana Goodyear,
> 'A Monument to Outlast Humanity',
> *New Yorker* (29 August 2016)

We open in south-central France at one of prehistoric humanity's most significant sites. Somewhere close to a giant rock arch, carved over millions of years as the lazy Ardèche river ate its way through the local limestone, a family group stands in a clearing. *Homo sapiens.* Four of them. The youngest – surely a male – is no more than four years old. They have paused, unsure of their next move; the father looks one way, the mother another. It has recently rained and may do so again. The air is thick, expectant. High above, the wheeling birds. Perhaps the humans are hungry. Who knows when they last ate? The boy-child seizes the moment of indecision and scampers into the dense thorny bushes and small evergreen oaks that cover this plateau above the river gorge. Just before he disappears bodily into the bottle-green scrub, the father catches his leg and pulls him back, sets him upright and cuffs him around the head. The boy starts wailing. This galvanises the adults into action. A look is exchanged, perhaps even a word or two. The decision is made. They gather their young, then turn and set off down the path towards the turnstiles and the Renault Espace that awaits them in the car park beyond.

Those people and that car park are here because, maybe as far back as 36,000 years ago, something astonishing happened in a cave overlooking this river: hundreds of animal paintings of an unprecedented sensitivity and elegance precisely and joyously daubed on to the cave walls.[1] This extraordinary burst of artistic expression makes the cave – now known as Chauvet – one of the first real places in the little-documented life of our species to that point. Yet these ancient paintings, which survived rock falls and thousands of years of obscurity, are now so vulnerable to human presence, to the humidity of our breath, that they have been permanently sealed off to all but a select few researchers. Instead, a complete reproduction of the cave complex, faithful to the smallest detail and with ersatz cave-bear bones strewn just so, now exists a couple of kilometres away.

I came to this educational theme park to think about a simple question. Simple, at least, in its formulation: what happened when *Homo sapiens* first encountered ice? And a follow-up: might I perhaps detect an echo of that initial enchantment? It seemed like a good line of enquiry since cave paintings are some of

[1] Such early datings seemed barely believable in the aftermath of the cave's discovery in 1994. Some researchers have doubted the paintings' age on stylistic grounds and others have questioned the surface contamination of dating samples. That said, many of the long-ago dates in this chapter are either provisional or vague, either because new evidence is emerging or because of differences in the interpretation of existing data (e.g. palaeoclimatological data, geological evidence, etc.) between source materials.

the most visible and famous relics of Ice Age life, ones that continue to exert a kind of primal tug, like the dream of a memory or a memory of a dream. And, underground, Chauvet II is impressive. Atmospheric. Looking at the daubs on the wall, you might feel a genuine connection to the cave painters. That they were in some meaningful way *just like us.*[2]

Ever since the first cave paintings were rediscovered, people have been speculating about their meaning; a long-dominant school of thought held that they performed a spiritual or even shamanic function for peoples living in deep connection with the natural world. Others have believed they are an expression of what we might now call magic, of a lost animistic knowledge, and, standing there in the shimmering black, you may intuitively feel the truth of this.[3] By contrast, above ground, where the self-service cafeteria, toilet kiosks and trim paths resemble nothing so much as a well-maintained motorway rest area, the idea of divining anything meaningful about their presence feels like a vain hope. What was once a site of wonder and awe, with an immense spiritual resonance, has been sanitised and packaged and equipped with a gift shop. The gap between past and present feels vast.

However, in the years since Chauvet II was created, our understanding of the world inhabited by the cave painters has advanced dramatically. New techniques in DNA extraction and analysis are offering an ever-more accurate picture of their lives, new interpretations are gaining ground and investigations around the world are radically decentring archaeology from its European orthodoxy. Significant revelations sometimes come only months apart, throwing received ideas of Palaeolithic life into turmoil.

[2] Since these replicas were painted between 2012 and 2015, these cave painters *were* just like us. But the line that the originals communicate some kind of shared and recognisable humanity is one that the Chauvet establishment promotes.

[3] Until the advent of gas and electric light, all art indoors, but especially in churches and places of worship, would only ever have been imperfectly seen. Art has always been shrouded in an 'aesthetics of darkness'.

It is more alive, more vividly present, now than at any point in recorded history.

And we might, I think, despite the banality of the non-place of Chauvet II, talk about the ice in the Ice Age's effect on humankind in several ways. First, there are the barriers it presented and the pathways it opened: after humans left Africa, low sea levels and giant glaciers played a major role in defining where we could go – and that affected who we became. Then there are its social and cultural impacts: the effects of the cold on the already complex Ice Age culture, as well as the echoes into the present day at places like Chauvet II – the weight of what you might call an Ice Age of the mind.

\*\*\*

Before any humans existed at all, the glaciers and ice sheets of the Pleistocene crept back and forth across the surface of the earth, scouring the millennia like tides. For over 2 million years, colder glacial periods – when ice was widespread across the northern and southern hemispheres – alternated with times of warmer temperatures and little ice called interglacials. The last glacial period began around 115,000 years ago (115 Ka), and the last glacial maximum (when ice coverage was at its most extensive) occurred between 26.5 and 19 Ka; then, around 11.7 Ka, the earth entered the interglacial period we are still living through today.

This ebb and flow helped to define the life of many species. With the moves from glacial to interglacial and back again, animal and bird populations would have found their territories expanding and contracting because of the climatic changes, in a rhythm like the inhalation and exhalation of breath. Areas where species and habitats persisted during harsh glaciations – relatively safe havens – are known as refugia. In refugia some would have thrived, some clung on to life and others, confronted by new environmental stresses or novel opportunities, adapted. To take a couple of non-human examples: during one of the early Quaternary glaciations, populations of European hedgehogs were confined to three distinct refugia – Iberia, Italy and the Balkans – and returned after the thaw to recolonise Europe as two distinct species, *Erinaceus europaeus* and *Erinaceus concolor*,[4] mixing yet never again becoming one undifferentiated population. Similarly, within the last 300,000 years a small and geographically isolated population of brown bears lived out an ice age in a northern coastal refugium where conditions favoured evolutionary adaptations to Arctic maritime conditions. They emerged as the sea-hunting, white-coated polar bear we know today.[5]

As for ancient humans, it's thought that *Homo sapiens* and *Homo neanderthalensis* – Neanderthals – had a common ancestor around 600 Ka. When this ancestral population, which had spread through Africa, Asia and Europe, became fragmented during a glaciation, the isolated groups evolved independently: in Europe they became Neanderthals; in Africa they eventually became us. *Homo sapiens* evolved around 300 Ka; then, about another hundred thousand years after that, we became anatomically modern – that is, capable of everything we can do today. Give one of these ancient humans a baseball cap, shorts and flip-flops and they would blend into the crowds at Chauvet II.

This evolutionary spark happened in sub-Saharan Africa, and from there humans spread south and north through the African continent. Though there are, in the words of one academic paper, 'pulses' of small-scale excursions out of Africa as long ago as 194 Ka, the fossil record supports the idea of a larger wave of movement, beginning some time around 70 Ka: this is when we definitively gained a foothold in Eurasia and beyond. Modern people passed through Egypt, crossing the isthmus of Suez and the Sinai peninsula, and fanned out in all directions. They travelled fast: as early as 65 Ka they reached Australia, which was then

---

[4] There is a third hedgehog species, *Erinaceus roumanicus*, which has only recently been recognised as distinct from the other two, so perhaps it's three species, three refugia.

[5] These pockets of favourable conditions, 'climatic islands' at unexpected latitudes or longitudes, are known as 'cryptorefugia'. It could also be said that the polar bear – so well adapted to subzero life – is these days living in its own refugium, the Arctic, hoping to wait out this interglacial and roam far more widely during the next ice age.

joined to New Guinea; by around 45 Ka they were in Europe and by 31 Ka they were established in the land of the midnight sun, above the Arctic Circle in Siberia.

Somewhere in this journey out of Africa we encountered ice.[6] In these millennia before the last glacial maximum, temperatures were falling and ice cover expanding. The Scandinavian Ice Sheet squatted on much of the British Isles and north-eastern Europe, eventually reaching almost to Moscow, and the Patagonian Ice Sheet crowned the Andes, while the northern third of North America was more or less covered: to the west was the Cordilleran Ice Sheet, and the Laurentide Ice Sheet to the east reached as far south as New York City.

On a fundamental level this ice dictated where we could go. Part of this was the space it created: because so much water was locked in the ice, sea levels around the last glacial maximum were perhaps 120 metres lower than they are today. What are now the British Isles were connected to the Netherlands by Doggerland, an area of tundra in which the Thames, the Rhine and the Scheldt all met to flow via a giant channel into the Atlantic. The first *Homo sapiens* to reach England simply walked there. Equally, a land bridge between Siberia and Alaska also existed, which we now know as Beringia, allowing small populations of modern humans to cross into the Americas from eastern Russia. During this period, too, some of the Indonesian islands were linked to the Indochinese mainland.[7]

Glaciers, meanwhile, patrolled the boundaries of the navigable land. Once humans arrived on North American soil after crossing the land bridge, for example, they would have found Beringia isolated from the rest of the continent by glaciers (Beringia, as with much of Siberia and northern China, was

---

[6] There was, and is, ice in Africa. The glaciers adorning the highest summits of East Africa would have been more extensive than they are today, and there are ski resorts in South Africa, Lesotho, Morocco and Algeria, but ancient peoples had little time for peak-bagging – that is, as we shall see in Chapter 7, a modern phenomenon.

[7] Evidence shows that in earlier glacial periods some parts of Japan were connected to northern China by land or ice bridges, allowing mammoths and probably even *Homo erectus*, an archaic human species, to cross over.

not glaciated because there was so little precipitation). As they spread south and east through the new land, glaciers controlled their passage. For a long while the dominant theory was that they descended via an ice-free corridor through Canada into the Midwest, around 14–15 Ka, but the weight of evidence is now shifting to indicate a much earlier human presence, and a route down the Pacific coast, skirting glaciers and island-hopping south.

However, if ice opened up new lands, it also cut them off again when it melted. Great Britain regained its island status around 7–8 Ka, after Doggerland suffered an inundation, possibly when a chalk ridge retaining a huge glacial lake collapsed, cutting off the natives and initiating the long and latterly fractious history of isolation from the European mainland. The Russo-American rapprochement on Beringia ended around 11 Ka and things have rarely been as cordial since.

What clues to our existence in the deep past might lie hidden under these post-glacial seas? If you consider how often human settlements have hugged the lowlands and coasts, what remains above the water potentially presents a very limited picture of Ice Age life. A hint of what might have been lost can be found at Cosquer cave, near Marseille in France. Discovered in 1985 by a scuba diver in the Mediterranean, its 175-metre-long access tunnel begins at a depth of 37 metres below the surface of the sea and slopes upwards to reveal an airy chamber filled with prehistoric handprints and paintings of horses, great auks, seals and other animals. When Cosquer was painted, beginning around 27 Ka, it would have been several kilometres from the coast in a range of limestone hills; it is the only painted cave yet found that is accessed underwater, and, even though roughly 80 per cent of its extent is now lost to the waves – walls that may also have been densely decorated – it is one of the most important sites of prehistoric art in Europe. Cosquer demonstrates just how radically ice changed the landscape we lived in.

Somewhere in our progress across Asia we were united with our cousins the Neanderthals, who were well established across the Levant, Europe and central Asia. We met, probably learned all sorts of things from each other, definitely had sex.[8] As the peak of the Ice Age closed in and temperatures continued to drop, southern and western Europe became a refugium for *Homo sapiens*. By the time of the last glacial maximum, winter temperatures in western Europe were falling to −30 °C and the summer average might have barely touched 10 °C. However, if it's true that western Europe was a safe haven for us, it was not so for our cousins. Nobody can say for sure how *Homo sapiens* supplanted the Neanderthals, or why the latter became extinct, but it's entirely likely that the cooling and increasingly unstable climate played a part. One theory is that Neanderthals, while well adapted to cold in many ways, lived an incredibly active lifestyle fuelled by large amounts of meat; as temperatures dropped and food became more scarce, their 'metabolic demands finally outstripped the ability to supply adequate energy for maintenance and reproduction', putting individuals, and then the species, under terminal stress.

Some of the youngest Neanderthal fossils have been found in Gibraltar. Perhaps, one day soon, evidence will be unearthed in Russia, China or elsewhere in Europe of Neanderthals even more recent than these; but these Gibraltan remains do, somehow, feel like evidence of a last stand against the cold at the very southernmost tip of Europe.

***

It's natural to think that humankind's first experience of ice was shocking or entrancing: just look at babies or toddlers encountering snow for the first time. It must have been quite a surprise to see water, which is rarely still in nature, frozen. Water become bone, as the Saxon riddle goes. And it was probably also very strange and unwelcome to be in climatic conditions conducive to ice's formation. No less a figure than Sigmund

---

[8] Every living person not purely of sub-Saharan African heritage has some Neanderthal DNA. (Sub-Saharans do too, but this seems to have arrived with them much later, through interacting with Eurasian *Homo sapiens*.) Some of the DNA we inherited from them, which might have been beneficial to us in this new cold world, were Neanderthal versions of genes connected to keratin production (skin, hair and nails), circadian rhythms and metabolism – though tracing single genes' effects is incredibly complex, and we did not take on the most obvious anatomical adaptations such as short arms and a thick chest.

Freud turned his analytical eye to this trauma. In a paper from 1914–15 – a flight of fancy so esoteric it was never published – he speculated that ancient humans experienced the Ice Age as a kind of Fall from Eden, something so psychologically damaging it was the source of all the modern neuroses. 'Mankind,' he wrote, 'under the influence of the privations that the encroaching Ice Age imposed upon it, has become generally *anxious*. The hitherto predominantly friendly outside world, which bestowed every satisfaction, transformed itself into a mass of threatening perils.' In the struggle for survival, hysteria, obsessional neuroses and the tyrannical rule of the primal Father would also be born.

Whether you take or leave Freud is up to you – and this particular idea of his is a humdinger, not even remotely grounded in observable reality – but in his day he was at the forefront of thinking about the human mind.[9] Freud was always rummaging around in the past to explain the present, whether childhood events or the Ancient Greece of Oedipus, and it's intriguing that at this middle point of his career he was harking back to the Ice Age to formulate theories about the modern human condition. In his telling, the Ice Age becomes, like Oedipus, a foundational myth.

The father of psychoanalysis was not the only one exploring such thoughts. Archaeology was coming of age just as psychoanalysis, the archaeology of the psyche, was being born, and other scholars of the mind were also responding to the new revelations about humanity's deep past. The idea that the hardships of the Ice Age changed our brains was widespread in the 1900s. Since Freud's ill-fated paper it has never entirely gone away. We still commonly look upon the Ice Age as a kind of mythic foundational period for humankind.[10] That tantalising *just like us* that Chauvet peddles, with its threadbare tableaux of cavepeople

[9] And, actually, the idea of transgenerational trauma – operating both psychologically, in affected communities, and even potentially in our genetic inheritance – is now being taken very seriously. But not that far back.

[10] 'Fred, will you turn up the heat,' Wilma complains at the start of an episode of *The Flintstones*, as she paces the floor of her rocky des res. 'It feels like we're back in the Ice Age.' 'Wilma, the Ice Age isn't due for another thirty thousand years,' replies Fred.

in furs, shabby megafauna and informational displays. But this proposition is now sliding out of date and being replaced with a more nuanced appreciation of global humanity's development – and of our relationship to the cold climate.

We now know, for example, that figurative art was most certainly born elsewhere.[11] In 2021, archaeologists announced that a painting of a pig in a remote cave on the island of Sulawesi had been dated to *at least* 45.5 Ka. The life-size Sulawesi pig in red ochre is the oldest known animal cave painting, and it joins a small corpus of Indonesian paintings from 40 Ka or earlier, all found very recently, that destroys the long-held supposition that figurative art of this very earliest period was only made in Europe. There is also a developing understanding of the Eurocentrism that has shaped our appreciation of the deep past. Since the very beginning, archaeology's contours have largely been defined by white European men. In the early days especially they were metaphorically grubbing around in their own backyards and – surprise, surprise – if you look for things primarily in France, Spain, Germany or the UK, that is where you will find them.

To this we must add the 'preservation bias'. A cool, dry cave, returned to year after year, is a concentrated and conspicuous well of activity and a good shelter for artefacts through the ages, whereas more expansive or temporary living in warm climates leaves fewer traces. Likewise, many cultures would not have had access to rock walls or large bones, and may have chosen to make tools or express themselves using less durable materials, or in ephemeral ways. Ancient DNA lasts much less well in the heat. In this sense, the Ice Age ice has been beneficial to archaeologists (and we will come back to ice finds in the next chapter).

However, the richness of the finds across a relatively small geographical area, from around 45 Ka, nevertheless makes a persuasive case that a whole host of skills and capabilities coalesced in a sudden and startling way, and the fabric of human

[11] Art also existed elsewho: most archaeologists believe that certain cave paintings and a rock etching in Spain, which predate modern humans' arrival in Europe, are the handiwork of Neanderthals.

existence changed. Exhibit one might be the Venus of Hohle Fels, a six-centimetre-tall mammoth-ivory sculpture of a woman with accentuated breasts, belly and thighs, which was found in 2008 in a cave in the Swabian Jura mountains in south-western Germany. Dating from 35–40 Ka, it is the oldest depiction of a human being ever found. Discovered in the same cave and of a similar age is a griffon-bone flute: with five finger holes and a notch at the end, it is one of the most ancient musical instruments in existence. And, in a cave only twenty (modern) minutes up the road, another amazing find: the Lion-man of Hohlenstein-Stadel is a mammoth-ivory sculpture of a man's body with a lion's head that again has been dated to around 40 Ka. Around thirty centimetres high, it took an estimated 400 hours to carve and represents an imaginative leap into a new realm of unreal, perhaps spiritual beings.[12] As such, according to Jill Cook, the curator behind the British Museum's *Ice Age Art and the Arrival of the Modern Mind* exhibition in 2013, it indicates 'the activity of a complex super brain like our own, with a well-developed pre-frontal cortex powering the capacity to communicate ideas in speech and art'.

It's important to emphasise here that these European humans were no different from humans elsewhere: they had no special genetic endowment over their contemporaries. The lights of culture had been blinking on and off globally for tens of thousands of years, from South Africa to Indonesia and doubtless many other places as yet undiscovered. We began our journey out of Africa with the neurological potential to adapt to the challenges we met. This has led many archaeologists and academics to turn to environmental pressures to explain this concentrated flourishing of culture and innovation in Ice Age Europe: the climatic and social may be intricately intertwined.[13]

\*\*\*

[12] Another early theriandrope = part human, part animal – can be seen on the walls of Chauvet; later in the Palaeolithic they become more numerous.
[13] Others also point to the influence of Neanderthal culture, since the so-called creative explosion was confined to areas of prior Neanderthal habitation.

As the Ice Age cold deepened towards the last glacial maximum, central and eastern Europe became increasingly inhospitable. One tangible reaction to this was the invention of a significant piece of new technology: the needle. The earliest examples of needles in Europe date from at least 35 Ka. They were made from bone and were used to sew together hides using animal sinew or gut – *haute couture* animal skins that kept people warm at night and protected them when out hunting on the icy tundra (it is thought needles would have been taken on multi-day hunting trips, in case a repair to vital thermal layers was necessary). Needles are qualitatively different from the stone axes that various human species had been making for some 2.5 million years. Both tools required conceptualisation, abstraction and forward thinking – the externalisation of thought – but the process of shaping the needle and boring the eye, followed by the delicate craft of shaping skins and sewing them together to make a composite piece of clothing, is by leaps and bounds a far more difficult and sophisticated thing to do. Awls – simple points to punch holes in skins – had already existed in South Africa and other places for over 20,000 years, but new selection pressures operated on existing technologies and modes of thought. The needle came about due to a life-or-death environmental imperative: cold.[14]

In the long run, well-fitting clothes were not enough to mitigate the full effects of the falling temperatures, and the centre of gravity of Europe's *Homo sapiens* population shifted south and west. Many eventually settled in south-western France and the northern Spanish coastal strip. This refugium would both protect and change their societies and culture. As increasingly frosty conditions hemmed European *Homo sapiens* into smaller and smaller areas of liveable land, like tadpoles in a shrinking pond, population density increased dramatically. This would have created socio-political problems, and the default hunter-gatherer

[14] In 2020 it was announced that Denisovans, an archaic human species, had created a needle even earlier than this, around 50 Ka, in the equally chilly Altai mountains of Siberia (a place we will return to), which shows that groundbreaking inventions often happen independently several times over.

response to territorial challenges – migration – would not have been an option. Instead, they had to find new ways to live together, mediate disputes and solve problems. This is the context of the appearance of painted parietal (wall) art at Chauvet and other caves. 'The invention of material forms of representation went hand in hand with a major social transformation,' writes one academic. 'Art would have played a role in conflict resolution as the social geography of the region came to be characterized more and more by relatively closed social networks,' adds another. All the major European cave-art sites are located in this refugium.

One function of the art was social: in larger groups, communication becomes more important. People need to collaborate, bond or negotiate with each other, and to recognise or forge a common purpose with people who may almost be strangers. Ritual and tradition bond people together in a shared understanding of the world and the forces that shape it, underpinning or reinforcing the essential practical tasks of survival. Many portable pieces of art and decorative elements, it is suggested, fulfilled this role.

Cave art, however, was informative in intent – because, although the population was increasing, it was also atomising. Since food and resources were scarce, any more than a certain number of members would have committed a tribe to impossible amounts of travelling just to find enough food to keep everyone alive: only small family or tribal groups could have survived day to day. But smaller populations run into difficulties in maintaining skills. They also are in danger of becoming inbred.

This is where large caves like Chauvet, Altamira in Cantabria, Spain, and Lascaux in southern France – where cave painting reached its apotheosis either side of the last glacial maximum – come in.[15] Many believe that such sites, in addition to possible spiritual or ritual uses, hosted 'aggregation' events: every year, many small tribal groups would have travelled from far and wide, drawn by the season of the sun and familiar landmarks along the way, to congregate in the large public chambers of the cave and swap knowledge about hunting grounds, pass on skills and mix

[15] These sites began to be painted from circa 36 Ka, 36 Ka and 17 Ka respectively.

genes before dispersing once more. The art would have played its part in these processes. Some of the paintings at Chauvet are naturalistic; others seem to borrow techniques from modernism, Cubism, cinema and other movements that wouldn't be born for over 30,000 years. Some of it you might call 'realistic', except that realism also comes with a set of cultural assumptions alien to the Ice Age; but the paintings mainly feature predators and prey depicted in an accurate, identifiable way. They are beautiful, yes, but also precise and useful, displaying an intimate, detailed understanding of the animals we depended on for survival.

Only recently, a revolutionary theory about the role of some cave paintings has been advanced. It had long been noted that the animals on the walls of Lascaux are shown in their rutting coats and displaying mating behaviours, even though the red deer, horses and aurochs (based on analogies with modern species) did this in different seasons. It is, according to Paul Pettitt, an archaeologist at Durham University, a 'calendar of rutting, of sex and of creation'. Similarly specific scenes are also present in other caves. Then, in 2022, it was revealed that an amateur researcher, supported by Pettitt and others, had cracked the code behind mysterious notations next to the images: these dots, lines and 'Y' shapes indicated the lunar month in which there were important events in the life of the animal depicted – migration, mating or, in the case of the 'Y', birthing. At these times the animals would be numerous or vulnerable, and especially suitable for hunting.

This notation – which the discoverers call 'proto-writing' – pushes the paintings beyond representation and realism and into something like an instruction manual. They are, to use a complicated term, *exosomatic memory*: a way of inscribing information outside the brain, to educate and pass on knowledge from group to group and generation to generation, just like books are now.

Not only did this Ice Age art fulfil an important social function, creating harmony and bridging between groups, it might just have been a vital store of information, a survival tool and a crucial step in our development. In the teeth of an eternal winter, at a critical point in our cultural evolution, we created beautiful, useful art.

# 2

# The Revenants

## *Time travelling via ice*

*How strange it is, to be standing leaning against the current of time.*

W. G. Sebald, *Vertigo* (1990)

*The past is never dead. It's not even past.*

William Faulkner, *Requiem for a Nun* (1951)

If the last chapter presented ice as a life-threatening force and an evolutionary challenge, this one will examine ice's powers as a medium of communication and preservation, one that bridges the gap between the distant past and today.

When we think about ice as a messenger through deep time it is probably ice cores that first come to mind. These long cylinders of ice drilled out of glaciers or ice sheets contain a record of conditions when each layer of ice within them was formed: local temperature, snow accumulation, volcanic and solar activity, and the chemical composition of the atmosphere can all be unlocked from within. How does this work? A Danish palaeoclimatologist, Willi Dansgaard, theorised that the isotopic composition of ice could be used as a proxy measure of global temperatures at the time it froze. Around 0.27 per cent of naturally occurring $H_2O$ contains unusual isotopes of hydrogen and oxygen: $^2H$, also known as deuterium, has one extra neutron, and $^{18}O$ has two. This makes them fractionally heavier, and since it takes more energy for these heavier water molecules to evaporate, fewer of them leave the surface of the ocean during periods of low temperatures. In colder climates they are also more likely to fall as precipitation before they reach the polar ice caps and freeze; each of these factors means layers of ice formed at the poles during the Ice Age contain a lesser proportion of these isotopes than layers formed today. (Curiously, this also means that the world's oceans during ice ages were ever so slightly heavier.) Thus, by determining the ratios of the different isotopes of water molecules trapped in ice cores drilled from the world's great polar ice sheets, and measuring them against a control, we can infer the temperatures in those regions in the distant past.

Dansgaard's first proof of concept came in 1952 from analysing rainwater collected in beer bottles in his garden, emptying the samples as cold and warm fronts passed over Copenhagen. Sure enough, the warmer clouds were dropping proportionally more of the heavier molecules. Over the years he collected water samples from around the world, including from icebergs calved from glaciers; in 1966 he was given access to an ice core from the Greenland Ice Sheet that reached right down to the bedrock, containing frozen data reaching back 110,000 years, to the beginning of the last glacial period. Once analysed, this revealed the large and abrupt temperature rise at the end of the last Ice Age, and several smaller but significant variations. By combining this temperature data with contemporaneous information about atmospheric composition extracted from the tiny air bubbles trapped within the ice, a link between atmospheric gases and temperature was made. This was a groundbreaking contribution to the debate about human-powered climate change.

Ice cores aside, there are other ways in which ice can convey *human* messages from long ago. Glacial archaeology is the study of the remnants of cultures revealed in terrestrial ice. In practice, most of this is glaciers, but it includes many other kinds of ice.[1] The term was coined in 1968 by a man named Oddmunn

---

[1] These include, in ascending order of size: ice patches (small, stationary accumulations of ice); ice caps (large chunks of ice sitting on a high massif, usually feeding several glaciers); and ice sheets (super-large bodies of ice sitting on land, also called continental glaciers).

Farbregd, who had been researching Iron Age burial mounds in Oppdal, Norway. It first appeared in a student newspaper, and if I mention its provenance it is only to demonstrate that glacial archaeology was, for quite a while, a low-key field of interest. Previously, it was not clear that it even existed at all: thanks to their extraordinary condition, any ice finds were generally assumed to date from the not too distant past. We knew about the preservative power of ice, but simply did not think about it in this context, it seems. Systematic study of objects found on or around ice patches and glaciers had started in 1914 – again in Oppdal – when the university museum began working with local reindeer hunters to record their discoveries. However, it was not until 1937 that it was understood that the arrows and other artefacts were actually emerging from within the ice – that they were appearing because the ice was melting. This realisation linked the discipline to changes in climate, and turned glacial archaeology into perhaps the first truly native academic discipline of the Anthropocene.

Not all of the subjects of this chapter, which range from the prehistoric to the ancient to the merely long dead, are the fruit of glacial archaeology. There are other quirks of environment and time – ice accidents – that have brought them into proximity with the present day. But each is a conduit to distant lives we otherwise never could have known.

\*\*\*

Thursday 19 September 1991: two German hikers in the Ötztal Alps are walking at an altitude of 3,200 metres, not far from a path and only a couple of kilometres from a well-used mountain hut, when they spy a man's bare back protruding out of an iced-up gully, almost as a swimmer hauls him or herself out of a pool of water. Supposing him to be relatively recently lost, they alert the warden at the nearby Similaunhütte, who, unsure of which side of the Austria–Italy border line the body has fallen, contacts the

Similarly, 'glaciology' is generally speaking the study of all types of ice phenomena in the natural world, but is usually used to refer more narrowly to glaciers only.

authorities in both countries. It is the seventh corpse to emerge from an Austrian glacier in 1991, surpassing the total number of bodies found in all the years between 1952 and 1990, so it seems, at the end of the long hot summer, bizarrely routine. At this point it is still presumed that it dates from the First World War at the earliest and is possibly that of a Veronese music professor who went missing in 1941.

When, two days later, Innsbruck-based archaeologist Konrad Spindler reads the short notice in Saturday's newspaper, he is not all that interested: not one of the summer's six previous bodies had dated from before the 1950s. A follow-up article quotes the famous alpinist Reinhold Messner (astonishingly, he was walking in the area and examined the still-icebound body), who says the dead man's footwear reminds him of 'the Eskimos'. This is more interesting to Spindler; but, on the other hand, Messner has recently announced he has tracked down the yeti in the Himalaya, so this tantalising promise of antiquity is more than likely a red herring.

Bad weather hampers the recovery. It is only six days after its discovery, after the body has been removed from the remaining ice by pneumatic drill, helicoptered to the nearest road and then taken by undertakers – as the law decrees – to Innsbruck's Forensics Institute that Spindler sees it for the first time. It is immediately clear to him that the as-yet-unnamed corpse is unimaginably old – at his estimate, 4,000 years or more. A first-year archaeology student, he says, would be able to date the axe taken from the man's grasp to at least the early Bronze Age. (In fact, it will turn out to be copper – older – and extremely rare.) He likens his feelings to Henry Carter's when opening the lid of Tutankhamen's sarcophagus, but this find is, if anything, more important than that. Nothing like this has ever been found; no protocols have been observed, the site has been turned over and the iceman's body manhandled – his stiffened left arm had been fractured by an undertaker manoeuvring him into a coffin for transport down to forensics – because people could not conceive of the possibility that he was of archaeological significance. Now he is safe in a freezer, the real work starts.

The corpse is nicknamed 'Ötzi the Iceman' after the mountains in which he was found. But who is he really? He is, as multiple newspapers point out, the ultimate 'cold case'. The detective story has been running for over thirty years and is still ongoing.[2]

Spindler's initial estimate of Ötzi's age was quickly superseded: carbon dating fixes his life at around 3,200 BCE, more than 5,000 years ago. More remarkable still was the state of his 5,000-year-old possessions, which provided incredibly detailed information on how he had lived. These included deerskin shoes with cow's-leather laces, a sheep- and goat-skin coat, a deer-hide quiver for his arrows and a bearskin hat. Ötzi used woods including yew, ash, hazel, birch and lime, and birch tar to fix flint arrowheads to viburnum sapwood shafts. A mat of rushes served as a kind of cape, and fresh maple leaves as insulation to transport embers, and he carried mosses and funguses with antiseptic and other qualities in his 'first aid kit', which he stowed in his rucksack. Ötzi had fleas and Lyme disease and digestive complaints, and he also had high levels of arsenic and copper in his hair, which suggested he may have been involved in copper smelting. Sixty-one tattoos decorated his skin, where charcoal had been rubbed into incisions at pressure points similar to those targeted by acupuncturists today. In his stomach was his last meal, of red-deer meat (possibly smoked); in his colon, his penultimate meal, of einkorn wheat and ibex. Einkorn grains are known to have grown in the Vinschgau valley, close to where he was found, and analyses of his wooden tools, as well as his dental ceramic, confirmed he lived on the Italian side of the Alpine ridge. The copper in his axe blade was found to have originated in Tuscany, many hundreds of kilometres to the south, while the flint from his

---

[2] Even Ötzi is not outside the scope of cryopolitics. When he was discovered he was assumed to be Austrian, and taken to Innsbruck, where he lived for six years. Later it was determined that – by a matter of metres – he had lain on the Italian side of the border, so he was moved, and currently resides in Bolzano. But these mountains had been divided up according to the watershed at the end of the First World War. And with the melting ice, the watershed has changed. In 2013, water from his resting place was shown to drain north, into Austria. Thus he is a 'cryopolitical subject' whose 'emergence reveals new spatiotemporal dimensions of geopolitics within which narratives of origins and belonging are constructed'.

dagger was sourced in the mountains by Lake Garda, to the west –
discoveries that were entirely consonant with the growing body
of evidence that the Copper Age had seen a great expansion in
long-distance trade and ties between communities across Europe.

Around these facts many hypotheses have been built to
explain the circumstances of Ötzi's death, but the truth may
still be emerging. Initially, he was thought to have died in the
late summer or autumn, when the high mountains would have
been more hospitable to travellers or shepherds; then a theory
was advanced that he had died in the valley and was later carried
up, in some kind of ceremonial burial befitting a high-status
individual. Then undigested hop hornbeam pollen was found in
his stomach, confirming he had died in springtime. And some
of the latest research has proved, using pollen and moss samples
taken from Ötzi's digestive tract and around his grave site, that in
his final hours he rapidly climbed, descended and then climbed
the mountain again, passing from temperate spring lowlands to
the still snow-covered heights.[3]

What was he doing up there, and why the frantic up-and-down
just before he died? A flint-tipped arrow lodged in the sinews of
his shoulder provides a chilling answer. Ötzi was very possibly on
the run from mortal enemies: he was hunted to death.

Picture, then, an injured man huddling in a straw cloak,
clutching his bow, axe and knife as a freezing Alpine spring night
falls. He is well dressed and equipped with expertly selected and
adapted materials, and he is a practised and skilful traveller over
the ice of the high mountains. But today his luck has run out.
Perhaps he had stopped to rest and eat on a rocky ridge poking
out of the ice (new studies on glaciers close by suggest that only
the very peaks of the mountains nearby would have been truly
ice free), only to have been attacked; his shoulder is periodically
dripping blood red on to the snow, though it is a head wound
he also sustained in the fight that will kill him. That night he
expires. His body lies there for a period of time and the exposure

---

[3] The contents of his digestive system have been called a 'gastro-intestinal chronotopograph' –
a gut map of the terrain he traversed in his final few hours.

freeze-dries the flesh, helping its long-term preservation; later, perhaps as spring turns into summer and snow melts from under him, he falls into a gully, where he is covered in snow. Over the years, this compacts, cocooning the body in ice. Over the long course of the millennia, the ice levels dip every now and then, and his top half resurfaces intermittently for brief periods. This melting also disperses his possessions, and those bits that remain submerged are more perfectly preserved.

The above summarises some aspects of many of the long and painstaking investigations into the find, which reveal a cultured member of a highly mobile Copper Age civilisation in deep and technologically advanced harmony with its natural environment. Overall, it is an astonishing yield of information about Ötzi's life and times. Little or none of the organic materials that afforded these insights would have survived if he had not been caught in the ice. It is incredibly lucky – lucky for us – that Ötzi did not fall into the glacier adjacent to his gully: like an icy cradle, the gully kept him immobile, safe and whole. Ötzi survived 5,000 years of solitude, then his manhandling and his exposure to twentieth-century air, and is now kept in what is essentially a giant freezer in the South Tyrol Museum of Archaeology in Bolzano, where he reclines at −18 °C and is viewable by museum visitors through a round reinforced window, a porthole to another dimension or time. He is constantly misted with water, which freezes in a thin, transparent layer of ice, to keep him in the style to which he has become accustomed. The ice has reclaimed him, and, for now, he has nothing more to say.

\*\*\*

The Iceman's discovery put glacial archaeology firmly in the spotlight. These days, it is an exciting field of study, albeit in a bittersweet way. It is, in two profound senses, a race against time. Given the speed with which glaciers (and ice patches, etc.) are now receding, soon there won't be much left to melt: 'The time during which glaciers spit out their treasures will be short and unique,' a Swiss geographer told *Le Temps* newspaper in 2016. The other urgency stems from the fragility of the glaciers' cargo.

In contrast to Ötzi in his gully, those who fall into glaciers tend to be carried along in the flow and, given that glaciers carve valleys out of solid rock, soft humans are light work. Bodies are torn apart and reappear bit by grisly bit. Then, once thawed and exposed to the air, previously icebound finds quickly discolour, deform and decompose.

To give just one example, in 1820 a party climbing Mont Blanc led by a Russian doctor, Joseph Hamel, lost three guides when an avalanche swept them into a crevasse. Forty-one years later, the Bossons glacier near Chamonix began to disgorge clothing, scientific instruments, fragments of bone and skull, a foot and even a complete arm. The relics had travelled at the glacial speed of approximately twenty centimetres a day to arrive at the terminus around eight kilometres away. One of the guides who had survived the accident, Joseph-Marie Couttet, was brought in to identify the remains. Piece by piece the septuagenarian went through them, until he reached the arm: 'This is Balmat's hand, I know it well,' he said, breaking down with emotion. 'I would never have dared to believe that, before I left this world, I'd be given the chance once more to shake the hand of one of my brave comrades, that of my good friend Balmat.' As metaphors go, that handshake (which is surely apocryphal) is perfect. Ice had disrupted the normal flow of time and the past had returned to reintroduce itself to the present. That eerily well-preserved arm was preternaturally caught between the living and the dead, still moving, zombie-like, until it resurfaced and could finally be put to rest.

This corporeal destruction, wrought in the blink of an eye (in glacial terms), emphasises how special Ötzi is. But although he is pre-eminent, he is not the only so-called 'ice mummy'. One very basic definition of a mummy is a preserved corpse that retains some of the flesh or soft tissues that clothe its bones. They are most commonly thought of as intentional: bodies that have been prepared, embalmed and laid down in an attempt to make the temporary permanent, in a gesture towards the eternal. However, this is not always true. Many environments can produce or preserve mummies: deserts, peat bogs, caves, human-made containers or structures, and certainly ice. Of the ice mummies in existence, very few are embalmed, but some are; some are freeze-dried and others drowned in ice (Ötzi is both); and the vast majority are coldly conserved for the long term by accident rather than design. 'Ice mummies' therefore denotes a rather ragbag collection of bodies, a motley corpus of corpses unified only by the ice that has placed them in suspended animation, precluding their burial, preventing their decay and delaying the natural end of their story.

After Ötzi, the 1990s continued to be a busy time for ancient ice mummies. The next major revelations would come from Russia. In 1993, a young archaeologist called Natalia Polosmak was preparing to dig on Ukok, a high plateau surrounded by mountains on the Siberian steppes, where China, Russia, Kazakhstan and Mongolia meet. The name has been supposed to mean 'the end of everything', but the region is also known, betraying its long history of animal herding, as the 'pastures of heaven'. The plateau is little changed in thousands of years, and these days it is home to the snow leopard, as well as to remarkable archaeological finds of what is now called 'Pazyryk' culture. Polosmak's work digging into the icy tundra would shed light on a dazzlingly rich society and revolutionise our understanding of the lives of these people of the steppes.

Before we get to Polosmak's find, some context: the Pazyryks were a nomadic, pastoral horse-riding tribe, one of the many similar and interrelated tribes that proliferated in the first millennium BCE across the vast grasslands that separate Europe from Asia. Often, these peoples are known by the umbrella term 'Scythians', after a tribe that lived between the Black Sea and the Danube, thousands of kilometres west of the Pazyryks, who came into contact with the Ancient Greeks.[4]

[4] Many researchers now believe that the real Scythians – the most famous and best-documented ones – originated near Pazyryk territory in the Altai mountains: some of the earliest Scythian-style finds are there. In addition, a study of ancient DNA in *Nature* from 2017 found evidence of significant and ongoing gene flow from east to west Eurasia early in the Iron Age (first millennium BCE) – that is, the tribes were interbreeding, 'plausibly explaining the striking uniformity of their material culture'.

Much of our knowledge of the Scythians (both the Scythian Scythians and the collective peoples) comes from Herodotus, who devotes almost a book of *The Histories* to them. 'The whole region I have been describing', Herodotus writes, 'has excessively hard winters; for eight months in the year the cold is intolerable; the ground is frozen iron-hard, so that to turn earth to mud requires not water but fire. The sea freezes over, and the whole of the Cimmerian Bosphorus; and the Scythians . . . make war upon the ice, and drive waggons across it.'

For the Ancient Greeks, people who could survive in such conditions were necessarily brutal and base. But the warlike Scythians did themselves no favours. 'The Scythian custom is for every man to drink the blood of the first man he kills,' states Herodotus.

> The heads of all enemies killed in battle are taken to the king; if he brings a head, a soldier is admitted to his share of the loot; no head, no loot. He strips the skin off the head by making a circular cut around the ears and shaking out the skull; he then scrapes the flesh off the skin with the rib of an ox, and when it is clean works it in his fingers until it is supple and fit to be used as a sort of handkerchief.

And yet, even by contemporary estimations, this savagery was not quite the whole story. As well as their bows and arrows, the tribes were known for their sophisticated decorative art, portable objects made out of precious metals, petroglyphs and tattoos in the characteristic 'Animal Style'. The nomads transported silk and other precious goods from China westwards, and bartered with the Greeks; and they were respected all around for their horse riding and the magnificent horses they bred.

But nomads travel light. The Scythians left few traces other than their burial mounds, countless islands in the sea of ice and grass that are known as 'kurgans'. After they had died out, there was little, for centuries, to challenge the view, extant since Herodotus, that the steppes were uncivilised, dangerous wastelands, places to build walls against (as the Chinese eventually did) or travel through quickly. Then, in the seventeenth and eighteenth centuries, finely wrought Scythian gold jewellery and precious stones, which had been looted from the kurgans, began to appear at Tsar Peter the Great's court in St Petersburg. Methodical study, however, would not happen for another century or more. And this would encounter a significant barrier, and an enigma: ice.

'It is only by digging that one can know the tundra for what it is: an immeasurable and unchangeable ice vault which has endured, and will continue to endure, for hundreds of thousands of years,' wrote a zoologist called Alfred Edmund Brehm in 1896. And this is what, by Brehm's time, people had started to do. The trailblazing archaeologists of the steppe were, like Polosmak, Russian. In 1865, a certain V. V. Radlov happened upon kurgans filled with a concrete-hard mixture of ice and gravel. Inspired, perhaps, by Herodotus ('the ground is frozen iron-hard, so that to turn earth to mud requires not water but fire'), he lit a blaze on top. Thus penetrating deeper, he found many of them were empty – their contents perhaps already now the property of Peter the Great – and was disappointed.

The next significant digs happened in the 1920s, led by archaeologists Sergei Rudenko and Mikhail Gryaznov. Working on five large kurgans in the Pazyryk valley, Gryaznov refined the fire-lighting excavation technique, liberally dousing the iced-up tombs with hot water. Over the course of several seasons the duo discovered and documented four embalmed human bodies and three skeletons, plus twenty horse bodies and thirty-four horse skeletons. The most striking of all was a tattooed, musclebound chieftain. While parts of the body had deteriorated, the ice had kept much of it fresh.

These finds defined Pazyryk culture and gave it its name, but this great boon to archaeology was also a puzzle. Kurgans could be dug only where the ground was not frozen. None of Rudenko and Gryaznov's digs in the Pazyryk valley was in permanently frozen soil; nor were the nearby tombs explored by Natalia Polosmak almost fifty years later: they were dotted around, located precisely where the soil was *not* frozen.[5] Yet the contents

---

[5] Polosmak found that Ukok permafrost generally started around three metres down. This, not unrelatedly, happened to be the depth of the burial pits: 'Even modern iron spades rebound from the frozen ground,' she wrote.

seemed to owe their survival to ice. Some of the human bodies were preserved by ice, but were found under horses that had rotted to skeletons; in other places the grave robbers had clearly hacked through thick layers of ice to reach the loot. In fact, the tombs that had been disturbed were often the most icebound. One of them was almost full to the brim. The whole situation seemed illogical and unlikely, and in some cases downright impossible.

Through careful study of the distinct layers of ice and the construction of the kurgans themselves, they identified the peculiar flukes of circumstance that had led to the icy preservation. The freezing of the ice tombs had taken place in many phases, as Rudenko later explained, and ice mainly affected the larger kurgans. These were capped by rock cairns that could be well over twenty metres wide, which generated a colder microclimate beneath, creating a permanent, lens-shaped layer of permafrost and ice around and above the burial chambers.[6] Because of these peculiar conditions, any water that crept into the burial shaft and other spaces also froze. And the ones that were totally icebound? In a leap of intuition, Rudenko realised that, by putting holes into the roofs of the burial chambers, the looters had opened them to the weather: 'The main practical effect of the robbing was to allow rainwater to penetrate the tombs, which filled with ice.'

The bitter irony was that the best-preserved tombs, those most fully encased in ice, were also those that had been looted: rich as their yields were, the two pioneering archaeologists were certain that much had been lost.

This was the background to Natalia Polosmak's work in the 1990s. Polosmak was an archaeologist from the Russian Institute

---

[6] 'Permafrost' describes rock or sediment that remains below 0°C for two or more years, sometimes freezing the earth to a depth of hundreds of metres. Permafrost can be up to 90 per cent ground ice by volume, but, curiously, the term can also refer to subzero rock that contains only a fraction of a per cent of $H_2O$ by total volume. The word was only coined in English in 1943 by a Russian-born US geologist, Siemon W. Muller, in a report for the US military, and it did not have its first public outing until 1947. Before that, people called it 'rock ice', which has a nice ring and a simple heft to it. Both names rightly suggest that, pre-Anthropocene, it did not move much. But 'rock ice' in particular captures how physically hard permafrost can be.

of Archaeology and Ethnography in Novosibirsk. She had spent many winters with her books and artefacts, 'wondering what the Pazyryk people had really been like. In my imagination they were standing around me, their eyes imploring, "Natasha, you have to tell people about our lives."' A scholar of Rudenko and Gryaznov, Polosmak understood the icy paradox of the grave robbers' business. Flying to the Ukok plateau in 1993, at the start of her fourth season prospecting for Pazyryk artefacts, Polosmak landed in an area very close to China. It did not take long for the soldiers guarding the border to direct her to one of their 'favourite' kurgans, a medium-sized mound just within the frontier fence. Half fallen in and with a large hole at one end, it had clearly been disturbed.

The team began to dig and, soon enough, they discovered an interloper, a body in a stone coffin, simply arranged, left by a later civilisation; as a rule, authentic Pazyryks were entombed in three-metre-long wooden coffins, in double-walled subterranean cabins made of hewn larch logs. And although this death-cuckoo's eternal rest had been disturbed by grave robbers, the signs were nevertheless good: the ice covering what was below – a lid to a main chamber? – appeared untouched.

In a *National Geographic* article in 1994, Polosmak described the initial excitement of the find. How her dog Peter the Great (Pete for short) licked the now-exposed ice as it melted. How helpers hauled in buckets of lake water, which they heated with blowtorches and she then poured into the kurgan one mug at a time. 'When you spend day after day in the ice vault,' she wrote, 'first one thing, then another, appears gradually in the ice mass like in a transfer picture – you cannot recognize them [at] first, then you can see them more and more clearly, and finally they give you the joy of discovery.' Soon, the top of the casket emerged; then a couple of short-legged tables, with mutton and horsemeat laid out upon them, a symbolic last meal to see the occupant safely into the afterlife. As Polosmak continued to pour on hot water, she made a kind of foul-smelling broth as the meat, which had begun to rot before freezing, thawed.

Slowly the larch casket emerged . . . then a jawbone . . . and then . . . then, it became clear, melting out of the ice, the body of a woman, lying on her side, as if asleep.

Nobody had expected a woman. Let alone a tall woman (around five foot six or 1.67 metres), still young, and heavily tattooed with horses and dragon-like creatures, wearing a felt headdress decorated with golden cats and swans that took up a third of the length of her coffin – all in finest Animal Style. Surrounding her, gold leaf shimmered in the slush, along with other fineries that would in normal circumstances have long decayed. A delicate ceremonial vessel made out of translucent yak horn, a jug decorated with cats that still contained ancient yoghurt. She had a small hand mirror and saddles decorated with winged lions, and had been buried with coriander seeds and, according to some reports, cannabis.[7] Covered in a blanket of marten fur, she was wearing woollen trousers and a silk top. Her robes were still pliant and soft.

Six elaborately harnessed chestnut mares (they still had clumps of hair) had been sacrificed and laid outside the north wall. Horsehair stitches were visible on her torso: her insides had been removed and her mummification carried out with the enormous care usually reserved for Pazyryk royalty. And her eyes had been scooped out and the sockets stuffed with fur, again part of the preservation process.

Soon, the ice maiden was named the 'Princess of Ukok'. She was simultaneously twenty-five and 2,400 years old, and, in all her pomp and circumstance, her interment was broadly similar to that of other high-status Pazyryks. But she was the first woman to be discovered buried in this way, and her accoutrements were so much more complete. It was a sensation. The richness of her

---

[7] Herodotus described the Scythians' love of 'hemp seed', which they would put on heated stones to release its vapour and, transported, they would 'howl aloud'. Other Scythians had indeed been found with such paraphernalia, but an MRI analysis published in 2017 revealed that the Princess of Ukok had died from breast cancer, so the cannabis may have been medicinal. The coriander seeds would also have been burned, and their aroma possibly used to mask the corpse smell – her body had perhaps been transported for weeks to be interred in the pastures of heaven.

possessions filled in huge gaps in the archaeological record and told a bright, colourful story of Pazyryk life. Her grave proved that steppe nomads had enjoyed a sophisticated material life filled with fine things. Its contents also underlined their vital role as a link in a trading network that connected Europe to Asia. Her polished bronze hand mirror, for example, was of Chinese origin, and the fibres in her yellow silk blouse came from as far away as India; the yak horn and the coriander seeds, meanwhile, indicated trade with Persia. Among Rudenko's finds is the world's oldest knotted-pile carpet, which is decorated with patterns and animals, as well as pottery in an Ancient Greek style.

The Pazyryks, then, were not simply the vicious savages Herodotus, the Chinese and the Persians feared. Archaeologists have not found cups made from the skulls of enemies. Or at least, not yet. The accumulation of evidence from the icy ground has allowed a different interpretation – has permitted them to tell their own story. As a prominent anthropologist of the nomads, Lev Gumilev, once wrote: 'To measure an alien culture by the number of secure monuments is entirely wrong. There may be a magnificent civilization built on the basis of non-persistent materials like leather, furs, tree and silk, and a primitive one that uses stone and noble metals. The former will leave no trace while the latter will abound in artefacts.'

These days, philologists think that the Eurasian steppes were the birthplace of all Indo-European languages, now spoken by more than 3 billion people worldwide – languages that spread due to the steppe peoples' mastery of horses and very early adoption of the wheel. We owe the Pazyryk, their ancestors and their kin a lot.

\*\*\*

Why are there not more ice mummies? For one thing there is the aforementioned difficulty with glaciers which, although much frequented and the site of numerous accidents, tend to destroy the evidence.[9] There is also the cold, hard truth that it is very

---

[8] The Victorian scientist James David Forbes wrote in 1843 of finding three recent and not-so-recent fatalities exposed to the air during a single glacier traverse. The final one

difficult to intentionally bury a body in ice. Traditionally, Inuit communities did not bury their dead, leaving them instead covered by a walrus- or seal-skin shroud and placed in a cave or crevasse, or surrounded by rocks or blocks of ice to keep predators away. Sometimes these graves kept bodies well drained and aerated by the dry Arctic winds, unintentionally preserving them for the long term. However, only two such burial sites, containing fourteen mummies dating from the fifteenth century, have been found to date, showing just how rare these circumstances are. Before the arrival of Christian Russians in Siberia, the indigenous Yakuts rarely buried their dead, instead suspending them in trees or placing them in wooden coffins on aerial platforms known as 'arangas'. Generally, in the high Arctic permafrost regions, only the bodies of foolhardy southerners – whalers and polar explorers – tend to be found below ground, and not very far below it at that, showing that old habits truly do die hard. And in Ötzi's region of the South Tyrol, even in the twentieth century bodies of people who died in the cold season were frequently stored for anything up to a few months, until the ground thawed enough to permit interment. One account tells of the dead 'kept in rooms cold as freezers' until transport and digging were possible; another that they were kept protected on the roof or freezing in the attic until burial.

Most ice mummies that make the news are accidental, irregular deaths and consequently exceptional finds.[9] Perhaps the most famous accidental ice mummy – quite as celebrated as Ötzi, though at the opposite end of the seniority spectrum – is George Mallory, the British mountaineer who died near the summit of Everest in 1924. His body, still clad in tweeds, was recovered

was 'nearly the whole skeleton . . . in detached bones laid in order upon the ice, – the skull lowest, next the arms and ribs, and finally the bones of the pelvis, legs and feet, disposed along the glacier so that the difference between head and feet might be five yards'. This freakish arrangement puzzled him, though it now seems easy enough to understand: the ice had been unusually gentle with its victim, laying out the bones as it receded like a suit on a bed ready to be worn.
[9] That said, a 2014 study of ancient tuberculosis dug up 140 Yakuts buried in permafrost between the sixteenth and nineteenth centuries – the largest sample of frozen mummies ever taken.

from the eternal snows of the Himalayan death zone in 1999. Thanks to the incredible state of preservation, experts were able to reconstruct Mallory's attire, and found that, contrary to George Bernard Shaw's judgement that the era's expeditions were peopled by underequipped amateur toffs (a 'Connemara picnic surprised by a snowstorm', he is reported to have remarked about a photo of the British climbers in 1921), his clothing compared relatively favourably with modern Everest-ready gear. It's not known whether Mallory was on his way up or coming down after successfully scaling the peak. His Kodak Vest Pocket camera, were it ever found, might provide proof: Kodak has said that, thanks to the subzero temperatures, it may still be possible to develop the film contained within, revealing that hoped-for summit shot. But for now it remains lost in the icy wastes.

Altitude is a natural place for corpses to freeze, as has also been shown in Peru. In 1995, just a few years after Ötzi and the Princess of Ukok, an archaeologist and his companion climbing in the Andes discovered a bundle on the ice close to the top of Ampato, a 6,288-metre-tall extinct volcano. Within, the body of a young girl, fourteen or fifteen years old, who, in the fifteenth century, had been the victim of a child sacrifice, a ritual known as *qhapaq hucha* in which the very purest in Incan society – children – were singled out and put to death so they could act as messengers to the gods. *Qhapaq hucha* took place according to a ceremonial calendar, to ensure good weather and harvests, or, exceptionally, to address a specific disaster such as a volcanic eruption or the death of a king, and it seems to have been known that the high-altitude cold preserved: since the children were effectively deified by the ritual, many *qhapac hucha* subjects would regularly be visited long after death.

After a sharp blow to the head that had cracked her skull, Juanita had probably started her afterlife buried in a chamber excavated into the mountain. This is how other *qhapaq hucha* victims in equally high places have been found, either freeze-dried or eventually encased in ice. Indeed, in the weeks following Juanita's discovery, an eight-year-old boy was also unearthed on Ampato, buried on a rock slab excavated in the side of the mountain peak.

But Juanita had been rudely ejected from her burial nook when a neighbouring volcano erupted, showering Ampato's summit ridge with hot black ash and causing a portion to collapse.

It was an incredible stroke of luck that Juanita was found only a short time after being forcibly disinterred, since the ice almost completely encased her still. The feathers on her headdress were still bright, the textiles wrapping her still bore the colourful stripes of the Cuzco upper class, and, though her face had dried out, the rest of her skin and flesh were still frozen. In the lab, her skin, tissues and organs were examined; there was even blood present in her heart and lungs. Analysis showed that in the months before her death she had been put on a diet of maize and meat, to prepare her for the sacrifice. And with six or eight weeks to go she had been given increasing amounts of alcohol and coca, probably to stupefy her when the time came.

The Incas were aware that the bodies of those chosen for *qhapaq hucha* would freeze and would endure, but could they have guessed that Juanita and many others would be discovered again, 500 years later? In death Juanita has become a guide to the political, societal and spiritual regime of her civilisation, one that, like Ötzi's, did not possess the power of writing. There is a visceral irony in the thought that this poor girl, killed by her elders, has become our link to the long-dead civilisation that condemned her.

In all these diverse cases, spanning thousands of years and several continents, ice has given earthly remains a life far beyond when a heart stops beating and a civilisation dies, and has allowed us to take an empathetic leap across the millennia. It has helped modern researchers to believe in, to feel, the humanity of those who are long dead. What more of our shared past might be revealed as the upper ice world melts and as the permafrost subsides and collapses underneath us? For better and for worse we will surely soon find out.

# 3

# The Revellers

## *The Little Ice Age, sport and frost fairs*

*For all the perception of physical mastery, skating is still strange and dreamlike. Dreams of flying are the nearest you get to the feeling of being on ice.*
Jenny Diski, *Skating to Antarctica* (1997)

*Birds froze in mid-air and fell like stones to the ground.*
Virginia Woolf, *Orlando* (1928)

*Behold the wonder of this present age*
*A frozen river now becomes a stage*
*Question not what I now do close to you*
*The Thames is now both fair and market too*
Anonymous, frost fair poem (1684)

Here we pass definitively from prehistory and protohistory – from a foundation story featuring ice as an existential threat, and ice as a messenger from the deep past – into the annals of recorded time. There will be lots to say about the Ancient Greeks and Romans, Levantine civilisations and knowledge in the Arab world, but we will meet these later, when looking specifically at food, medicine or other themes. We'll now jump to a period when ice, while still a hardship, became an inspiration and a source of fun. And who better to introduce it than one of the foremost chroniclers of any age, Samuel Pepys.

For Samuel, Monday 1 December 1662 started like any other day Pepysing around London. After getting up, he went by coach to the Duke of York's chamber, where the duke, the Lord High Admiral of the Navy, thanked Pepys for his close attention to various mast contracts. Thence he went to the Sandwiches' to talk with the lord's lawyer about a little business. All very ho hum. But then, after that, passing through St James's Park, he encountered something out of the ordinary. 'I first in my life, it being a great frost, did see people sliding with their skeates, which is a very pretty art,' he wrote. On the very same day the diarist John Evelyn wrote:

> Having seene the strange, and wonderfull dexterity of the sliders on the new Canall in St. James's park, perform'd by divers Gents & others with Scheets, after the manner of the Hollanders, with what pernicitie & swiftnesse they passe, how sudainly they stop in full carriere upon the Ice, before their Majesties: I went home by Water but not without exceeding difficultie, the Thames being frozen, great flakes of yce incompassing our boate.

Pepys and Evelyn could not have known it, but they were living during a significant cold period now known as the Little Ice Age. For hundreds of years, lower temperatures, particularly across Europe and the North Atlantic, brought widespread heavy frosts, and the cooling climate had huge social and economic impacts. Some historians believe that the ensuing crop failures and bad harvests created existential challenges to some of the world's great powers: the so-called 'General Crisis' of the seventeenth century saw instability and revolution from the Mughal Empire to China, Russia and Poland, as well as threatening the Spanish monarchy and the Low Countries. Another cultural historian has argued that these same food shortages helped to break the centuries-old feudal system, improving life for millions – but also that they drove dramatic colonial expansion. Essentially, so the thinking goes, Europeans chose to trade and raid rather than starve, aggressively accumulating produce and riches from across the globe. But, as the skating shows, this was also a period in which ice became mass entertainment – something we'll explore in the rest of this chapter.

***

Before around 1300, Europe was marginally warmer than in modern times. Records of harvests often document a huge abundance of crops; Britain had vineyards (thanks to the Romans), and olive and fig trees grew well north of their current natural limits. In the Alps, the treeline was perhaps 200 metres higher than it is today, and Norse burials in Greenland are evidence of a thriving trading outpost. (Indeed, their very presence also shows that the ground was sufficiently unfrozen to receive bodies.)[1] But in the fourteenth century a cooling began. Britain's vineyards withered, the Norse left Greenland and things did not grow as they had previously.

In around 1570, an abrupt second onset – really what you'd think of as the 'core' Little Ice Age – arrived, bringing 'A strange and wondrous succession of changes in the weather', as an archivist in Lucerne, Switzerland, wrote in 1614.

This had its effect on the collective imagination – 'Europe where the sun dares scarce appear / For freezing meteors and congealed cold,' wrote Christopher Marlowe in *Tamburlaine* around 1587 – but it is also amply attested to in clerical documents recording, for example, reduced crop yields and tithes because of bad growing seasons. With rivers icing up more frequently, it also hit river tolls in the Low Countries, to take another case.

How far average temperatures dropped we do not exactly know. The most enthusiastic estimates have pegged the fall to as much as 2 °C; more recently most now put it at under 1 °C, or even around half that – but the average probably masks large regional variations and more frequent occurrences of extreme weather events. Europe's cold snap was to last until the mid-nineteenth century.

[1] This has been called the Medieval Warm Period or Medieval Climatic Optimum, and it appears confirmed by evidence and data in Europe, though these are either sparse, lacking or indeterminate for many other parts of the world.

The reasons for the cooling during the Little Ice Age remain unclear and disputed, or at least multiple. From around 1645 to 1715 a prolonged period of diminished sunspot activity occurred, known as the Maunder Minimum. This had some effect on global temperatures, but its duration alone clearly exonerates it from being the sole culprit of the Little Ice Age. A more involved theory is that the population decline in the Americas caused by Columbus and other Europeans (imported diseases are estimated to have killed 56 million people), and the attendant mass reforestation as cultivated lands were abandoned, significantly lowered atmospheric $CO_2$ levels.

During the period of the Little Ice Age there was a large amount of volcanic activity, too, and it's true there is often measurably colder or more erratic weather after volcanic eruptions, because ash and tephra ejected into the atmosphere block the sun's rays, sometimes for several years. But as with the sunspots, given their rather specific and relatively short-lived effects, this cannot be the whole story.

The probable major causes of the Little Ice Age were small and normal variations in the earth's orbit and distance from the sun, or changes in the course and strength of the Gulf Stream – tiny shifts in angles and trajectories, the proverbial butterfly's wings beating on the other side of the world, that had big ramifications. But the records of where cooled, by how much and when are partial and incomplete. Data from glaciers, palynology (pollen and growth spores), dendroclimatology (using trees' growth rings to provide clues to climate and atmospheric conditions) and the archaeological record are all proxy measures of temperature, and subject to multifarious and often unknowable local factors.[2] They are lone voices whose polyphonies become intelligible only in hindsight.

One thing everyone can agree on is that it was not a real ice age. Real ice ages are marked by big global temperature shifts lasting

[2] Some evidence puts the coldest sustained period in North America's recent history in the nineteenth century – after European temperatures began to climb – and in Africa and Asia reports are more often of drought.

thousands of years. Temperatures can be lower by tens of degrees, not just decimal points. Whole ecosystems are destroyed and seas and rivers and land are replaced by ice. New lands emerge where once was sea. And real ice ages leave a large impression on the world's great ice sheets. The last real ice age lasted tens of thousands of years, and is starkly documented wherever there is ice old enough in the ice-core record. 'Compared to the changes in the proper ice ages, the so-called Little Ice Age is a very short-lived and puny climate and social perturbation,' wrote one group of researchers in the journal *Astronomy & Geophysics*. In the grand sweep of climate data, then, the stuttering glacial advances of the barely half a millennium of the Little Ice Age are trivial. Call it, at most, an 'anomaly'.

Ice age or not, it had a marked effect on human experience. If crops fail, famine provokes unrest; cold brings uncommon parasites and diseases to which weakened populations have little resistance; when rivers ice up, ships cannot sail, and food and money are not received. Water sources disappear. These are all life-shaping events. In 1626, in southern Germany, a hailstorm followed by arctic temperatures led to the arrest, torture and execution of more than 900 men and women suspected of producing the calamity through witchcraft. At the beginning of his book *Global Crisis: War, Climate Change and Catastrophe in the Seventeenth Century*, Geoffrey Parker presents an impressive collection of testimonies of the Little Ice Age. For example, from an East India Company official in Surat, India, 1631: 'The times are so miserable that never in the memory of man has the like famine and mortality happened.' Or from the diary of Lu Shuyi, in southern China in 1641: 'Jiangnan has never experienced this kind of disaster.' By the 1640s settlers in Massachusetts were expressing surprise at the 'frost so great and continual', and the excess of frozen water in some parts of the world in the 1640s was reflected in droughts in Mexico, Indonesia, Egypt, Senegambia, Niger and Angola. And there was Hans Heberle, writing from Ulm in Germany in 1660: 'It was so harsh a winter that no one could remember another like it ... only after Easter could peasants go to their fields and begin to farm.'

So Samuel Pepys and John Evelyn were only two voices among many describing the impact of the Little Ice Age. But in the cacophony of misery and hardship theirs stand out. Their brief accounts of skating testify to a shift in our engagement with ice. Ice so far in this book has been something formative in our environment, a medium through which the past communicates, or simply a thing that happened around us. Here our relationship to it becomes dynamic and additive.

Given that the Little Ice Age monopolises a good portion of recorded history, it will be the backdrop to a lot of the other events in this book. But in this chapter I want to concentrate on one aspect of it: the carnival, chaos and the birth of icy revelry that accompanied the frozen winters of the period. When Pepys and Evelyn saw ice skating, they saw fun.

\*\*\*

How many firsts do we get in this world, moments when a remarkable thing takes place that we have never seen before? Pepys's words make it clear this was his first encounter with skaters, but they also show that the concept was not new to him. Ice skating had been around for a long time: the first written record in English came from the pen of a monk named William Fitzstephen, a clerk to Thomas Becket in Canterbury in the twelfth century. In his *Life of St Thomas*, written in the 1170s, he notes, on a visit to London:

> When the great marsh that washes the Northern walls of the City is frozen, dense throngs of youths go forth to disport themselves upon the ice. Some, gathering speed by a run, glide sidelong, with feet set well apart, over a vast space of ice. Others make seats of ice like millstones and are dragged along by a number who run before them holding hands. Sometimes they slip owing to the greatness of their speed and fall, every one of them, upon their faces. Others there are, more skilled to sport upon the ice, who fit to their feet the shin bones of beasts, lashing them beneath their ankles, and with iron-shod poles in their hands they strike ever and anon against the ice

and are borne along swift as a bird in flight or a bolt shot from a mangonel [a kind of siege engine or catapult].

We can dig back much further than this. Northern Europeans have been strapping bones to their feet to glide quickly over the frozen wastes since around 2000 BCE, simply as a form of fast and efficient transport. Archaeological finds across the Nordics and Russia point to the possibility of ice skating emerging in multiple different locations around the same time, though one study in 2008 named Finland as ice skating's probable country of origin. The authors, Federico Formenti and Alberto E. Minetti, deduced that Finland's flat topography and extensive network of long, thin lakes – in winter, the highest concentration of natural skateable ice in the world – meant that the Finnish would have gained the greatest economy of movement by developing bone skates. But this remains only conjecture: another theory holds that ice skating was invented some time during the second millennium BCE in the steppe zone stretching from the northern Pontic area towards the Hungarian plain. A 2007 study estimated that ancient bones may have been only 25 per cent as efficient as modern skates, but also finds they 'were probably the first human powered locomotion tools to take maximum advantage of the biomechanical properties of the muscular system'.

Antique bone skates were somewhat shaped for the purpose, with protrusions cut off, and a flattened surface to stand on. Many had holes drilled fore and aft for leather thongs to attach them to one's shoes. And bone was a natural choice of blade material. 'The oily external surface of the animal bones makes a natural wax which limits resistance to motion,' Formenti told *National Geographic News*, after testing replica bone skates on an ice rink in Italy. The long metapodial, metatarsal or radial bones of cows or horses – which in humans would be hand or foot bones – were ideal for making the blades. Poles were used, however, as the shape of the bones did not aid forward movement, as do modern skates.

But why do ice skates skate? For a long while it was thought that the glide was produced by the pressure of the blade turning a small amount of surface ice into lubricating water. However, it was soon discovered that this pressure was nowhere near sufficient and another theory was put forward: friction between the blade and the ice heated and melted it, enabling the glide. The idea that friction can cause slipperiness is satisfactorily counterintuitive, and no more than I would expect from such a confounding substance. And it is true – but it is not the whole story. Now it is believed that a very thin layer of molecules at the ice's surface has fewer bonds between molecules (only two or three instead of four in the layers beneath it) which lets it move more freely, dynamically producing a liquid-like layer of rolling molecules as the skater passes above.[3] It is this effect, along with the friction, that creates the slide.

In China, by the time of the Song Dynasty (960–1279), ice skating was popular, but as a form of entertainment rather than purely as a mode of travel (ice skating is also known as 'ice frolicking' in Chinese). By the Qing Dynasty (1644–1912), skates had also become a military technology, after Nurhachi (1559–1626), the father of the first Qing emperor, established a skating cadre within his mountain forces. Skating troops would parade each winter: 200 soldiers, selected from a 1,600-strong battalion trained to fight on icy terrain, performed manoeuvres in front of the royal household on skates with either single or double iron blades. There were also up to a thousand speed skaters in competition, a figure-skating exhibition and a giant ice-based game of football with several dozen participants.

The proceedings were memorialised in pictures and words. 'Skaters moved on ice like shooting stars or lightning,' a Qing Dynasty document records.

Qing ice warriors were required to cover huge distances – reportedly up to 350 kilometres daily – on their skates, and then

[3] This is true only for ice that is near-ish 0 °C. When the temperature gets very cold, the molecules seem to bond more tightly, or behave differently, and the sliding stops – as any polar explorer might tell you. See for example Captain Scott's diary for Saturday 3 March 1912: 'The surface, lately a very good hard one, is coated with a layer of woolly crystals . . . [that] cause impossible friction to the runners. God help us, we can't keep up this pulling, that is certain.'

be capable of fighting. However, it is not the Chinese but the Dutch who are credited with inventing the metal skate blade in the 1500s and who refined it to a recognisably modern shape. The Dutch made skating a popular form of mass entertainment, and also immortalised it in art.

*Lidwina's fall on the ice.*

The earliest known icescape in Dutch art, a woodcut known as *Lidwina's Fall on the Ice*, from 1498, is also the first known representation of ice skating. Lidwina was born in Schiedam, just west of Rotterdam, in 1380. When she was fifteen she collided with someone while skating on the frozen river, and fell and broke a rib. From that point on, according to the story of her canonisation, she became progressively more unwell, began a continual fast, became paralysed and sloughed off skin and body parts, which her parents kept in a vase – all sorts of normal things that happen to medieval would-be saints. Miracles began to happen at her bedside and she became a healer and holy woman, and lived to the age of fifty-three. Lidwina of Schiedam is now the patron saint of ice skaters.

In the woodcut, Lidwina is portrayed prone on the ice, her left foot in its still-bladed boot protruding at an awkward angle. She is being cradled by two women and another is coming across the ice to her aid. In all probability intentionally, her swoon imitates that of Mary in *The Descent of Christ from the Cross* by Roger van der Weyden from around 1435. It is unsurprising that the first known representation of ice skating appears in a religious picture – not because ice skating has any particular link to the holy but because Western art until the mid-sixteenth century was dominated by religious themes, with portraiture and classical and allegorical subjects trailing behind. Winter was simply not considered as a thing in itself. Neither were the lives of peasants, nor the landscapes in which they existed.

Pieter Bruegel the Elder (b. 1525–30, Breda?, d. 1569) almost singlehandedly changed this – 'shedding the vestiges of traditional limitations, concentrating exclusively on the everyday aspects of winter activity and winter scenery', according to eminent critic Wolfgang Stechow. Bruegel, in a sense, invented winter. It is as if, before paintings like *Hunters in the Snow* and *Winter Landscape with Ice Skaters and Bird Trap*, winter was not notable or worth painting, and in them he is showing us the season for the first time. These famous works were both painted in 1565, after the hardest winter for more than fifty years, one of the first of the deepening trough of the Little Ice Age's second coming.[4]

*Hunters in the Snow* was originally part of a 'Labours of the Months' cycle, an artistic tradition dating to medieval times that presented a sequence of pictures depicting each season's occupations. However, the particular subject of *Hunters in the Snow* was novel: in the foreground there is hardship, in the form of the eponymous hunters trudging through the snow, heads lowered, their dogs thin and hungry. They are returning only with the dejected corpse of a fox. In the river below them (and

---

[4] Bruegel's *Census at Bethlehem*, one of the first wintry depictions of the Nativity story, was painted the following year.

below decidedly un-Low Countries mountain peaks), a water wheel is frozen stiff. The skies are, to borrow from Walter de la Mare's poem 'Brueghel's Winter',⁵ 'ice-green'. Perhaps it is the solstice, the still point of the turning world, but everything is tending towards inertia; it is difficult to believe that life will renew. If Bruegel does have a secular impulse, it's because God has forsaken the world, or so it feels here. De la Mare again:

But flame, nor ice, nor piercing rock,
Nor silence, as of a frozen sea,
Nor that slant inward infinite line
Of signboard, bird, and hill, and tree,
Give more than subtle hint of him
Who squandered here life's mystery.

But not everyone is despairing in the cold. There is a cheering element in the middle distance where, under the ice-green firmament, tiny figures play ice hockey and curling on a frozen lake; three small children chase a larger boy across the ice, and a man tows a woman in a red dress. Small anecdotal details of leisure and play, painted with familiarity and affection. In *Winter Landscape with Ice Skaters and Bird Trap*, the scenes of winter fun are more prominent, occupying the centre of the picture.

The contemporary popularity of ice scenes was astounding. There are still at least 127 copies of Bruegel's *Winter Landscape with Bird Trap* extant, which surely must put the total number of originals and copies in the thousands – a blizzard of pictures that would have been commissioned and received by a far smaller population than live in the Low Countries today.

It is more than tempting to see a relationship between the climatic changes of the late sixteenth century and the emergence of the winter landscape in painting. Just as the turn away from religious subjects might be associated with the seismic events in Christian life – the widespread iconoclasm after the Protestant

⁵ Bruegel changed the spelling of his name early in his career and his several sons and grandsons who also painted played with the 'e', 'u' and 'h'.

Reformation – so the weather that was descending on sixteenth-century Europe demanded new forms of representation. Changes in our relationship with the divine, with each other and with the non-human: all fit subjects for art. Bruegel was responding to what was happening around him.

But, for me, that does not completely explain their popularity. Ice scenes would not be so cherished if they were only a record of frozen miseries. Instead, they offered – even for their contemporary original audiences – a reminder of the transformative magic of snow and ice, and a record of the sense of community and the fun that icy pastimes bring.[6]

Heavily indebted to Bruegel is Hendrick Avercamp (c. 1585–1634), who is generally acknowledged as the Dutch Golden Age's master of the ice scene. His first dated pictures came after the extremely hard winter of 1607/8,[7] and his works received popular acclaim in his lifetime. They continue to delight, but they are also an important historical record. The catalogue to the Rijksmuseum's exhibition *Hendrick Avercamp: Master of the Ice Scene* in 2009 states: 'After four hundred years our understanding of the long, hard winters of the Golden Age is still largely shaped by Avercamp's drawings and paintings.'

This is, in part, because of Avercamp's synthesis of landscape – or rather icescape – and the 'world picture' genre. His *Winter Landscape with Ice Skaters* and other similar paintings depicted people from across the Dutch social spectrum arranged in panoplies across frozen rivers and canals, from the rich and noble wrapped in luxurious furs and carried in sleighs to washerwomen breaking holes in the ice, beggars trying to survive the bitter cold and the frozen corpses of horses being devoured by dogs and crows, not to mention, in the background, another reminder

---

[6] Compare Charles Dickens's *A Christmas Carol*. Dickens was born in 1812 and the first eight Christmases of his life were snowy. But by the time he wrote his great Christmas story in 1843 the Little Ice Age was coming to an end and white Christmases were not such a regular occurrence. So *A Christmas Carol* was already nostalgic even to its first readers.

[7] This was the so-called 'Great Frost', the self-same that features in Virginia Woolf's *Orlando*, quoted in the epigraph to this chapter.

of the mortal difficulty of a big freeze, the almost ever-present gallows in the shimmering winter light.[8]

There are bare bottoms. There is lovemaking. There is stink and death and drunkenness and revelry. *'Slibberachtigheyt van 's menschen leven'* is a very pleasing Dutch phrase that translates to 'the slipperiness of human life'. In the seventeenth century, ice scenes and ice skating came to symbolise this precarious chase for joy – the skater in danger of slipping through the ice seen as analogous to the hedonist courting the risk of falling into sin. In Bruegel's and Avercamp's paintings there is plenty of slipping up, both metaphorical and literal, one feels.

To look closely at an Avercamp ice scene is to look at existence enchanted, transformed into a fusion of *Where's Wally?*, *Downton Abbey*, Hieronymus Bosch and *Holiday on Ice*. His people are rendered in lively poses via impossibly fine, deft brushstrokes, while the air around them, suffused with the soft luminosity of the weak winter sun, seems coldly alive too. Avercamp skilfully reproduces ice and snow's effect on light and colour with silvery greys and delicate glows of peach and aquamarine. The ice, usually bare and shining coolly, reflects a not-quite-double of the people upon it. The Rijksmuseum catalogue notes that when Avercamp depicts the tracks of the skaters, he does so by scratching into the wet paint on the canvas.

Avercamp is decidedly not as 'serious' a painter as Bruegel, and nothing like as serious, for example, as Rubens or Rembrandt, but his pictures speak loudly both about his personal situation and about what it feels like to be alive. Avercamp was very likely both deaf and mute, and he lived with his mother all his life; his pictures seem to hint poignantly at both these facts, showing as they do a communal warmth he probably never fully experienced. Was he left out in the cold? If he was an outsider looking on – which is the sense you get from the ice scenes, with their elevated viewpoint and high

[8] Dutch towns at this time enjoyed considerable autonomy, including the right to independent jurisdiction up to and including the death penalty, so he may have just been reflecting what was actually there. But in compositions so carefully assembled and rehearsed on paper beforehand every element seems deliberate. To the modern eye, these memento mori are striking.

horizon – he nevertheless fully celebrated winter's joys, capturing the 'ice fever' that gripped the Netherlands in his time and has done ever since. If Bruegel made winter visible, Avercamp turned it into a performance. Central to that was ice skating. The sense of liberation and amusement in the skaters, seen from afar as they carve out their patterns or rock from foot to foot as they glide casually across the ice, is palpable, something anyone who's ever been on ice skates might recognise.

There is little that is bleak about an Avercamp. Was he able to concentrate on the festive aspects because his success (and, as the son of a pharmacist, his relatively comfortable background) insulated him from the undesirable effects of the big freeze? Somehow his pictures manage to contain the tension between the fierce cold and the festive fun. Or perhaps it is ice itself – an uncertain and paradoxical substance – that holds these polarities in balance. One exact contemporary of Avercamp wrote a couple of lines summing up ice's ambiguous properties:

Of iron shoes in winter time in Holland goes this talk:
On water not like water you walk and do not walk.

In Avercamp's pictures there are also several people playing colf, a game that – risking the ire of the Scottish nation – many Dutch people strongly believe to be the origin of golf.[9] In colf, which simply means 'club', players attempt to hit a small ball, in times past made of elm or beech wood, with an iron- or lead-headed stick, on a long course to an agreed point in the fewest possible strokes. There are of course plenty of other club-and-ball sports that might have been proto-golf, but it is colf that one scholar in particular, Steven J. H. van Hengel, advances.

He dated the first known game to 26 December 1297. Held at Loenen aan de Vecht in the County of Holland, to celebrate the end of a six-month siege of a castle where a suspected murderer had been hiding out, it was subsequently re-run every year for

[9] There were many wayward medieval and early modern spellings – colven, colffven, colven and others – which are commonly standardised to 'colf'.

over 500 years until 1831.[10] The course can be walked to this day and measures around 4.5 kilometres for the four 'holes'. After experimenting with replica early colf-type clubs and balls, Hengel reckoned a good stroke might travel a hundred metres, and par for this course might have been around 60 or 70 – not dissimilar to a modern eighteen holes.

*A colfer, c.1700, in an English pen-and-ink drawing after a Dutch engraving.*

There was nothing in the rules of colf that dictated it be played exclusively on ice; yet most of the well-known paintings and engravings depicting it, which date from the mid-sixteenth

---

[10] This 'first' golf game is disputed. But Hengel did not claim it as an origin story, simply using it as evidence that colf was being played around this time – a long time before golf was in Scotland. We have to pick times and places and call them beginnings, I suppose, and this seems no less likely than an English public schoolboy picking up a football one day and running with it, spontaneously creating the game of rugby.

century onwards, *are* on ice, which may give a false impression. For this, Hengel offers a very player-oriented explanation: in all the Low Countries there was only one public land-based course – in Haarlem – where the grass was mowed and kept short, which consequently meant that colf was impossible to play in the summer (early golf in Scotland was also an autumn and winter game, for the same reason). Ice presented an even better surface: frozen rivers or canals were a convenient alternative to losing your ball in the long grass and having to pack in the fun halfway around the course.

Another thing in ice's favour as a colf surface was that, as the national craze grew, it became a nuisance. Grubby urchins played in alleys, drinkers in taverns, villagers in fields and sailors on docks, blocking streets, injuring people, spreading mud and frightening cows with their wayward clubs and balls. Gambling, also, was epidemic. Countless edicts against colf were handed down by judges from the fourteenth century onwards, trying to ban the sport within city walls. All of this, except the gambling and the potential hazard to innocent bystanders (one would imagine, judging by the crush on the canals in Bruegel's and Avercamp's works), might be averted by playing on a nice wide stretch of ice outside city limits. Colf was a sporting sensation, a passion, and ice was an outlet that let people pursue their passion without fear of offending proprieties or getting into trouble.

Around 1450 colf migrated, probably thanks to Dutch fishermen travelling to towns like St Andrews on Scotland's east coast (Hengel does generously allow that the Scots probably 'invented' the hole). Then around 1700, in the Low Countries, it ceased to exist, seemingly very suddenly. For this Hengel can offer no ready explanation, except to point to the rise of kolf – a similar stick-and-ball game but played between two sticks on a course or court around twenty metres in length. An indoor version of kolf still exists today.

\*\*\*

Before the Little Ice Age, it was not unknown for the Thames in London to freeze. In 1824, the catchily titled and not unambitious

*A Dictionary of Chronology, or the Historian's Companion; being an Authentic Register of Events, from the Earliest Period to the Present Time, Comprehending an Epitome of Universal History, with a Copious List of the most Eminent Men in all Ages of the World* attempted to compile a definitive list of such moments. It records, in 150 CE, the Thames icing up for almost three months, while in 695 CE, according to its author, Thomas Tegg, eyewitnesses spoke of a six-week freeze and booths erected on the ice. In 1086, a great fire destroyed much of London, blamed on wayward home heating as people tried to keep warm during a long hard frost; and in 1205 the London weather was so cold that frozen ale and wine were sawn into chunks and sold by weight. Tegg records that it wasn't only the Thames that was affected by savagely low temperatures. In 359 CE 'the Pontus Sea [off modern-day Turkey] was entirely frozen over for the space of twenty days, and the sea between Constantinople and Scutari'.[11] And in 1207, 'The Mediterranean was frozen over, and the merchants passed with their merchandise in carts.'

With the coming of the Little Ice Age, the freezing frequency increased. Between 1400 and the removal of the medieval London Bridge in 1831 (we'll come back to this later in the chapter), there were more than twenty winters during which the Thames froze over completely. In 1537, King Henry VIII and Jane Seymour rode in a sleigh on the icebound river from Whitehall to Greenwich, and at Christmas in 1564 (the year of *Hunters in the Snow*) Queen Elizabeth I practised archery on the ice. Doubtless there was ice skating too.

In normal, liquid times, the river was at the centre of London's commerce. When it froze, the ice became a trap squeezing the life out of the city and all normal business was replaced by the business of surviving. 'The ploughman's hands are held in his pocket as well as the shopkeeper's,' as *The Great Frost*, an anonymous pamphlet written after the winter of 1607/8, puts it.

---

[11] Many of these far-flung and historically distant 'frosts' listed by Tegg might be treated with a good pinch of salt. But these things really can happen: during the winter of 1620/1, the Bosporus froze hard over, so that it was possible to walk across the ice between Europe and Asia, a phenomenon described by Geoffrey Parker as a 'unique climatic anomaly'.

The short tract introduces two characters, a London 'Citizen' and a 'Countryman' visitor, essentially doing what British people have loved to do since time immemorial: talk about the weather. The former complains about the 'frozen vacation', while the latter bemoans the 'cold doings' of the 'slippery world'.

The ice had set in during the week before Christmas 1607, and it quickly captured the Thames: 'The frost hath made a floor on it, which shows like grey marble roughly hewn out,' says the Citizen. After a while, people – on their enforced frozen vacation – became more daring and began to cross the river upon the 'pavement of glass' (the Citizen again). Watermen, meanwhile, who had traditionally made their living ferrying customers from bank to bank, began to charge at the quays for passage on to the ice; enterprising watermen on the other side would then charge people for the privilege of landing again. By early January 1608, people had taken 'tumultuous possession' of the ice and it had become a football pitch and an archery range. A kind of shanty town came into being in which entertainment, food and drink were bought and sold. On 8 January the famous gentleman of letters John Chamberlain wrote:

> Above Westminster the Thames is quite frozen over and the Archbishop came over from Lambeth on Twelfth Day over the yce to the court. Many fantasticall experiments are dayly put in practise, as certain youths burnt a gallon of wine upon the yce and made all the passengers partakers: but the best is an honest woman (they say) that had a great longing to have her husband get her with child upon the Thames.

And so the trap of the ice became a liberation of sorts.

The Citizen recalled archery, football, drinking and people being shaved upon the Thames. He added: 'It is a place of mastery, where some wrestle and some run; and he that does best is aptest to take a fall. It is an alley to walk upon without dread, albeit under the most assured danger.' This was no longer the London people knew, but a strange, almost magical city containing all the slipperiness of human life. There being no such thing as police, the watermen kept the peace, and polite society mixed with ruffians, faeries and beasts in a midwinter night's dream.

In 1608, the river kept its 'freeze coat' on until February. Then the ice began to break up, and the party did too. Life began to flow more normally again.

The winter of 1607/8 was London's first generally celebrated frost fair. Over the next 200 years, such fairs would become a tradition: whenever the river froze solid for long enough, frost fairs reimagined the city as a fluid, transgressive place – deregulated, impermanent, liberated from normal etiquette and powered by a funfair economy. Order was inverted and everyday rules suspended.[12] *He that does best is aptest to take a fall... Fantasticall experiments... On water not like water you walk and do not walk.*

The next frost fair took place in 1620, and later ones were held in 1683, 1688, 1709, 1715, 1739, 1788 and 1814, each blurring the line between risk and fun, and, in addition to lewder activities, providing a space for debate and intellectual discussion. They were also tremendous – if short-lived – sites of commerce and hustle.

Perhaps the coldest and the greatest was that of 1683/4, when the river 'congealed' up to eighteen inches thick from the beginning of December until 5 February.[13] It was known as the 'blanket fair' because watermen placed drapes over crossed oars to make tents.[14] Boats were used as sledges, hackney carriages gave trips across the ice and traders set up booths and shops. Samuel Pepys skated with Nell Gwynn, the king's mistress, and Charles II himself visited and sampled some of the whole ox roasted on the river. John Evelyn wrote in his diary that there was 'bull-baiting, horse and coach races, puppet plays and interludes,

---

[12] Compare Tom and Jerry in 1939's *Mice Follies*, in which Jerry and Nibbles flood the kitchen and then freeze it using tubes from the icebox, turning it into a skating rink. What follows is a delightful and affectionate ice dance between the two foes, who in the heat of the moment forget their enmity, at least temporarily.

[13] In English 'congealed', as in solidified, was another way of describing the process of freezing all the way through to Francis Bacon's time and beyond. And, to this day, if you buy fish fingers in France you would still be sure to put them in the *congélateur* when you get home.

[14] 'The Watermen for want of Rowing Boats / Make use of Booths to get their Pence and Groats' ran a poem printed in 1714.

cookes, tipling, and other lewd places, so that it seem'd to be a bacchanalian triumph, or carnival on the water, whilst it was a severe judgment on the land'. And an anonymous printed poem declared: 'Folk do tipple without fear to sink / More liquor than the fish beneath do drink.'

Other attractions at the frost fairs over the three centuries they existed included bowling, throwing at cocks (throwing weighted sticks at a tied-up cockerel, until it died), bear fights, sex and 'Dutch Whimsie' – being spun around in a chair or a boat tied to a pole, the antecedent of modern playground roundabouts.

The bawdy rhyming couplet quoted above is hardly Shakespeare, but its very existence is remarkable since, like many other frost fair souvenirs, it was printed on the iced-up Thames itself. Printing presses were star attractions at every frost fair after 1683, doing brisk business and adding to the lively, seditious atmosphere, just as they had at London's coffeehouses.

Coffeehouses, which became popular in London and other English cities in the mid-seventeenth century, had a reputation for intellectual debate: they were 'penny universities' where, sharpened by caffeine instead of dulled by drink, patrons could carry out their business, read the latest radical pamphlets or hear dissenting voices speak. But by the 1680s King Charles II, once the father of the licentious Restoration, was cracking down on this freedom of expression. Like pirate radio stations broadcasting from derelict sea defences, or casino ships moored in international waters, the frozen river was, however provisionally, outside the law. One historian describes them as offering a 'heterogeneous and shifting space' for printed items to circulate.

*Frostiana*, a compendious and beautifully titled book about all things icy, had its frontispiece printed on the river during the 1814 fair. In one memorable passage about the unnatural Little Ice Age winters, it describes how, in 1809:

> a boy in the service of Mr. W. Newman, miller, at Leybourne, near Malling, went into a field, called the Forty Acres, and saw a number of Rooks on the ground, very close together. He made a noise to drive them away, but they did not appear alarmed;

he threw snowballs to make them rise, still they remained. Surprised at this apparent indifference, he went in among, them, and actually picked up twenty-seven Rooks; and also in several parts of the same field, ninety Larks, a Pheasant, and a Buzzard Hawk. The cause of the inactivity of the birds, was a thing of rare occurrence in this climate; a heavy rain fell on the Thursday afternoon, which, freezing as it came down, so completely glazed over the bodies of the birds, that they were fettered in a coat of ice, and completely deprived of the power of motion. Several of the Larks were dead, having perished from the intenseness of the cold. The Buzzard Hawk being strong, struggled hard for his liberty, broke his icy fetters, and effected his escape.

Given its subversive credentials, it's not surprising that the frozen Thames attracted the attention of one of the eighteenth century's sharpest voices, Jonathan Swift. In 1714, with the death of Queen Anne, he had found himself in political trouble and had fled London and sought sanctuary in Dublin (never to return, though he was not to know that). His close Tory allies, the Earl of Oxford and the Viscount Bolingbroke, were either imprisoned in the Tower of London or on the run, accused of (or indeed actually plotting) treason. And in 1716, he published a little-known pamphlet in which the image of the frozen Father Thames during the hard winter of 1715 (which he cannot have actually seen with his own eyes) becomes a metaphor for the malaise he believes is affecting the English and Irish state:

Where gentle Thames in murm'ring Streams did flow
Hills rise of Ice and Mountains stand of Snow
The liquid Rumbler's mild obliging Flood,
Long having run, and ran for England's good,
With Horror rigid stops its Course, and grieves
To feel Rebellion floating on its Waves
Frighted th'ingrateful shocking Weight it bears
Hears Treason's Voice but stagnates as it hears.

Frost fairs of course posed other, more immediate dangers to the people that visited them. One anonymous pamphlet from 1683 tells the story of two women who dress as men so they can skate without chaperones. They are accosted by two ice-skating men dressed as women and are raped. In 1715, an uncommonly high tide lifted the ice fourteen feet, spilling into Thames-side cellars, while the fair carried on above. And in 1739, a particularly deadly year in the records, a daredevil 'flying man' plummeted to his death from high above the frozen River Severn after his tightrope snapped while he was entertaining crowds at the Shrewsbury frost fair – showing that, while some laws could be broken, the law of gravity still had to be observed. That year, too, a storm on the Thames tore boats from their moorings and drove them through the ice, resulting in many deaths. Also during the fair a famous itinerant hot-apple pedlar named Doll fell through the ice, and her fate was recounted in a contemporary poem:

> The cracking crystal yields: she sinks, she dies –
> Her head chopt from her lost shoulders flies;
> Pippins she cried, but death her voice confounds,
> And pip, pip, pip, along the ice resounds

Later at that same fair, a whole section of the Thames ice collapsed, taking stalls and people with it.[15] Then in 1788 a frozen-in ship that had been anchored to a Rotherhithe pub shifted in the night, pulling loose a beam and levelling the house, killing five sleeping people.

Eighteen-fourteen was London's last frost fair and, in hindsight, it has the feeling of a last hurrah. After the river had frozen, festivities began between London and Blackfriars Bridges on Tuesday 1 February. Printing presses were again rolled out and an elephant was marched upon the ice. On Saturday morning came the first signs of a thaw, which spurred the presses into working double time – at least one of them in service of the river itself, which had a letter to write:

---

[15] 1739 does seem to have been an especially savage year. A painting by Jan Griffier the Younger of the frost fair seen from on high has tiny people clambering over giant pile-ups of ice, looking for all the world like angry storm clouds as seen from an aeroplane above.

To Madame Tabitha Thaw

Dear dissolving dame,

Father Frost and Sister Snow have Boneyed my borders, formed an idol of ice upon my bosom, and all the Lads of London come to make merry: now, as you love mischief, treat the multitude with a few cracks by a sudden visit, and obtain the prayers of the poor upon both banks.

Given at my own press, the 5th Feb. 1814,

Thomas Thames

By Sunday morning, most people had packed up and cleared off, but some revellers were reluctant to let the party end. Some sources mention several drunken people being dunked as their tent got carried away on loose ice and was dashed against the bridge; another reports that above Westminster Bridge two men were standing upon ice that became detached in the flood tide and, in waving to get help, they overbalanced the floe and were drowned.

Why no more London frost fairs after 1814? Undoubtedly by the mid-nineteenth century the climate was changing, but perhaps the main reason was London Bridge itself. The medieval bridge, erected in 1209, had nineteen arches within its span (the current bridge has three) and large protective starlings at the foot of each, which slowed the water in shallows above the bridge and in places created a weir-like flow – all of which made the river more likely to freeze. Then, when ice formed, the small arches would trap ice floes carried by the lazy current, further encouraging a total freezing over. In 1831, the dismantling of the medieval bridge began and this, along with the creation of engineered stone embankments (Victoria Embankment was completed in 1870), eased Thomas Thames's passage and meant that the river has never frozen solid here since.

The frost-fair era of danger and fun, of throwing at cocks and of haircuts, roasting oxen and seditious pamphlets on the ice, all the slipperiness of human life, was over.

# 4

# The Buccaneers

## *Adventure capitalism and Sir Humphrey Gilbert*

*Everything begins in mysticism and ends in politics*
Charles Péguy, 'Ève' (1913)

*All that glisters is not gold*
William Shakespeare, *The Merchant of Venice* (1600)

*What a glorious failure! What a victory!*
Hillel Samson, *Sir Humphrey Gilbert: A Record and a Surmise* (1921)

In early 1597 William Barentsz, a Dutch explorer, took part in probably the most northerly game of colf ever played. With a shipful of men he had become trapped in the sea ice somewhere in the archipelago of Novaya Zemlya in the Russian Arctic and been forced to overwinter. One April morning, having not much else on, the mariners left their self-built hut (polar bears had made a lair of the icebound ruins of the ship) and took to the ice where, according to the diary of Gerrit de Veer, one of Barentsz's officers, 'we made a staffe to plaie at colfe, thereby to stretch our jointes, which we sought by all the meanes we could to doe.' Actually, they were pretty busy, shooting Arctic foxes for their meat and

fur, avoiding said polar bears and doing exercises to keep warm –
all the busyness of keeping alive – but colf formed part of this
latter regime to keep the blood moving.

Aside from the colf, in this episode Barentsz (from whom the
Barents Sea takes its name) was playing his part in a new chapter
in the history of ice, a chapter that had flourished in the century
before his voyage. This was the search for a northern sailing route
to the Orient, which seemed to promise to whomsoever could find
and control it a competitive advantage in the race to trade with
the nations of the Far East. The pursuit of this wealth became an
obsessive quest, both for the brave and foolhardy sailors and for
the nations they represented, a stubborn and destructive fixation
that extended into the Arctic the political and economic battles
between the western European powers. In time it would almost
seem that besting the ice had replaced the riches of the Orient
as the goal. The obsession would last, on and off, for almost
500 years, and still we live with it today.

Yet what riches from this endeavour did arise? None – or, at
least, none in the fashion that the sailors and their paymasters
envisaged. Chasing an illusion of fantastic wealth, they hit a
solid wall of ice. Ice, in volumes previously unseen and even
unimaginable, became a formidable obstacle to these dreams
of conquest. Ice blinded them to reality: the harder and more
unpleasant it got – the more the ice menaced their hopes – the
more the sailors believed that success was just around the corner.
The tenacity of the delusion – or, put another way, the strength
of the adventuring spirit – is startling. However, these repeated
confrontations with the impenetrable northern ice, and the
inability to find a northern sailing passage, might, in this nascent
period of European colonial expansion, have diverted some
explorers on to new and profitable paths.

To explain how Barentsz came to be enjoying his Arctic colf,
we need to go back a few hundred years. Since Marco Polo's
voyages over land to Cathay (China) in the thirteenth century, the
spices and all the other treasures the Orient seemed to promise
had been tempting Europeans to look east. But the trade routes
known as the Silk Roads were a long and complicated daisy chain

along which only tantalisingly small amounts arrived; then, in 1453, Byzantine Constantinople fell to the Ottoman Empire, disrupting this flow of goods. This spurred concerted maritime campaigns among many European nations to find a seagoing option. Their goals were principally India, China, Japan and the Moluccas, also known then as the Spice Islands (and now as the Maluku Islands, part of Indonesia); a direct sailing route would permit cargo in larger amounts, and allow foreign powers greater control of the trade.

It was only in 1498, when the Portuguese Vasco de Gama rounded the Cape of Good Hope and reached India, that the existence of a sea route south of Africa from the Atlantic into the Pacific was confirmed. But this was a long, slow and dangerous passage. What if there was a way of getting there faster? Time is money, after all, and money is, well, money.[1] Why not try going the other way?

Instead of heading south and east, some went west and north.

West, because sailing west to get east was an almost magical idea that was very much in vogue. It had, in 1492, seemed to meet with great success when Christopher Columbus left Spain and arrived at the island of Guanahaní (which he renamed 'San Salvador') in the Bahamas. He had been in search of a shortcut to the Orient across the South Atlantic, and was so convinced that he had succeeded that he named its inhabitants 'Indians'. Ignorant of his flawed geopositioning, others believed it too.

North, because a northern route was more direct from northern Europe, and less hot, and because the northern Atlantic had the advantage of containing fewer Spaniards. Once pointed north, sailors were faced with a choice: some of them turned their ships back east, heading around Norway and above Russia searching for navigable waters: a north-east passage. This was what Barentsz was hoping to find, but, as he proved several times during the 1590s, the seas above Russia all too easily turned into

---

[1] Here I would refer the reader to David Mamet's satire on capitalism *Heist* (2001), in which Danny DeVito's character, the fence Mickey Bergman, says: 'Everybody needs money: that's why they call it *money*.' My unscientific thesis is that this lucre-as-the-be-all-and-end-all attitude can be traced back half a millennium to this time of nascent venture – why not call it 'adventure'? – capitalism.

a colf course. Others bet their reputations, their fortunes and their lives on a *north-west* passage, which surely would, it was presumed, offer a way through to Japan, China and India above what we now know as North America.

Which route – north-west or north-east – was more likely to lead to the untold riches these sailors so fervently desired? The merits of either lay completely in the realm of conjecture. Information on the far north was scant. There was a well-known and pioneering voyage by Pytheas, a Phocean from Marseille, who around 325 BCE sailed north and found 'Thule',[2] and provided the earliest descriptions of a frozen sea. The water was, he wrote, 'curdled', and he also witnessed something he described as 'sea lungs' – possibly describing the movement of ice as it rises and falls on the surface of the water. But after that there were very few known antecedents: the Vikings, of course, are now celebrated for sailing through northern seas in open-decked boats, and for having outposts on Greenland and in North America as early as the eleventh century; but their sagas were not widely known. Pytheas, wrote Fridtjof Nansen, a much later polar explorer, set 'his mark more or less upon all that was known of the farthest north for the next thousand or fifteen hundred years'. So when seafarers like Barentsz pointed their ships towards the top of the world, they were doing so more in hope than with sound judgement. Perhaps the very fact that there was no solid information fuelled the northern obsession: the icy wastes spoke of possibility, opportunity, hope.

One of the pioneers in the northern quest was a man called Sebastian Cabot, a Venetian seafarer born in the mid-1470s who spent much of his life in the service of foreign powers, including England, where it seems he was living in 1492: 'newes were brought that Don Christopher Columbus Genovese had discovered the coasts of India, whereof was great talk in all the Court of King Henry VII,' Cabot said later in life. 'All men

---

[2] Pytheas in all probability reached northern Norway, not far off the Arctic Circle. For later explorers Thule would become the mythical source of all the cold in the world.

with great admiration affirmed it to be a thing more divine than humane, to sail by the West into the East where spices grow.' Only five years after Columbus had seemingly proven magic possible, Sebastian Cabot in all probability sailed on the first recorded voyage in search of a northern-western spice route under the captainship of his father, John Cabot. Rather than reaching the known countries of the East, they rather came across 'new found lande' – becoming, as far as we know, the first Europeans to reach the American continent since the Vikings.[3]

The following year, Cabot senior quested for the north-west passage once again (again possibly accompanied by his son), but no evidence exists of where he got to, and it is presumed he was lost at sea and swallowed by the briny deep. Ten years later Sebastian Cabot launched his own attempt. As he travelled north he encountered 'monstrous heapes of ice swimming on the sea, and in maner continuall day light, yet saw he the lande in that tract free from ice, which had been molten by the heat of the Sunne'.

In this short description there are several remarkable things: first, the ice itself, existing in quantities previously undreamed of and – *swimming* on the sea like a whale – wholly unlike the water that surrounds it. Second, the continual daylight, something which the sailors had been apprised of by Pytheas, yet still fantastical in itself. And then the ice-free land beyond, a shining illusion that might keep alive one's hopes of an easy passage. It was a common misconception that in the furthest north the midnight sun would melt all the ice: even into the nineteenth century many believed that beyond a fortifying ring of icebergs there was an Open Polar Sea, a giant polynya[4] that, once reached, would make further progress simple.

---

[3] Newfoundland, while still an island, was closer than Columbus got: in 1492 the Genovese sailed no further than the Caribbean, visiting the Bahamas, Cuba and Hispaniola. Only on his third voyage, beginning in 1498, did he touch the mainland, in what is now Venezuela.
[4] An elegant borrowed Russian word that denotes a large patch of open water completely surrounded by ice. Polynyas do exist, although on nothing like the scale of the imaginary Open Polar Sea.

On this voyage, Sebastian turned back and, unlike his father, survived to bring tales of the ice back to Europe. The descriptions must have been scarcely believable, otherworldly, tantalising: so little was known of the icy north, and the chances to visit so rare, that it seems less, in this era, like a real place and more an image that operated on the mind. The very few that did see the sights with their own eyes sold this image to the non-seafaring, who in turn financed the expeditions that might open up the hoped-for passage. This fixation of spirit thus had a great effect not only on sailors like Cabot, but on the lives and fortunes of nations thousands of kilometres away from the ice, the majority of whose people would never, ever visit the extreme north. The icy blanks at the top of the world became a repository to be filled with all our hearts' desires.

Unfortunately, these tempting visions collided with the hard reality of ice. The trouble with the north-east and north-west passages, these desperately desired shortcuts, was that, as much as everybody wanted them to be, they were not there. They existed only in the imagination.

Nevertheless, the false premise at the base of every voyage – that a breakthrough was possible, even imminent – remained unexamined, in the face of mounting evidence to the contrary. Why? Centuries before, a perspicacious anonymous writer in Old Norse wrote this summation: 'The answer to your query as to what people go to seek in [Greenland] and why they fare thither through such great perils is to be sought in man's threefold nature. One motive is fame and rivalry . . . A second motive is curiosity . . . The third is desire for gain; for men seek wealth wherever they have heard that gain is to be gotten, though, on the other hand, there may be great dangers too.'

These vainglorious and nakedly capitalist impulses – which ring loudly across the centuries – would lead European sailors into a centuries-long collision process of reconciling desire with reality. Their goal, the ice-choked north-west passage, is a prize we are still striving for today.

***

If the far north was an imagining or at best a paper-thin construct, one of the places in which it took life most tangibly was in a book called the *Principal Navigations, Voyages and Discoveries of the English Nation*, by Richard Hakluyt, the younger of two cousins of that name, which was published in 1589 and much expanded upon afterwards. The 1812 edition I ordered at the British Library came in five leather-bound folio volumes in sturdy cases, each one almost too heavy to pick up. For several days, after the librarians had huffed and puffed them on to a trolley, I would trundle them to a desk and read through these early accounts of seafaring, often in the translation provided from the original Latin, and wonder at, given how little they had to go on, how ready these men had been to set sail.

After Hakluyt I looked at maps of the period. Maps, in this golden age of mapmaking, were a key tool in the global merchant's arsenal for two reasons. First, and most obviously, maps facilitated global trade: the better charted the journey to the faraway lands one wanted to trade with (or to claim one owned), the safer and surer the voyage would be. As also, more importantly, would be the expected return laden down with riches. Second, maps were a way of visualising value. Maps acted as proof that the goose laying the golden eggs on the other side of the world really existed. They were beautiful boasts, prime examples of ego massaging: my colonies are more bountiful than yours, my ships faster and my patronage more able to attract the most skilled craftsmen.[5] Later, Sebastian Cabot would be employed by King Henry VIII as a cartographer.

Hakluyt and the maps were as interesting for how they charted the borders of knowledge as they were for their stories and geographical features: they proved how little these adventuresome sailors knew. Almost everything they 'knew', including the north-east and north-west passages themselves,

---

[5] This created a curious tension, in that half the point of accruing riches was to display them, but intelligence about sailing routes and colonies was highly sensitive. Trade secrets, I suppose. In the mid-sixteenth century it was Spanish government policy not to publish maps delineating the country's possessions.

was in fact hypothetical. How much there seemed to be that one could write – five folio volumes! – about things one did not know. And how much one could draw! Even the era's best maps contained giant lacunae in the knowledge of trade routes, countries, oceans, the globe itself, gaps that cartographers like Cabot would fill with dragons, gods and sea creatures, as well as with numerous ignorant and unflattering depictions of people from other parts of the world: dog-faced men with the feet of ostriches, pigheaded men and giants with flapping ears. The illustrations were the product of the innate human inability to leave a blank space, evident both in the colonial impulse and in the cartographer's craft.

Like William Windham's account of the glacier above Chamonix, they took me to the edge of what could be described, to where ice – a physical limit, ambition's rebuff – forced ships to turn back, ensured that maps remained blank.

It's telling that one sixteenth-century expedition into the north-west passage named a newly found peninsula 'Meta Incognita'. Not quite *terra incognita* nor yet *mare incognitum*, the name suggests there might be anything there. The ice world belonged to a different category, was outside the natural order of things.[6] Yet the actors within Hakluyt's pages always seemed to face this unknowability with a certain attitude. Call it courage or gumption or daring, foolhardiness or ignorance masked by overweening hubris.

Without a doubt the era's most important mapmaker was the Fleming Gerardus Mercator. His revolutionary map of 1569 flattened the earth by straightening out the lines of longitude that otherwise would naturally converge at the poles. This unconventional unpeeling meant that, for the first time, a compass bearing remained constant whether it was taken from a real-world

---

[6] In the sixteenth and even seventeenth centuries, even less was known about the polar south. A 1690 polar projection by the Dutch mapmakers Hondius and Janssonius shows a total blank covered merely by the words *'Terra Australis Incognita'* – 'unknown southern lands'. James Cook was the first to circumnavigate the Southern Pole during his second voyage between 1772 and 1775. But he was repelled by ice before finding solid ground. The charts of his voyage replace *'Terra Incognita'* with 'The Ice Sea'.

location or a two-dimensional map. While good for navigators, the flaw in this was that, by straightening the converging lines of latitude, countries and seas, though conformal (the right shape), were distorted in size. The further they lay from the equator, the bigger they now appeared.

In the Mercator projection, the Arctic is stretched, unrealistically wide at its southern extremes, and as you travel further north increasingly, incredibly so. This was a problem that Mercator recognised: 'The chart cannot be extended as far as the pole, for the degrees of latitude would finally attain infinity,' he wrote, on a legend to one of his maps.[7]

Mercator's North Pole was therefore an unattainable space, a fantasy realm – like the northern passages themselves. But in depicting the ice this way he accurately, if unwittingly, represented the prominence of the region in the contemporary psyche, and sketched a map of how the North Pole and the north-west passage had disproportionately obsessed navigators and adventurers before him, and would for centuries to come.

***

When King Henry VIII acceded to the throne in 1509, he proved himself less interested in the New World than his father, preferring instead to spend his time marrying and provoking religious schisms. Fewer English expeditions set sail and other nations took the lead. Jacques Cartier, a French mariner, made several expeditions north in the 1530s and 1540s, succeeding in mapping the Canadian coastline and exploring the area around what is now Québec City. The Spaniard Francisco de Ulloa also tried for the north-west passage, but from the Pacific rather than the Atlantic. He sailed from Spanish-held Acapulco in Mexico up the Gulf of California, but he did not leave temperate waters,

---

[7] To show that he did not truly believe that the poles were infinite, a small circular map of the Arctic viewed from above the pole – the first such thing – was inset into the 1569 map's corner. It showed four countries around an open polar sea, and a giant magnetic rock at the centre. By 1606 he had improved upon it and indeed coloured it in, but given that the 1606 map still refers to four-foot-tall polar pygmies, it was still basically nonsense.

let alone prove that a hypothetical 'Strait of Anián' existed to connect west and east through the 'frostie zone'.[8]

Sebastian Cabot had left for Spain in 1512, but in 1521 returned to England to mount another exploratory voyage north. This had the support of the king and of Cardinal Wolsey, but never managed to weigh anchor. One difficulty was that these expeditions were incredibly expensive, relying on a combination of royal permission and patronage along with significant private backing to get off the ground. But London's merchants had as yet seen no return on their investments in earlier expeditions and were beginning to realise that such big financial speculations were best shared.

In 1551, Cabot became the co-founder, and first governor, of the 'Mystery, Company, and Fellowship of Merchant Adventurers for the Discovery of Unknown Lands etc.', which was England's first major joint-stock company.

A joint-stock company was a chartered organisation that allowed shares to be sold to raise capital for large and risky ventures such as transatlantic exploring – a forerunner, in other words, of modern corporations. That the word 'adventurer' here was synonymous with 'investor' – someone who *ventures* capital – should make clear the company's mercenary aims. The Company of Merchant Adventurers anticipated the East India Company, founded in 1600 to drive British colonial endeavours in the east, and the Virginia Company, founded in 1606 to colonise North America. Thus the beginnings of speculative imperial capitalism are intimately bound into the expeditions into the ice.

The year 1553 saw the Company of Merchant Adventurers' first investor-backed voyage seeking a north-east passage to the Orient. Organised by Cabot and commanded by the Company's other two founders, Richard Chancellor and Sir Hugh Willoughby, it was both a great success and a terrible failure. Chief pilot Chancellor quickly became separated from the other

[8] What we now call the Bering Strait is thousands of kilometres north and its existence was not confirmed until 1728.

two ships in a North Sea squall, and, after waiting for a week at a rendezvous agreed upon for just such an eventuality, gave up hope of rejoining his captain-general, Sir Hugh.

Under the command of Willoughby, who was a less experienced sailor, the *Bona Esperanza* and the *Bona Confidentia* sailed to Nova Zembla, then, in awful conditions, began to retrace a route back towards home. Somewhere off the Kola Peninsula, the location of present-day Murmansk, they became icebound. After winter had passed, they were chanced upon by Russian fishermen, who discovered the crews frozen in various postures in their quarters and the mess. When they broke into Willoughby's cabin they found him, frozen, sitting upright, alone.

It must have been a terrible end: 'it is ascertained he was still alive at the end of January 1554,' wrote one nineteenth-century source. 'Probably before his decease he was even several times rejoiced by the sight of the sun at midday; but what a scene of horror it shone upon! Two frozen-up vessels full of stiffened corpses, and only partly discernible through the snow which had drifted over them.'

I do not know how much William Barentsz, forty-three years later, knew of the demise of Willoughby and his men, but his fateful voyage prospecting for the passage in 1596, when he in turn became icebound, was his third in as many years, so he had a good idea of what he was getting himself into. He persevered – survived – longer than any previous voyager, and with his men proved that it was possible to live through a Nova Zembla winter by colfing and other pursuits. While they sheltered in the hut they'd named *Het Behouden Huys* (the 'Saved House'), only the cabin boy died. However, in June 1597, with no sign of the ice relinquishing the ship, the scurvy-ridden men made their escape in open boats. Barentsz died at sea, but twelve of the sixteen original crew survived.[9]

9 As for the plight of Willoughby and his men, the latest theory is that, since flora and fauna were relatively plentiful, they might have been OK if they hadn't battened down the hatches and blocked the stove flues to say warm – as a result consigning themselves to death by carbon-monoxide poisoning from the sea coal they were burning.

Back in 1553 with the Company of Merchant Adventurers, Chancellor endured an easier and luckier fate than Willoughby – this time. He steered his vessel into the White Sea above Russia, where he docked at Kholmogory, travelled by horse-drawn sleigh to Moscow and was received at the court of Ivan the Terrible. Thanks to him, the Company, while very far from getting to India, was able to begin importing Russian furs and other goods, and to search for an overland route to Persia. When the Company finally received its charter in 1555, it was rechristened the Muscovy Company – a name that recognised this significant achievement, and also formally acknowledged the corresponding failure to break through the barricade of ice.

The celebrated Arctic naturalist Barry Lopez nicely sums up these early attempts at the Arctic passages: exploration was, he wrote, 'an arrangement between bankers and dreamers, carried out by tough, sagacious pilots and resourceful crews'. When you look at the tiny spaces they carved out and inhabited, between success and failure, life and death, I think 'dreamer' – both in the sense of wishing for great things and also being disconnected from reality – is apt. Further than that, their situation, the balance of the decisions they made in a world fringed by the white unknown, is impossible to comprehend. The trident prongs of ambition, financial gain and fear that drove men like Willoughby and Chancellor on are irrecoverable, too vulnerable to anachronism. Chancellor, unlike the gentleman adventurer Willoughby, was a professional mariner. Yet still he was lost at sea in 1556, on the way home from Russia for the second time, another early victim of this impulse to go forth and trade.

*\*\**

Sir Humphrey Gilbert is almost the last significant name I want to mention in this period of early ice exploration. His is a curious case because he probably did more than anyone of his age to ensure the enduring appeal of the search for the north-west passage; but, despite his fervour, once he had set sail for the icy north his attention was diverted. Gilbert, born probably in 1537 or 1539 into a long-established Norman family in Devon, was the half-brother of Sir Walter Raleigh, though fourteen years his senior. At around the age of sixteen Gilbert was introduced into the court of the young Princess Elizabeth; from this time on, after she became queen in 1558 and beyond, he would serve her interests as devotedly as he did his own.

The corpus of writing on Gilbert's life dates from the early twentieth century, a time when a biography's subtitle could be 'England's First Empire Builder' and this still be thought an unabashedly good thing. But Gilbert, like empire building, was not as straightforward as that. Another, more honest subtitle was 'Elizabeth's Racketeer'.

Even in his day, he was a controversial figure: as member of Parliament for Plymouth in 1571 he was rebuked in a debate for being 'a flatterer, a lyer, and a naughtie man'. And although he styled himself an adventurer, tales of misadventure – getting lost in the fog off Land's End and the like – abound. For a long time he remained, as the editor of his writings points out, a 'dry-land sailor'; another historian called him an 'armchair sailor'.[10] In all his doings his heraldic motto, *Quid Non* ('Why not' – no question mark needed), and his famous sign-off, *Multare vel Timere Spurno* ('I scorn to change or to fear'), seem apposite.

Gilbert's obsession with the north-west passage probably began at Havre de Grâce in France, where he led his queen's soldiers covertly in support of the Huguenots in 1562. There he may have met some French geographers and certainly was around people with business interests in the Caribbean, any of whom might have sparked his interest. In 1566, 'in the loytering vacation between military stratagemes', an acquaintance, the soldier–poet George Gascoigne, went to see him at home, in Lime House just outside London, and was presented with a pamphlet – one that would form the basis of Gilbert's *A New Passage to Cataia* [Cathay] that was eventually published in 1576.

---

[10] This, while possibly anachronistic, was not meant entirely unkindly. Part of the point was that the state of English knowledge of navigation and geography was generally lamentable, and far behind the Spanish and Portuguese, and so being a scholar of such things, however prone to mishap, was not such a bad start.

This was a long and reasoned treatise advocating for exploration in the north, the first such tract ever written. In the published version he argued against a north-east passage on the grounds that 'the pearcing colde of the grose thick ayre so neere the Pole, will so stiffen and furre the sayles, and ship tackling, that no Mariner can either hoise or strike them.' The accompanying map cunningly showed no gap above Russia to the east; to the west, however, it advertised clear water above a severely truncated North America that conveniently led straight to Japan. Other arguments marshalled included the density of the mists in the north-east and something abstruse about unicorn horns.

But, as a dry-land sailor, what could he have known? Again the northern ice was a blank white screen on which to project whatever one chose.[11] There was some solid reasoning, based on the latest maps and theories, but, as so often, in the *Discourse* knowledge about the north and speculation were one and the same thing.

Speculation: above all, this is what Gilbert wanted to do. He petitioned the queen in 1566 to be allowed to mount a northern voyage, for which endeavour he desired she assign him the right to trade through the passage for forty years, paying nominal customs. He also asked for one-tenth part of all the lands discovered, which he undertook to hold in her name, and also that he should be governor for life of all these territories. Not a big ask, then. It's likely that the queen fobbed him off, guessing

---

[11] Compare this to Lewis Carroll's *The Hunting of the Snark* from 1876:

> He had bought a large map representing the sea,
> Without the least vestige of land:
> And the crew were much pleased when they found it to be
> A map they could all understand.

> 'What's the good of Mercator's North Poles and Equators,
> Tropics, Zones, and Meridian Lines?'
> So the Bellman would cry: and the crew would reply
> 'They are merely conventional signs!'

> 'Other maps are such shapes, with their islands and capes!
> But we've got our brave Captain to thank'
> (So the crew would protest) 'that he's bought us the best –
> A perfect and absolute blank!'

that the Muscovy Company would object on the grounds that it already held a charter to exploit these routes. (It did, and it did.)

Instead of northwards, she sent him to wage a colonial war in Ireland, where, even by the standards of the time, Gilbert proved himself a sadistic and bloodthirsty warrior. The Irish, while ferocious, were out-organised and technologically outclassed, and Gilbert's viciousness matched the English superiority: if a castle did not yield straight away, he would kill every person in it; Irish lords who came to surrender were made to walk to his tent between two lines of heads severed from their countrymen, women and children. The campaign set a precedent in its attitudes to foreign conquest, if not in its specific barbarous techniques, that Gilbert and others would replicate elsewhere. For these atrocities and other sordid assignments, Gilbert was knighted in 1570.

In Ireland, Gilbert met Martin Frobisher, a Yorkshireman who possessed an innate talent for seafaring, and it was probably Gilbert and his *Discourse* that inspired Frobisher to take up the cause of the north-west passage.[12] Finally, in May 1576, with the backing of the Muscovy Company, which had swung its favour from east to west, Frobisher sailed 'Northwest, for the search of the straight or passage to China', and probably penetrated further north in Canadian waters than anyone previously. During the voyage he 'found' and named Frobisher Bay, where his shipmaster reported 'great iland[s] of yce'. The ship returned safe and sound laden with animal skins, an Inuit they had kidnapped and a large piece of black rock, which was pronounced by an alchemist – in defiance of several London goldsmiths – to contain gold.[13]

This was motivation enough to finance another voyage: in 1577 Frobisher again reached Frobisher Bay, this time seeing 'many

[12] Another story is that, many years earlier, Frobisher may have met a Portuguese mariner who claimed to have sailed the passage, while both were languishing in a Lisbon gaol – Frobisher had been privateering off the coast of Guinea.

[13] It was this 1576 expedition that resulted in a part of Baffin Island being named Meta Incognita. It was said that Queen Elizabeth herself came up with the name. This seems doubtful, since it appears in the shipmaster's account of the voyage. But if it was Elizabeth's idea, we might think the quick-tongued queen had sharp Latin: *meta incognita* might well mean something like 'unlimited boundaries' or 'unlimited potential'. Disappointing, then, that the potential for gold mining had no end but also no beginning.

mountains and great Islands of yce: a thing both rare and wonderful and greatly to be regarded', and brought home more than 200 tons of the black rock. But this heavy haul was declared to be inferior to the first lump; it was locked in Bristol Castle and the Tower of London and they went again: another year, another voyage, more tons of precious black ore. Yet again this proved worthless – just pyrite, fool's gold. Frobisher's reputation would take several years to recover.

'*All that glisters . . .*' etc. Perhaps the only thing glittering up there was the ice.

***

What I take from this story, over and above the folly of collecting hundreds of tons of worthless rock in situations of considerable peril, is that the cause of the north-west passage faded quite markedly once something more easily and immediately profitable caught the eye. 'There is no evidence that at any time after 1576 Gilbert had any idea of pursuing a search for a north-west passage or had any hope of a passage through temperate latitudes,' states the editor of Gilbert's collected writings. Gilbert had believed in and dreamed about the north-west passage for decades, but by the time his pamphlet was published his sights had shifted. After his sorties in Ireland, he had grasped, perhaps more acutely than most of his English contemporaries, that *terra incognita* was potentially more valuable than simply being a reprovisioning opportunity on the way to India, or somewhere to establish a trading station: it might, in itself, be something to exploit.

Gilbert finally got out of his armchair and made a trip across the Atlantic in 1583, five years after being granted a six-year patent on the attempt. His vision for this venture was that it would unite a great number of different individual and corporate interests eager to chance their arm in the 'new found land'. Sir Humphrey's schemes and petitions had always included some territorial benefit to himself and, as a benevolent governor, he would effectively rent out land to them (that he did not own) and create new markets (that he would control) for English goods overseas. From all of this – and from the mineral rights too – both he and the English crown would take a cut. This was frontier capitalism at its best.

On Monday 5 August 1583, Gilbert arrived at St John's, Newfoundland, and took possession of it for queen and country. Fishing vessels of many nationalities used its small harbour during the short open season, and men would land there to salt and dry their catches before returning to sleep on their boats. Before Gilbert, it had belonged to nobody, but the English had at least been senior occupants, or perhaps the playground bully: they generally had bigger fishing boats, and they also had the shortest voyage, so they were the first to arrive each year.

A ceremonial turf cutting, symbolically transferring ownership of all the land lying within 200 leagues to Gilbert, his agents and his queen, established the first English colony on American soil. Nobody thought to ask any indigenous people what they thought about being dispossessed of their land rights for evermore, but the other fisherman weren't displeased – it was reason for a party and someone else was paying for the grog. It seems the northern ice had proved itself too unyieldingly hostile, too *difficult*, when there were easier riches to be taken.

Forever is, however, always provisional. Gilbert, it seems, didn't do much governing and barely established a settlement beyond the canvas of his tent. Many of his crew had been recruited straight from England's prisons, and soon the more dyed-in-the-wool criminal elements were trying to hijack boats and go pirating, or running off into the forests never to return. Others were sick (they were shipped off quickly, directly to England), and some of the more salubrious of his newly christened subjects were homesick. In any case, fishing vessels were leaving every day: the season was ending and ice would be returning to the bay.

After less than three weeks, which included some prospecting and reprovisioning, Gilbert upped stakes and weighed anchor. Not long afterwards, the largest ship of his remaining three, the one carrying most of the comestibles, ran aground on a sandbank and was lost. Then a sea monster, like a lion with glaring eyes, was sighted (perhaps those maps were right). On 9 September 1583, somewhere near the Azores, a storm hit the last two ships.

Sir Humphrey, captaining his beloved *Squirrel* – a decidedly puny eight-tonner compared with the hundred or so tons of the *Golden Hind* and the 120-ton (though lost) flagship *Delight* – was repeatedly close to being overwhelmed.

As night fell, he was spotted abaft, sitting and reading a book on deck (some say it was Thomas More's *Utopia*, a fitting title for a man ever in search of an illusion); every time the *Golden Hind* drew near enough, he would wave and shout, 'We are as close to Heaven by sea as we are by land!'

And then he disappeared into that darkness from which there is no return.

Much of the early exploration and mapmaking of what is now northern Canada was driven by the north-west quest, by men who – unlike Gilbert! – were trying to force a passage through the ice but failed. Many of the geographical features – Davis Strait, Baffin Island, Hudson and Frobisher Bays, the Parry Channel and others – of the complicated archipelagos of northern Canada take their European names from those who laboured their way to them between the sixteenth and the nineteenth centuries. Gilbert and his *Discourse* played their part in keeping the north-west dream alive for generations to come. It was, like the alchemist's vision of transmuting base materials into gold, impossible yet irresistible, an obsessive endeavour that would attract the finest minds and lead them into failure. In each case the adventurer started off hopeful of riches, but ended up, at best, with a load of old rocks.

This failure was mainly, but not exclusively, English. There were of course Barentsz, Cartier and Ulloa; later, in 1619, a Danish–Norwegian expedition set out with sixty-five men in two ships. After fighting through Hudson Strait, they landed and spent the winter on shore in Hudson Bay. Ravaged by famine, cold and scurvy, only three men survived, returning to Bergen in a single ship in September 1620. In 1679, the Frenchman René-Robert Cavelier set sail in *Le Griffon* for the north-west passage via the upper Great Lakes, but on 18 September he turned back towards Niagara. The ship, and its cargo of furs, vanished, with all six crew. Its final location and ultimate fate are still unknown.

In 1776 one of England's finest sailors, Captain James Cook, came out of retirement and gave it a shot; but, like the Hollywood Mafioso persuaded to do 'one last job', it did not end well. Cook was trying to sail through the passage from west to east, but found his maps hopelessly inaccurate. He was repelled by ice in August 1778 and, turning towards happier hunting grounds, he headed south, where he was killed, on Hawaii, on Valentine's Day 1779.

The most terrible and famous disaster was the 1845 expedition under the English Captain Sir John Franklin. He sailed in two ships, the *Erebus* and *Terror*, with 129 officers and men, confident he would chart the last unnavigated channels, but after being sighted in Baffin Bay by two whaling vessels, in July 1845, they were never seen again. In 1848, under pressure from Franklin's wife, Jane, the Admiralty mounted the first of many investigations and searches into their disappearance. Artists, novelists and politicians, not to mention the press, all weighed in with sensationalist speculation about what might have happened.

The truth, more gruesome than anyone imagined, is still being uncovered. In April 1848, the *Erebus* and *Terror* were abandoned and with Franklin already dead the survivors set out overland to trek back to European settlements; it is believed all died hundreds of kilometres from their goal. In the years and then decades after their disappearance, a couple of frozen bodies were found and brought back to England, plus a few relics – ships' cutlery, handwritten notes on scraps of paper left under a cairn – but no ships were found. In 1850, the body of a petty officer named John Torrington was discovered, mummified and frozen, on Beechey Island, near the ships' recorded winter mooring. Two other crew members shared his shallow, permafrost grave.

In the 1980s, they were exhumed, and modern autopsies of the ice-preserved bodies found that lung damage (from tuberculosis or pneumonia) and lead poisoning (probably from badly tinned food) may have contributed to their deaths. Botulism has also been proposed as a cause. The other sailors died from scurvy, hypothermia, starvation . . . and cannibalism. By 1854 reports had been gathered from Inuits of forty or so white men who had resorted to eating each other, before perishing, in a camp near the mouth of the Back River in what is now Nunavut State in Canada's northern Arctic.

The catastrophic loss was a deep embarrassment for the British government which, as a consequence, ceased backing Arctic exploration. *Erebus* and *Terror* were only found in 2014 and 2016 respectively.

It was during the search for Franklin and his men that west and east were finally connected through Canada, by an Irishman called Robert McClure, though much of this was accomplished by trekking over the frozen sea after abandoning his ship to the pack ice. A full waterborne journey through a north-west passage was first completed by Roald Amundsen – also first man to the South Pole – who dodged the pack ice in a tiny herring boat between 1903 and 1906.

*** 

'There is more to twenty-first century Arctic politics than melting ice, navigable sea routes, and *mare liberum*,' it was declared in 2006, by the two academics in the paper that coined the term 'cryopolitics'. Since then, other academics and theorists have used the term to encompass Arctic security, environmental protection for indigenous peoples, the history of cryo-exploitation, scientific work on glaciers, governmental actions on climate change, cultural issues and many other things. But cryopolitics is something the nations of the temperate world have been playing at ever since rival seafarers pitted themselves against each other to force a way through the north-east and north-west passages. Capitalist geopolitics did not wait for the ice to melt. These white parts of the maps were contested spaces 500 years ago: you might well say that cryopolitics was born in the cryocommerce and cryocompetition of the sixteenth century.

If the problem with the north-west passage in former times was that it was not there, the problem with it these days is that, because the ice is melting, it is. And everyone still wants it.

The first single-season transit of the north-west passage was achieved in 1944, and the first cargo ship not accompanied by icebreakers passed through in 2014. Because of the melting ice it is now a navigable prospect for commercial ships and the world's powers are jockeying for position to exploit the newly viable possibilities. Canada believes that the various routes that constitute the north-west passage between the Canadian mainland and its Arctic islands count as internal waters and therefore fall under its sovereign control; others believe it is an international strait, and in 2019 US secretary of state Mike Pompeo called Canada's claim 'illegitimate'. Meanwhile, the Chinese have taken to saying things like: 'There will be ships with Chinese flags sailing through this route in the future,' and 'The Chinese side will make a suitable decision according to various factors,' sending a strong, if gnomically ambiguous, statement of intent. Elsewhere in the Arctic, Russia is planting flags on the seabed in an attempt to extend its sovereignty and exploration rights.

'This isn't the fifteenth century. You can't go around the world and just plant flags,' responded one Canadian official. He might have been a century or two out, but actually it doesn't sound much different from Cabot, Frobisher, Barentsz and Gilbert at all.

# 5

## The Scientists and Gourmets

### *The new science of cold and pagophagia*

> *Whosoever will be an Enquirer into Nature let him resort to a Conservatory of Snow or Ice.*
> Francis Bacon, *Sylva Sylvarum* (1626)

> *The pure Walden water is mingled with the sacred water of the Ganges.*
> Henry David Thoreau, *Walden* (1854)

> *The universe is under no obligation to make sense to you.*
> Neil deGrasse Tyson, *Astrophysics for People in a Hurry* (2017)

When the TV-friendly astrophysicist Neil deGrasse Tyson posted the aphorism in the epigraph to this chapter on Twitter, it struck a chord with modern readers adrift in a sea of social media, getting thousands of likes and retweets. Expressing both a cosmic indifference and the human instinct to challenge – *to make sense of* – things in the face of this indifference, it launched a thousand memes. But our disorientation, in our information-filled, technologically complicated, increasingly incomprehensible environment, pales in comparison to the situation of those mariners in the sixteenth and seventeenth centuries. No Google Maps or GPS existed to lead them to untold riches on the other side of the ice. However much money or hope they poured into their quests for the north-west passage, the universe did not owe them success. It did not give an inch: what they found in the north was ice. Ice as barrier. It impeded their progress and was lifeless. As they saw it, it was, in both natural and economic terms, *unproductive*. And when it seized and crushed their ships, it became a mortal danger, an implacable enemy.[1]

In the mariners' accounts collected by Hakluyt it's easy to spot some of the tropes that would dominate temperate thought about icy regions in the centuries to come: we witness the birth of what one might call the heroic attitude towards ice. There are also a few signs ('Islands of yce: a thing both rare and wonderful and greatly to be regarded') of the beauty and awe that turns an intimidating meeting into a sublime experience – one we shall explore further with the Romantics later on.

What I find funny, though, is that the sailors did not seem tempted to try to explain the ice. To them it was elemental, just there because it was very cold – tallying, I suppose, with their experience of winter wherever it was they called home. Instead they reserved their curiosity for more showy things, such as pyrite, or unicorns' (actually narwhals') horns. The paucity of European knowledge about the globe's northern extremes was mirrored in the level of understanding of ice itself.

However, others began, during the late sixteenth and seventeenth centuries, looking for new ways of explaining natural phenomena. What we now call the Scientific Revolution swept away received ideas about the natural world, some of which had remained current since the Ancient Greeks, through empirical

---

[1] For native Arctic peoples, ice is of course just an everyday thing, and they find shelter, nutrition, transport, all of life's necessities in their environment. Their contributions have historically been minimised and erased, but Europeans have ignored these lessons at their peril. To take an extreme example, Captain Robert F. Scott had had bad experiences using sledge dogs, in part because the men in his British expeditions were not accomplished skiers. On his doomed Antarctic trip, he chose to take ponies to the South Pole, which were fed with fodder brought from England and laboured in the snow. Whereas his rival, Roald Amundsen, had learned the secrets of dog handling from Inuits he met during his north-west passage crossing, and his men skied much of the way to the pole, pulled by dog teams. Scott and his party's ignorance, or refusal to take heed, of time-honoured techniques slowed their progress and left them vulnerable.

observations, systematic experimentation and inductive thinking. Rather than in the icy voids, these natural philosophers ('scientist' was not coined until the nineteenth century) found their *terra incognita* in the laboratory. Their journeys exploring the nature of being made the universe a more comprehensible place, and I am not the first to see the sympathies between the two kinds of exploration: 'The polar regions of physics appeal to the fighting spirit of scientists in the same way that the extreme North and South Poles appeal to the explorer,' wrote the Norwegian scientist Heike Kamerlingh Onnes much later on.[2]

The scientific story of ice starts, more or less, with questions posed by Sir Walter Raleigh to Thomas Harriot in the late sixteenth century regarding the best way to stack cannonballs on the deck of a ship. This was a problem concerning the efficient packing of spheres, and Harriot, a noted mathematician and astronomer, was the man to answer it. Harriot believed all matter consists of tiny particles – he was an 'atomist' – so it is tempting to think that, for him, the cannonballs on the deck of a ship were both a juicy mathematical problem and a macrocosm of the inner workings of the world itself.

Almost two decades later, Harriot was consulted by Johannes Kepler, the famous astronomer, about optics. Harriot's sphere-packing problem clearly captured Kepler's imagination: in 1611 he published *A New Year's Gift; or On the Six-Cornered Snowflake*, which attempted to answer the question of why frozen water always fell from the sky in tiny six-pointed flowers.

That snowflakes had six sides had been widely known in China as far back as 135 BCE,[3] but the knowledge had never travelled as far as Europe, and *The Six-Cornered Snowflake* was the first sustained enquiry into the form and structure of snowflakes – or, for that matter, any substance – and was the foundation of the science of crystallography. In it, Kepler wondered if the

[2] This was in 1904. Onnes was involved in a risky quest for absolute zero in his laboratory, just as Roald Amundsen was conquering the north-west passage for the first time.
[3] Possibly the Chinese had used lenses to magnify the flakes, but in dry and cold conditions snowflakes, made up of multiple individual snow crystals, each in turn made up of millions of infinitesimal ice crystals, can easily be large enough to be seen with the naked eye.

snowflakes' six-sidedness was immanent in some way, or if it was occasioned by outside influences; and he considered the way seeds are packed into a pomegranate as a possible model for what was happening on a smaller scale – just like Harriot's cannonballs. The shape of the snowflake is, as Kepler guessed, a direct consequence of the unseeable structure of ice, and his understanding was validated by the discovery of molecules and atoms and by deeper investigations into crystallography.

But that was not until much later. After Kepler, René Descartes penned a very precise description of ice crystals and snowflakes that he had observed falling in Amsterdam one February night in 1635, which again insisted on their perfect six-sidedness. 'These were little plates of ice, very flat, very polished, very transparent, about the thickness of a sheet of rather thick paper . . . but so perfectly formed in hexagons, and of which the six sides were so straight, and the six angles so equal, that it is impossible for men to make anything so exact,' he wrote. Descartes made these precise observations with the naked eye only, but the European (re)discovery of the shape of the snowflake benefited from a new piece of technology: the microscope. When it was invented, around 1620, it was possible to see, for the first time, whole worlds in a single drop of water or shaving of ice.

Robert Hooke, the celebrated natural philosopher and member of the Royal Society, was among the first to share these worlds. His beautiful illustrations of snowflakes in *Micrographia* (1665) and elsewhere were drawn using guidelines etched into the paper with a compass and razor, for strict circularity and six-sided symmetry. Such geometric perfection, he thought, was proof of God's hand in the world; imperfect flakes had been rendered so by their descent through the elements and their jarring arrival on earth.

Ice, snow and liquid water featured prominently in seventeenth-century experiments in part because water is such a vital and ubiquitous substance, but also because ice was central to the enigma of cold. 'The phenomenon of freezing of liquids was considered to be the principal effect of cold,' writes one historian of the period. But what exactly was 'cold'? Was it a thing in itself, a quality or an effect, or did it really reside in Thule somewhere in the imaginary north? Humans had been able to manufacture heat for hundreds of thousands of years, but cold remained a mystery. How did hotness or coldness vary, were they relative or absolute, and how could one measure them? Since Aristotle, many ideas had been proposed, but in the seventeenth century a new 'corpuscular' theory was gaining favour: Descartes had proposed that light was made up of tiny particles, and many thought of heat and cold as both similarly consisting of submicroscopic corpuscles that attached themselves to things.

Robert Boyle is recognised as one of the fathers of modern chemistry, and is most famous for his law governing the volume and pressure of gases, but he was also a pioneer of the emerging science of cold. His *New Experiments and Observations Touching Cold* (1665) collected together all his thinking and practical work on the subject, which had fascinated him for the best part of two decades. With his insistence on examining all the various phenomena of cold, accumulating data and testing the existing theories as to its nature, he was working in the experimental tradition of Francis Bacon (whom we will come back to later). Boyle argued that human senses were unable to accurately measure cold, and by introducing a thermometer into his experimental apparatus he gained objective measures of how hot and cold substances were, as well as the temperature changes caused by various chemical reactions. He did not get everything right, and many of his experiments raised more questions than they provided answers, but his perceptions and rigour did much to advance our thinking about the natural world.

Ice was the key material and chief subject in Boyle's *New Experiments and Observations Touching Cold*. Across the hundreds of experiments he either undertook or reported on, he measured its strength and how quickly it melted in contact with various other substances, looked at its effects on different materials and sought to understand what exactly freezing was – a process which to him seemed to change the texture of other substances in mysterious ways. Boyle used the testimonies of Gerrit de Veer, from the ill-starred Dutch Novaya Zemlya expedition, and of Captain Thomas James, a Welshman who in the 1630s had become the latest in the long line of sailors to founder among the icy perils of the north-west passage, mining them for any intelligence he might glean from the world's icy frontiers. And he froze everything from vinegar to urine and from oil to wine, noting that aqueous liquids were more readily frozen than 'subtle' or 'spirituous' liquids. Boyle also debunked the commonly held notion that the freezing of water indicated the highest degree of cold: in several places he mentions that mixing ice with certain salts lowered ice's temperature even while liquefying quantities of it. Although this was not news (Bacon alludes to experiments with ice and salts in the 1620s – and we'll see more of this in the next chapter), it was a fact that would later prove very useful.

A particular puzzle was why ice expanded when freezing, forcing corks out of bottles or even shattering the bottles themselves. The Accademia del Cimento (Experimental Academy) in Florence had even caused thick brass spheres to rupture thanks to water freezing within. This was a problematic phenomenon if one believed, in essence, that cold was the absence of particles that made something hot. If ice was bigger than water, then surely something was being added to it? And then, how come ice, no matter how bulky, floated on liquid water? Boyle put ice under a microscope to see if its expansion and buoyancy might be caused by air bubbles trapped within: 'A piece of ice that to the eye looked clear like crystal, being put into a microscope, appeared even there free from bubbles; and yet the same piece of ice being presently removed, and cast into common water, would swim at the top,' he wrote. Although he subscribed to certain aspects of the corpuscular theory, perhaps Boyle's most important insight was that cold was the lack of heat, a privation, rather than a separate thing in itself – which, indeed, it was.

What we now know is that the crystalline structure of ice makes it less dense than water in its liquid state. As water freezes, individual molecules join together to form regular tetrahedral lattices through a process called hydrogen bonding, in which positively charged hydrogen atoms in one water molecule are attracted to the negatively charged oxygen atoms in *other* water molecules. Hydrogen bonds are relatively weak – not nearly as strong as the bonds between the O and the two Hs *within* the $H_2O$ molecule – so when the temperature is high, the majority of water molecules can escape these hydrogen bonds.[4] But when the temperature drops and energy leaves the system, more and more water molecules get trapped by hydrogen bonds that, eventually, form continuous, regular three-dimensional lattices: ice![5] The net result of the lattices is that the molecules in ice are more spaced out than the previously dense, disordered molecules in water.

So it is that ice, very unusually for a solid, floats upon its own liquid form.

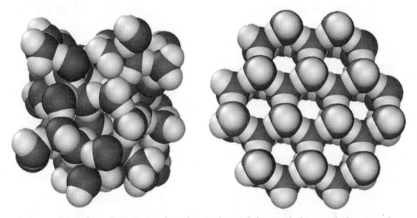

*Dense, disordered $H_2O$ molecules in liquid form (left), and the regular, spacious hexagonal lattice of ice.*

Water is in fact at its densest at around 4 °C; after that, the hydrogen bonds begin to gain the upper hand, distancing the molecules from each other, and it actually expands until it is frozen. This means that in a frozen pond there is a temperature inversion and the water is warmer at the bottom than near the top. In the eighteenth and nineteenth centuries it was still commonly believed that seawater could not freeze, a fact that appeared to be

[4] Water, in fact, always contains some hydrogen-bonded molecules, but the large majority of liquid water molecules are still very free to move.
[5] The two hydrogen atoms in a molecule of $H_2O$ are bonded to the oxygen atom at an angle of around 108°, which is just right for building tetrahedral structures (think of the shape of jacks in the retro children's game, or of certain kinds of concrete sea defences). It is these lattices, which appear hexagonal in 2D, that give snowflakes their six-sided appearance.

confirmed by Captain Cook in the 1770s, when he noted during his travels in the Antarctic that icebergs consisted of fresh water.[6] As Captain Cook's mistaken surmise shows, misapprehensions persisted for hundreds of years after Boyle's work. But, by seeking to understand ice, Boyle and his contemporaries began to understand the fundamental laws of physics, and of matter itself.

*New Experiments and Observations Touching Cold* was a bestseller, and reached far beyond the select meetings of the Royal Society, but many of the experiments did not have much immediate relevance outside the laboratory, nor any obvious practical uses beyond the cause of furthering science itself. A major exception was the subject of ice and food. Boyle touched on this at various points in his tome, showing both how ice was already being used in the consumption and preservation of foodstuffs and also pointing to how ice would transform our relationship with natural produce in the centuries to come. He experimented with freezing eggs, apples and cheese, to observe how they reacted to being frozen and also how they fared when defrosted.

Thanks to Boyle and others in the seventeenth century, ice was becoming comprehensible. And it was also becoming, to a much larger number of people, *useful*. Boyle's food experiments, though tangential to his purpose, pointed the way to some of the most significant developments in using ice over the next few centuries.

\*\*\*

'Pagophagia' is the name for the compulsion to eat ice or iced things and, in a non-pathological sense, it is a desire we have forever been succumbing to.[7] The idea of using cold to preserve

---

[6] Icebergs are indeed freshwater as they are parts of a glacier or an ice cap that formed originally on land from precipitation, which have split from the main and 'calved'. Seawater freezes at lower temperatures than freshwater – typically around −2 °C (28 °F) depending on its salinity and other factors – and so sea ice, or pack ice as it's called when not landfast, is less common. Either Cook was not far enough south to encounter sufficiently low temperatures, or he grabbed hold of the wrong bit of ice.

[7] Pagophagia is, correctly speaking, an eating disorder characterised by the compulsive consumption of ice. It belongs to the family of pica disorders, whose sufferers compulsively eat non-nutritive substances – compare, e.g., trichophalgia, the consumption of hair. Definitions of what is 'too much' ice are vague, with some studies taking as a baseline a

foodstuffs seems almost as fundamental as the application of fire to make nutrients more readily digestible, and our delight in consuming cold things seems equally primal.

However, there was an obvious problem during those long centuries before the invention of the icebox: unless one lived at high latitudes or restricted one's pagophagia to only the chilliest of circumstances (and where is the fun in that?), ice was either completely unavailable or did not hang around long enough to be savoured. Indeed, the whole history of ice consumption in temperate climes might be read as one of first trying to conjure the ephemeral in the most unlikely conditions and then of delaying its inevitable disappearance.

Nevertheless, there is a long and rich tradition of ice exploitation and ice management in some surprising corners of the world, all of which are based around the construction of (primitive) ice and snow pits, or (more sophisticated) ice houses, to store and preserve the precious cold.

The earliest records yet found of ice houses are from Mesopotamia and date to the early second millennium BCE. Cuneiform tablets from the palace at Mari, which was located on the banks of the Euphrates in present-day Syria, describe ice houses dug twelve metres long and six metres into the ground. Into these would be placed snow – probably transported by land and river from the Liban mountains of Lebanon, or the Taurus and Zagros mountains now shared between Iraq, Iran and Turkey – that would be packed until it was so dense it turned to ice. These ice houses were lined with tamarisk branches, which both kept the ice cold and allowed any meltwater to drain away, extending the lifespan of the remaining ice. It was in great demand for chilling the drinks of the city state's elite, as well as for sacred purposes.

freezer tray of ice daily for several months. Quantities rise from there. A neurological basis to some cases of pagophagia was proposed in 2014, when iron supplements were proven in a study to reduce the ice-chewing lust in some sufferers. Apparently, for people suffering from iron-deficient anaemia, chewing ice may boost the brain's blood supply; however, it may also simply be that the ice numbs the sore lips and tongue that are also common symptoms.

These ice-preservation methods would remain substantially unchanged across cultures and for thousands of years: there are records of ice being stored similarly in China in the first millennium BCE and also by the Ancient Greeks and Romans, who probably acquired their pagophagia at the eastern extremes of their empires and transmitted the practice west. According to Pericles (495–429 BCE), 'The use of snow was very common in Greece, not only in the towns amongst the nobility and the people, but also in the armies amongst the soldiers,' and the Romans, too, often had ice stores at their settlements. Both civilisations developed sophisticated systems to cool their drinks: the Greeks used elegant double-walled amphoras called 'psycters', sort of like a modern thermos flask but with snow instead of a vacuum; the Romans had a tea-strainer-style device called a *colum nivarium*, often made of silver, to hold the ice or snow, through which the wine would be poured. This required an extremely high-quality product. Fastidious consumers would demand ice from deep down in the store, where it lay untainted by mud and straw on its journey to civilisation or by insulating straw or chaff at the edges, and it is said that the emperor Nero invented the practice of packing snow around a thin glass vessel filled with boiled water so that, when it froze, the resulting ice was pure and did not carry contaminating flavours.

Even in antiquity, ice had become a managed resource or a crop, a commodity in a system that aspired to provide year-round availability and put consumer convenience above nature. This aspect of the fashion was not to everybody's tastes: Elizabeth David, who at the time of her death had been working for many years on a colossal study of culinary uses of ice, writes that Pliny passed judgement on the 'degenerate custom of turning the seasons upside down, by the people who in summer used the snows of winter to chill their wine' – that is, on the morality of civilisation aspiring to control nature. These doubts would resurface in many contexts over the centuries.

After the Romans the widespread use of ice was lost in Europe. It was reintroduced during the Renaissance, as so many things were, from the Near East, where it had perhaps never gone away. By the late Middle Ages the great mountain ranges ringing the Mediterranean were providing snow to northern Africa, Lebanon, Syria, Turkey, Malta and Spain. And by the latter half of the sixteenth century, according to Elizabeth David, it had reached the Florentine Republic, the great Renaissance centre of wealth and culture. It was used to cool wine and to make what were known as 'sherbets'. These took their name from the Persian word *sharbat*, meaning 'sugary non-alcoholic drink', and described syrupy fruit- and flower-scented essences or pastes that, in Turkey, Persia and India in particular, would be mixed with cold water or snow and ice to create cooling drinks. The word is also the source of 'sorbet' and 'sorbetto'. Rich Florentines in this period also enjoyed an array of elaborate dishes indirectly cooled by snow. Contemporary records list recipes such as ice-encrusted fruit and peeled peaches in wine on ice, hashed chicken and ground-almond blancmange, iced fresh figs and innumerable jellies. Ice pyramids and obelisks decorated the tables.

It seems very likely that Robert Boyle saw ice houses in Florence when he stayed there in the early 1640s. Also in the 1640s, Boyle's friend John Evelyn travelled extensively through Italy, and fed Boyle's cryophilia with a report of Italian ice houses in his letters. Boyle gave a paper at the Royal Society in 1665, detailing how Italian ice houses were constructed. However, in his *New Experiments and Observations Touching Cold* Boyle restricted himself to a passing mention: ice is 'in *Italy* and some other Regions much employ'd, especially to cool drinks and fruits'.

From Florence, the fashion spread; Rome and Naples, too, were ice-mad cities, and across Europe economic, political and social systems were springing up around the cold white stuff. By the early eighteenth century, the trade in snow collected on Etna and other mountains around Naples was controlled by *banditti*, who ran protection rackets anticipating those of the Camorra. Ice became big in Paris in the reign of Louis XIV, who for years championed a certain Nicolas Audiger. Audiger had travelled to Rome in 1661 to learn the secret to becoming a master confectioner and distiller (that is, someone who concocted drinks, not necessarily of the alcoholic variety). In 1692, he published *La Maison Réglée*, giving recipes for fruit ices, *cresme glacée* – an early form of ice cream[8] – and ice-encrusted fruit. These concoctions were sold by confectioners and *limonadiers*, who were licensed by the king to sell lemonade, ices and other refreshments; one of the most famous, Café Procope, opened in 1686 by a Sicilian, is still trading today.

In Robert Boyle's Britain ice stores would have worked in just the same way as they did in Ancient Rome, with only cosmetic changes in materials and decoration. The first ones were probably constructed by King James I, who had two snow conserves dug in Greenwich, in 1619 and 1622, and then another built at Hampton Court in 1625. Each was lined with sturdy brick and sunken below ground, with a protruding roof structure in a cylindrical or domed shape. In 1660, King Charles II built an ice house in Upper St James's (now Green) Park. On this 'improvement' the poet Edward Waller wrote:

Yonder the harvest of cold months laid up,
Gives a fresh coolness to the royal cup,
There ice, like crystal, firm and never lost,
Tempers hot July with December's frost.

Charles II had spent several years in exile after the English Civil War at the court of France's Louis XIV and on his return to England was intent on recreating the elegance and extravagance he had seen abroad. That required ice: there was nothing more opulent, no greater show of riches, than serving chilled drinks to one's guests in the summer. Where exactly Charles's ice came from is uncertain. Most probably it was from the lakes in St James's Park and from the River Thames, both of which would have produced muddy, unappetising ice. Accordingly, it would not have been used *in* drinks or directly on food, but, following the Greeks and Romans, to cool containers from the outside. Thanks to Charles, 'ice houses became fashionable almost overnight',

---

[8] Variants of ice cream – made with dairy products, that is, rather than just flavoured ice – seem to have been invented in both China and Peru before they appeared in Europe.

according to the foremost historians of ice houses, but 'only the very rich could afford to construct them'. One of the first was built by Barbara Villiers, Duchess of Cleveland – one of Charles's many mistresses – at her house on Cleveland Row.

Ice houses reached their zenith in the UK during the eighteenth century, in the villas and townhouses of London's nouveaux riches, and the stately manors of the English shires, where their characteristically egg-shaped or domed sunken structures were sometimes dressed up as a kind of neoclassical shed, a picturesque ruin or a baroque folly, and sometimes covered by earth or disguised in fashionable shrubbery. A well-built ice house on a country estate could hold ice from one winter all the way through the summer, until the weather cooled again and ice became newly available, at which point the ice house would often be cleaned before being restocked. Some had shallow ponds for ice collecting located nearby, including the ice house at William 'Mer de Glace' Windham's Felbrigg Hall in Norfolk, which was built during this time.

*\*\**

By the early nineteenth century, demand for ice was rising, rising everywhere – in Florence and Seville, Rome and Paris and London, and even in small seaside resorts. The rich wanted more ice, and higher quality; the poor just wanted in.

The question, really, was supply.

Towards the end of the eighteenth century, ice from Greenland started arriving in German ports, taken there by whaling ships that customarily picked up large blocks of ice on their return voyages to provide drinking water (it would have been just as easy to hoist a ton or two of iceberg on to deck as it would a dead whale). Greenland ice was almost totally transparent and incredibly dense and pure, which was both a logistical aid (it melted less quickly in transit) and later a marketing USP. By around 1815 ice was arriving in London from Greenland, Iceland and Norway.[9]

[9] Elizabeth David, whose scholarship on this matter seems by far the most thorough, notes that in the English public imagination the Greenland Seas were only vaguely known – their location something of a trade secret for whalers – and Greenland itself was a huge and inaccessible mass of ice; a great thaw and breaking up of the ice sheet would occur in 1818, which began to clarify matters. This also reignited the English quest for the north-west passage.

Norwegian ice, like Greenland ice, was top quality, and was readily available in the numerous lakes dotting Norway's south-western seaboard. Norwegian ice traders employed the fastest and best ships, to minimise loss. Over the course of the nineteenth century many industries converted to steam shipping, but the natural ice trade was one of the last to use sailing ships. Why? Wooden hulls, unlike iron ones, did not rust from the inside.

One of the first commercial importers was a man called William Leftwich. Leftwich had started out as a confectioner, making ices, ice cream and sweet drinks, a trade that in London dated back to the 1750s and was historically controlled by Italians.[10] However, confectioning was vulnerable to the vagaries of the weather, and a mild winter would mean little ice laid up in store, leaving many customers wanting.

Leftwich became frustrated by the uncertain quantity and quality of ice he could get his hands on, so he chartered a ship, the *Spring*, to sail to Norway from Great Yarmouth. It returned laden with 300 tons of Norwegian lake ice, only to be stopped, on 8 May 1822, by customs officers on the Thames. The shipment presented a puzzle. How could this ice be classified as 'dry goods' if it was sitting there visibly melting? Was it a 'product' or a 'manufacture', and exactly how much of it was there to tax if every minute it diminished, surreptitiously escaping the scrutiny of Her Majesty's revenue officers to join the river below? They took so long that Leftwich, who was aboard, 'had reason to fear his cold cargo would turn to water; for ice was not mentioned on the list of customs duties', according to a Norwegian newspaper.

Tax was eventually imposed at 20 per cent – which did not stop Leftwich making a large profit and establishing himself as one of nineteenth-century London's dominant ice importers. Once docked, there were lively scenes as the capital's pastry-cooks and fishmongers learned of this priceless article 'not before seen . . . between May and November', and flocked to buy some.

---

[10] One of the first was a certain Domenico Negri, who set up in Berkeley Square in 1769 selling 'all sorts of Ice, Fruits, & Creams in the best Italian manner'.

By 1826, Leftwich was advertising in London newspapers, promising 'Ice six inches thick and remarkably clean', available for delivery in quantities of not less than eighteen pounds for '2d. per lb., or 14s. per cwt', as well as for pick-up from his office in Fleet Street or his ice well on Royal Park Mews, close to the Regent's Canal, where it would arrive on barges to be unloaded.[11]

It was in these middle years of the nineteenth century that ice ceased being a luxury available only to the wealthy, becoming available to the masses as a treat or even a domestic necessity.[12] By the 1850s there were numerous sellers of ices (without milk) and ice creams (with it) in London town, mainly still Italians. Increasingly, they relied upon Carlo Gatti, a Swiss-Italian café proprietor-cum-entrepreneur, for their raw materials. Gatti sold ices and perhaps originated the 'penny lick', a short and stout glass ice-cream bowl that ice-cream sellers would offer for a penny. Around 1860, he began to organise his own shipments from Norway and soon became kingpin of the London ice scene.

Because of the quantity of ice being imported, and the fierce competition, by 1877 the price of an ice cream had dropped to a halfpenny, and ice-cream mania was being remarked upon in the press. For example, *Street Life in London*, a magazine from that year, pours a large helping of racism on to its reporting from the 'slums': 'A very large number of the street ice-sellers are Calabrians, and are, therefore, semi-barbarous mountaineers . . . They can make more in selling ices in our thoroughfares than in cutting throats round and about Naples,' wrote the authors. 'In little villainous-looking and dirty shops an enormous business is transacted in the sale of milk for the manufacture of halfpenny ices.'

In the dawn hours of the morning, the Italians of the Spring Hill district of Clerkenwell would congregate at Gatti's ice house

---

[11] In 2018, Leftwich's giant ice well was rediscovered under the site of a former terrace of grand houses designed by Buckingham Palace architect John Nash. The 9.5 m × 7.5 m subterranean brick egg is the earliest known large-scale commercial ice store in town. It was probably constructed by brewers around 1780 before being taken over by Leftwich.

[12] No source is very clear on exactly where the ice came from – aside from the commonsense answer, muddy local ponds – before the Norwegian shipments. Leftwich literally and figuratively cleaned up.

nearby, purchase their raw materials and begin the day's churn; then, once the freeze was achieved, they would fan out across London to their sales patches, returning only late in the day. The ices were, in the magazine authors' considered opinion, 'absolute snare and delusion' – simply sugared and dyed with cochineal to be passed off as raspberry or strawberry, or flavoured with a little lemon extract or juice. By contrast, the more expensive ice creams were apparently 'wholesome and delicious'.

The authors conclude the article by admitting their grudging admiration for the sellers, albeit in a patrician and Victorian way: 'Nevertheless, and however questionable his antecedents may be, the Italian ice-man sets an example of steady perseverance, economy, and foresight which is at once the envy and the marvel of the English poor who live around.' So successful were the ice men that many could afford to winter under the warmer skies of Italy, and even to buy fine English shooting pieces with which to hunt. Their industry, finally, permitted many of them to buy a small bit of land in the hills of home and while away their retirement in comfort. Such were the rewards of satisfying Britain's pagophagia.

*\*\**

But the British did not just demand ice at home. In the nineteenth century, the sun famously did not set on Queen Victoria's territories and the temperamental colonial class were more in need of ice than anyone in the motherland.

In India, under the increasingly oppressive influence of the East India Company and then the British Raj, many in the local population were put to work to make ice: and they were not, like the mountain workers in Europe, simply harvesting it; they were producing it.

They did this using methods developed in the Persian desert, possibly thousands of years ago, which made use of a quirk of atmospherics and physics called radiative cooling. In normal conditions liquid water loses heat mostly via evaporation: as water evaporates, the escaping molecules draw energy from their surroundings, which cools the water that remains. But in the very dry conditions of, for example, the Persian desert, large amounts of heat are instead lost to the atmosphere through radiation, and water cooling is turbocharged. To take advantage of this, the Persians constructed large shallow basins in the desert served by underground canals or channels shaded from the sun by large walls. Overnight, radiative cooling would work its magic on the few centimetres of water exposed to the sky and, even if air temperatures did not fall below zero, in the morning there would be a layer of ice atop the pool. Once collected, the ice might possibly be eaten straight away in a *paloudeh*, a fruit sherbet containing starchy vermicelli-like noodles, rosewater and plenty of ice that was a traditional breakfast slurp. Or it might have been transferred to the neighbouring *yakhchāl*. *Yakhchāl* translates as 'ice pit', though these specimens were much more elegant than that: domed structures up to twenty metres tall, made out of a traditional mortar called *sarooj*, carefully combining sand, clay, ash, goat hair and other materials possibly including egg whites for maximum insulatory effect. Inside were stairs into a deep pit, where the winter's ice harvest could be stored into the summer, supplemented by any ice or snow brought down from nearby mountains.[13]

By contrast, in India, in the nineteenth century, people excavated long flat holes in the ground, and placed earthenware pans at the bottom as the sun set; then, after the coolness of the night – again, because of the very particular atmospheric conditions, temperatures did not need to drop below zero – they would transfer the thin layer of ice that had formed to an ice house, where it was stored in sacking and vines. The resulting loose-packed ice, nicknamed 'Hooghly Slush', might have been fine for cooling food, but, as well as being seasonal and in short supply, it was of poor quality and expensive and required huge amounts of labour to produce. One nineteenth-century source estimated that to make twenty-five to thirty tons of ice in a night

[13] The use of *yakhchāls* was widespread, only dying out completely in the 1960s, and more than a hundred of the structures survive. Their sheer number and quantity show that in Persia ice was a more democratic substance than it was in Europe.

would require 2,000 workers and 'acres of land for ice fields'. None of this convinced the British administrators that life in India was anything but infernal.

Little did anyone know, 25,000 kilometres' journey away in Boston, Massachusetts, a man called Frederic Tudor was planning to change everything.

Tudor's father had been appointed solicitor general of the United States by George Washington, but the family were by no means rich, and Frederic's interest in shipping ice was classic speculative capitalism. There were many fortuitous circumstances that put a favourable wind in his sails. For one thing, ice in the Massachusetts winter was in almost limitless supply. And it was free – Tudor initially cut it from lakes on his family farm, but it was so abundant and so unwanted that nobody really minded where you harvested it from. Winter labour was cheap, as was sawdust, an effective insulator that was a by-product of the timber industry. Another piece of luck was that Boston was a hub for global shipping: ships that had unloaded there needed ballast to return to pick up their next cargo, and so ice benefited from reduced shipping rates.[14]

Tudor's crazy idea of taking ice to the tropics was also based on a sound understanding of human psychology: 'In a country where at some seasons of the year the heat is insupportable, where at times the common necessary of life, water, cannot be had but in a tepid state – Ice must be considered as out-doing most other luxuries,' he wrote in a letter to a friend.

However, it was by no means a get-rich-quick scheme. His eureka moment had come in 1806, when he heard of an outbreak of yellow fever on the Caribbean island of Martinique (heat was generally supposed at this time to be the cause of many diseases we now know to be airborne). Tudor shipped over several tons of lake. 'No JOKE', a Boston newspaper assured its readers in February 1806. 'A vessel has cleared at the Custom House for

[14] Because ships returning to places such as the Caribbean and India needed something to weigh them down, sending ice to Calcutta was cheaper per ton than sending it to cities in the US's Deep South.

Martinique with a cargo of ice. We hope this will not prove a slippery speculation.' Unfortunately it did. Sources differ on the exact amount (what man is honest about his debts?), but Tudor lost up to $4,500 on the venture. His first shipments to Havana also left him in the red, and, though he did eventually tip into profit, he spent several months in debtors' prison in 1812 and 1813, in part because he had been swindled by his agent. Tudor also began to ship to Charleston, Savannah and New Orleans, opening up ice routes from the frozen US north to the steamy southern states, where he bet that the leisured elite would be a ready market.

Another experiment, to fill ships returning from the Caribbean with (ice-cooled) loads of Cuban limes, bananas and oranges, also almost proved terminally disastrous, since the fruit largely rotted, leaving him with a $3,000 loan at 40 per cent interest and nothing to sell to pay it off. Somehow he kept going, both domestically and internationally, though his diaries in 1821, scrawled daily with ANXIETY, ANXIETY, ANXIETY in block letters, prove that it was by no means plain sailing. Still, he was clever in his business practices, initially offering his product for free to stimulate demand and pricing aggressively, while shipping prefabricated ice houses around the US and conducting rigorous tests on insulation, both of which reduced ice loss.

Things began to look up when Tudor employed a man called Nathaniel J. Wyeth, who proved as entrepreneurial with ice cutting as Tudor was with the rest of the business. Wyeth invented and patented, among other innovations, a horse-drawn saw, which functioned like a plough for ice. It cut large, regular blocks that were much easier to transport and conserve than smaller chunks. Production almost tripled. Costs tumbled. Finally, in 1833, came the breakthrough. With the help of another Boston merchant, Tudor prepared a brig, the *Tuscany*, for India. On 12 May it sailed for Calcutta laden with 180 tons of ice cut the previous winter. After four months at sea, this first shipment arrived in the fierce July heat with 100 tons of pristine Massachusetts ice aboard (a wastage of around 44 per cent).

The reception among the Anglo-Indians, obsessed as they were with battling India's heat, was rapturous. Wrote one: 'How many Calcutta tables glittered that morning with lumps of ice? The butter dishes were filled; the goblets of water were converted into Arctic seas with icebergs floating on the surface. All business was suspended until noon, that people might rush about to pay each other congratulatory visits and devise means for perpetuating the ice supply.'

Tudor's time had come. He responded by building ice houses and requesting custom-inspection exemptions, import-duty reductions and retail monopolies, and by extending the trade intermittently to Madras and Bombay. By the 1840s more than 3,000 tons were shipped from Boston every year.

Reliably, around half of this survived the journey.

Around half of that survived to be sold.

Despite the shocking wastage, Tudor, who would become known as the 'Ice King', grew rich. A shrewd salesman from the start, he knew that he was not just selling ice, but rather selling cold, that indefinable absence of heat that had so confounded the natural philosophers centuries before. Cold was a luxury that everyone wanted – and if you are selling an absence, perhaps it is fitting that most of it melts away.

Tudor had long striven for a monopoly, but Indians were also getting involved in ice distribution. And in 1832, Tudor and Wyeth had parted ways, with Wyeth heading on an expedition to the Oregon Territory. Tudor's competitors successfully argued that, by 'going West', Wyeth had relinquished his patents. The genie was out of the bottle. From the mid-1830s others began to benefit from Wyeth's advanced ice-harvesting technologies.

Of these, one in particular, the Wenham Lake Company, grew to be an international phenomenon. The men behind it had been the first to export American ice to London, in 1842, and by the end of the 1840s they were prospering. In the window display of the Wenham Lake Company's office on London's Strand sat a block of gleaming, transparently pure ice from the eponymous lake in Massachusetts – replaced daily, to give a never-melting illusion. Queen Victoria gave Wenham Lake the royal warrant, and the celebrated scientist Michael Faraday proclaimed Wenham Lake ice outstandingly pure and clear because, in freezing so slowly, all the impurities and air had been gently squeezed out of it. In an early example of franchising, the Wenham Lake Company bought Lake Oppegård, near Oslofjord in Norway, and rechristened it 'Wenham Lake', so powerful was the brand.

It wasn't only the increasing competition that was making Tudor's life harder. Once he had proved ice's commercial value, lakeshore access was jealously guarded by landowners, and by around 1855 more than twelve companies were cutting ice from Massachusetts's lakes, with teams of horses, equipment, ice houses and even purpose-built ice railways. It was no longer a harvest but an industry, one watched with a kind of reluctant wonder by Henry David Thoreau.

In *Walden*, Thoreau's great meditation on the self and the natural world, the woods around his cabin are often described as being busy with people: many of the surrounding forests had been felled, some to provide wood for the railway tracks close by. Yet although he is not totally isolated, nor his living there by the water purely 'natural', he rejoices when winter descends and the pond ices over, leaving the landscape solely to him, a few muskrats and the owls.

His peace does not last. First come ice fishermen, cutting their holes, and then the ice harvester, who 'cuts and saws the solid pond, unroofs the house of fishes, and carts off their very element and air, held fast with chains and stakes like corded wood'.

And not just one ice harvester: during Thoreau's winter of 1846/7, a hundred men worked Walden Pond. They can, they tell him, remove a thousand tons of ice a day. Yet he does not seem put out by their presence; this seems to be, rather, where Yankee self-reliance meets good old American enterprise. Thoreau watches as the extracted ice is piled up and covered with insulating hay and boards, creating a 'solid base of an obelisk designed to pierce the clouds'. Thus the industry of men becomes transcendent, and when Thoreau learns that the ice is destined for India, his words fly even higher as he imagines that the 'pure Walden water . . . is mingled with the sacred water of the Ganges. With favoring winds it is wafted past the site of the fabulous islands of Atlantis and the Hesperides . . . melts in the tropic gales of the Indian seas and lands in the ports of which Alexander only heard the names.'

The reality of the ice trade to India was at once far more prosaic and far more politically charged. For a privileged class of Anglo-Indians, premium American ice – harder, clearer and less quick to melt than India-made ice – became a home comfort, soothing fevered brows and palliating the scorching climate they found so intolerable. A symbol of colonial luxury, it was a cog in the imperial system, all but unavailable to Indians and yet reliant on their labour. An ice-cold sundowner on the verandah brought by the help?[15] How civilised. The iniquities of the situation were obvious even to some of the most strenuous supporters of English imperialism, including John Ruskin, who wrote in 1884:

> Every mutiny, every danger, every terror and every crime, occurring under, or paralyzing, our Indian legislation, arises directly out of our national desire to live on the loot of India and the notion always entertained by English young gentlemen and ladies of good position . . . that they can find in India, instantly on landing, a bungalow ready furnished with the loveliest fans, china, and shawls – ices and sherbet at command – four-and-twenty slaves succeeding each other hourly to swing the punkah [fan], and a regiment with a beautiful band to 'keep order' outside, all around the house.

Tudor's ice trade to India probably peaked in the late 1850s, and he died a rich man in 1864.[16] His had been a crazy dream and he had ridden his luck in the early years, helped by relaxations in trade rules and other factors completely outside his control. But he also had worked incredibly hard to stimulate demand for his product where there previously had been none. His home nation in particular had become obsessed – so obsessed that in the latter

---

[15] Some colonial houses even employed a special servant to keep bottles chilled.
[16] Tudor is widely held as being America's first millionaire, but his life and finances seem nothing if not mercurial and chaotic. According to one scholar, most of the wealth he accrued was in the waterfront land he purchased to facilitate his trade.

half of the nineteenth century Mark Twain observed that 'the only distinguishing characteristic of the American character I've been able to discover is a fondness for ice water.'[17]

It wasn't only a fondness for 'ice water'. Tudor's trade transformed how people – Americans, initially – drank alcohol. Nineteenth-century Americans undoubtedly drank more hard spirits than Europeans, but, pre-ice, this generally meant a rather desultory – and warm – menu of brandy or gin and sugar or bitters, or punches imbibed out of large bowls. In the large hinterlands outside the cities, simple whiskey or rudimentary rum were the tipples of choice. By the mid-nineteenth century, ice-delivery services to businesses and homes in many US cities were well established; adding ice to the mix contributed not only cold, but texture, flavour and theatre too.

When a standard twenty-two-inch cube arrived at a New York bar it had to be cut into usable chunks. Tongs, scoops, picks, axes and mallets became necessary. Did you want your ice in cubes, cracked or shaved? Well, of course that depended on what you were drinking. And once you had a shaker, ice would even help you mix the drink. Ice inaugurated an increasingly baroque and complex drinking culture, where people did not share grog in great bowls but had their drinks – high-concept showstoppers whose fearsome spirit content was toned down by sugary cordials and plenty of dilutional ice – made individually for them.[18] Whether or not they were the originators, the Americans popularised these drinks across the rest of the world: 'American' bars in Havana, London, Paris and other world cities served 'American' drinks, catering for American tourists but also attracting young and fashionable locals. The cocktail would come to define a generation

[17]Though this is quoted, among other places, on a US government website, I have found it untraceable. It does, however, sound quintessentially Twain-esque.

[18] Though a quintessentially American drink, the earliest known use of the word 'cocktail' was in a London newspaper in 1798. Early British spirit drinks often contained ginger syrup, and a *Telegraph* article from 2012 suggests that the name might have been taken from the equine world. A 'cock-tail' was a horse with its tail cut short so that it stuck jauntily up into the air. There was apparently a practice, when selling a horse, of putting a lump of ginger somewhere unmentionable so that the beast was bright eyed and cock-tailed at least until money had changed hands.

of flappers and jazz – ironically at a time when America was living through prohibition.

The second way in which ice changed the way we drank alcohol was its use in the brewing industry. Lager- and pilsner-style beers are brewed using a 'bottom fermentation' method that requires low, stable temperatures, so lager brewing traditionally happened in the colder months only. With a large ice supply, brewers could make lager all year round. By the mid-nineteenth century the US had a large number of German immigrants and a plentiful ice supply, so it's not surprising that these lighter styles predominated. In the UK, meanwhile, 'top fermentation' ales and beers, which could be brewed at higher temperatures, remained the norm. In the 1870s, breweries including Carlsberg in Copenhagen and Heineken in Rotterdam were early customers for new-fangled icemaking machines.

These were a sign that a change was coming. Although the consumption of lake ice persisted, by the early twentieth century the natural ice industry was in decline in Britain, the US and across Europe. It existed as Tudor knew it for only a few decades. In some ways it was a victim of its own success, since the rapid industrialisation of the wider Boston area began to pollute the lakes and spoil the product.

Artificially produced ice, though not immediately as pretty to look at, began to be widely manufactured in the last decades of the nineteenth century, and soon became abundant and cheap. The first artificially produced ice east of Suez was used by the British Royal Navy for cooling gun turrets, but the Indians soon caught on. In 1878, the Bengal Ice Company was set up in Calcutta. Close on its heels came the Crystal Ice Company. Soon, it was curtains for the Indo-American ice trade.

Within a few short years, artificially produced ice would change everything. Artificially produced ice on boats meant that you could fish further, and for longer, and bring bigger catches back without the fish spoiling. Meat and fruit could move further, and more people could be nourished. The commodification of ice and cold would, in the late nineteenth century, become complete. Iceland on every high street would be just over the horizon.

But that is a story for the next chapter.

6

# The Sheep Shifters

*Manufactured ice, food preservation and the
birth of the 'coldscape'*

> *The petitioners do not apprehend it a natural thing
> or agreeable to the spirit of commerce to allow the
> Produce of the Earth or Water, designed for the food
> of the inhabitants of the place where such produce
> arises, to be taken from these inhabitants and carried
> to distant corners of the world.*
>> Petition to Perth Town Council about salmon
>> exports (1774)

> *Cold arrests all change.*
>> Thomas Sutcliffe Mort, speech to the Council of
>> the Agricultural Society of New South Wales (1875)

> *Ice is civilization.*
>> Paul Theroux, *The Mosquito Coast* (1981)

A question kept nagging at me as I researched the *yakhchāls*,
ice houses and other ice stores: what was actually in them? Ice,
of course, but what else? If there had been anything more, the
records were conspicuously – though not quite uniformly – silent.
The path I had traced was overwhelmingly one of consumption.
Food preservation had barely got a look in.

But food goes off. It rots. Bacteria colonise it, yeasts and moulds devour it. Its own enzymes break it down. Decay is intrinsic to existence and there's nothing you can do to stop it; you can only slow it down. Over hundreds, even thousands, of years, the goal of using ice to preserve food was pursued with increasing precision and vigour through technological revolutions, with natural and then manufactured ice, until, towards the end of the nineteenth century, it had become a linchpin of the global colonial system.

People have known about the preservative power of cool from the earliest times. We probably worked out that keeping mammoth steaks at the back of the cave would extend their edible life, but there are also human-made pits without any obvious function, dating from the Palaeolithic period onwards, that one writer has suggested could plausibly have been crude ice or snow wells – and if that's true then cold was something we engineered. In northern Alaska, the Iñupiat natives have traditionally used 'ice cellars' dug into the permafrost, possibly for thousands of years, for storing meat from seasonal hunts, year-round, in a bacteria-free environment.

By the second century CE the Greek physician Galen was noting that 'snow preserveth fish from corruption as also flesh from putrefaction', and there are reports of 'ice chambers' in Han Dynasty China (202 BCE–220 CE). Later, during the Tang Dynasty (618–907 CE), ice was used as a preservative so that fresh fruit could be eaten out of season.

However, the idea that ice could be used to prolong a foodstuff's life is one that did not seem, in the long history of ice and food in the temperate world, to be as prominent as the idea of consuming ice as a delicacy. But food preservation grew to be much more significant in the grand scheme of things than the predilection of rich people through the ages for chilling their drinks. It leads us towards manufactured ice, which, eventually, would kill off the use of lake ice around the world, and usher us into the modern age of 'cold chain' logistics.

The story starts, more or less, with an unfortunate misadventure. In 1626, according to John Aubrey's *Brief Lives*, Francis Bacon was out in his carriage with Dr Witherborne, a physician to the king, discussing whether low temperatures might preserve meat in the same way salt did. Witherborne was sceptical, so Bacon, to prove his theory, 'alighted out of the Coach, and went into a poore woman's house at the bottome of Highgate-hill, and bought a Hen, and made the woman extenterate [gut] it, and then stuffed the body with snow'.

How long the hen lasted is not recorded by Aubrey, but the early experiment in refrigeration did not extend Bacon's use-by date. 'My lord did help to do it himself,' Aubrey writes. 'The Snow so chilled him that he fell so immediately ill that he could not return to his lodging.' Afflicted, he was put to bed at the Earl of Arundel's in Highgate, but the bed was damp and he caught a chill.

Bacon was never cured: he died a few days later.[1]

Robert Boyle, following in Bacon's footsteps, must have been aware of the latter's interest in cold preservation, which, as we'll see later, also manifested in other ways. And indeed, Boyle mentions food preservation in ice once or twice in his *New Experiments* – the experiment principally being 'What does X taste like when defrosted?' Beef was, according to Boyle, 'insipid', and iced beer 'dispirited, like phlegm'. He also mentions meat being successfully preserved in ice in cellars in Modena – but there the trail begins to run cold.

Why did using ice to preserve food not assume greater importance in Britain and Europe earlier? My best guess is that, in most places, when there was ice there was not an abundance of food that needed preserving. And when there was fresh food – fruit, vegetables, meat – there was generally no ice. For technology to become useful there needs to be a coincidence of need and opportunity. It took 150 years for this to happen. (And even that's disregarding the countless years of knowledge in China, Ancient

---

[1] Whether or not the chicken debacle is in all details true is somewhat debatable, but Aubrey claims to have been told it by Thomas Hobbes, who as a young man worked as Bacon's amanuensis – not an unreliable source.

Greece and elsewhere.) The British were, let's say, a little slow on the uptake.[2]

There was at least one glaring missed opportunity. That came in 1763 when John Bell, a Scottish doctor in the service of Tsar Peter the Great of Russia, published *Travels from St Petersburg in Russia to Diverse Parts of Asia*, describing a journey across Siberia to Peking forty years previously. Bell arrived in November 1720 after sixteen months' travel, and that Christmas was presented with a 'large sturgeon and some other fresh fish' – the gift of a Jesuit priest, brought from a river several thousand kilometres distant. 'These can only be carried to such a distance in the coldest season, when they are preserved by being kept frozen among the snow,' Bell wrote. He also recognised the important principle of fast freezing: 'This method is practised with success in northern countries; for, provided the fish is immediately exposed to the frost after being caught, it may be carried in snow for many miles, almost as fresh as when taken out of the water.'

The book was well received, but evidently not by the sort of people who were interested in carrying large fish long distances and then eating them. The moment of action came over twenty years later, in 1785, when William Dalrymple, an official in the British East India Company, happened to describe to George Dempster, MP for the Perth Burghs, a phenomenon he'd observed during long travels in China: ice houses and snow stores lining the coast. It was customary, Dalrymple said, for Chinese fishermen to carry ice on their boats to preserve their catches at sea, and then on their onward journey overland to market. From the description Dalrymple gave, the Chinese ice houses were an efficient system for fishing boats to restock whenever and wherever they needed. Each store would be cleverly replenished by flooding local rice fields during winter and then harvesting the ice. This was, then, the beginnings of the industrialisation of fishing.

---

[2] Not just us: Elizabeth David reports that in France a monk, Father Berthier, experimented with putting fruit and vegetables in jars between blocks of ice in an ice house, but this was 'regarded as of little practical value'.

Dempster's were the right ears for this information to reach. As a former director of the East India Company, he knew something about long-distance trade, and as an MP he was a proud (and rich) Scot who spent time down south. He also had a salmon supplier. Spying a good wheeze, he fired off a letter to said Scottish salmon supplier on the spot. This man, a Mr Richardson, was sceptical, but he agreed to pack some freshly caught salmon in boxes filled with pounded ice and put them on a boat to London. When they arrived six days later, they were in excellent condition.

After this proof of concept it did not take long for Richardson to construct ice houses at various points between Perth and the mouth of the Tay, nor for others to join him.

But oh how close this was to not taking place! In October 1786, *Scots* magazine published a letter from Richardson lauding his compatriot for acting on the idea and admitting that he had 'made the experiment rather in consequence of Mr Dempster's earnest manner of writing, than in expectation of any good, but that it answered beyond expectation, and that, should any benefit result therefrom, either to the public or individual, to that patriotic gentleman Mr Dempster it owes its beginning in this country and to none else.' That Christmas he made Dempster a gift of £200, a huge sum, and sent him a fresh salmon every month of the season for the rest of his days. Richardson's gloss on events suggests that Dalrymple did not see a share.

Where previously only small supplies of fresh salmon could be sent down to London in the very coldest months, putting it on ice dramatically extended the window of its availability as a fresh delicacy. The creation of this luxury market brought money flooding in to Perth,[3] as well as port, cheese and groceries returning on any of the seven smacks that were constantly sailing from the town to London, a voyage that could take as little as sixty hours.

[3] The town's traditional main export was salted salmon, though salt was heavily taxed and in some years as difficult to get hold of as ice. In the 1740s 'kitted' fish – boiled salmon packed in barrels with vinegar – made an appearance. Both preserved the life of the fish but were inferior products.

It also created problems. Tensions grew between the fishers in the Firth, who used stake nets, and the line fishers and riverbank proprietors upstream, who as a consequence of the nets did not see so many fish coming their way. A few years after the introduction of ice houses and iced transport, catches dipped slightly and Richardson expressed fears that the river might be being overfished. Trading practices became more hard-nosed, the export market began to dominate and the local population fell out of the habit of eating salmon: selling salmon to locals which could otherwise be making big profits in London was 'subversive of every principle of commerce'.[4] The townspeople did not like this, but there was little they could do.

The changes in the salmon business were not limited to the Tay: after Richardson's triumph, small ice houses sprang up along many of Scotland's finest salmon rivers, so the fish could be chilled as soon after being caught as possible. Soon there were cavernous ice houses at Findhorn, at Tugnet by the Spey and south of the border at Berwick-upon-Tweed, and high-quality fresh salmon was reaching Billingsgate market in London from as far away as Aberdeen and Inverness. Then the decidedly more proletarian herring fisheries on the Forth caught on, and began to pack herring on smacks from Berwick next to their more refined cousins. The practice spread south over the course of the nineteenth century: Fleetwood, Hull, Grimsby, Great Yarmouth and other commercial fishing ports built industrial ice houses to chill their catches.

In 1795, another Scotsman travelled south, this one with the delightfully Dickensian name of Scrymgeour Hewett. Hewett married Sarah Whennel of Barking, a fishing port in Essex, and eventually took over her father's fishing boats, known as the Short

---

[4] Actually this quote dates to 1774/5, when, as the kitted-salmon market grew, the townspeople brought a court case against the Burgh for not specifying in new fishing licences that some be supplied to Perth market for locals to buy. The Burgh argued back: if the townspeople were not starving, why should they 'so insist on eating at a low price, and during the season when it is a rarity, the fresh salmon which can be sold at a very high price in London for the use of the luxurious table of the Rich and Great?' Ice would only accelerate this profit-first thinking.

Blue Fleet after the small square flag they flew. His son, Samuel, took the reins of the business in 1815 and the fleet expanded dramatically, most significantly when, in the 1820s, he began using ice: first expensive ice from Norway and then cheaper local supplies, which he collected from more than 3,000 local farmers whom he had persuaded to flood the fields and marshes around Barking in winter.

Samuel Hewett invented a system of fishing known as 'fleeting', in which fishing boats would stay out on Dogger Bank in the North Sea for weeks at a time, catching fish and packing them in ice. These were serviced by 'carrier' boats that would bring food, drink and more ice, and take the catches back to dry land. By the middle of the century, Samuel had the largest fishing fleet in the UK, up to 220 smacks crewed by 1,500 men, mostly far from land at the mercy of the North Sea weather. It must have been grim work, even with the presence of *copers*, boats from Holland and Belgium that hung around the fleets selling duty-free spirits and tobacco, often rendering the miserable, unwashed fishermen dangerously drunk.

Around 1860, Samuel Hewett and his son Robert decided that sailing all the way from Barking up to Dogger Bank was a waste of time, and relocated the Short Blue Fleet to Gorleston-on-Sea in Norfolk, where there was a capacious ice house and trains that could take his iced-up catch swiftly to the capital. Consequently, a good part of Barking's economy collapsed. There, as in Scotland, traditional livelihoods were streamlined and industrialised out of existence. Though there was little mechanisation in either place at this time – no fish farms, no bottom dredgers, not even steam-powered boats until the 1860s – this was the Industrial Revolution played out in miniature, fuelled not by factory furnaces or weaving looms but by ice. Mass production, poor working conditions and large inequalities, the priority of the market and alienation of workers from the fruits of their labour are all the classic symptoms.

The Hewett ice house in Barking reportedly held 10,000 tons of frozen Essex marsh water. In London ice was an object of ostentation, praised for its purity of form and literally the centrepiece of meals and social occasions; here, the muddy ice was an industrial technology, integrated into a process, hidden away.

\*\*\*

It is difficult to chart how the idea of ice as a preservative filtered into British polite society and domestic use. It wasn't until the first half of the nineteenth century, as far as I can make out, that ice houses on country estates began to be used to store dairy and products from the orchards or kitchen garden, alongside hooks for meat to hang next to the ice. A book by the architect John Papworth from 1818 stated that 'the ice house forms an excellent larder for the preservation of every kind of food that is liable to be injured by heat in summer,' while in 1834 another Victorian garden designer dispensed advice on how to achieve different degrees of cooling by placing items at different proximities to the ice. But this knowledge took time to percolate through. A garden encyclopaedia from 1850 advised: 'In England, many persons are deterred from forming an ice house by the idea that . . . ice is only useful for making ice creams and cooling wines: but . . . as a place for preserving meat, fish, fruit and vegetables, there is not a more useful appendage to a country house.' No doubt it was, at least in part, the introduction of larger volumes of pristine ice from Norway and the United States that triggered changes in Britain's perceptions and habits. The timing can scarcely be a coincidence.

In the US, though there were much greater natural supplies of ice, they were unevenly distributed in time and space, favouring the north and the colder months of winter. At the turn of the nineteenth century, most farmers still travelled to market by night (for the comparative coolness), butchers would only kill for a single day's supply of meat and fishmongers tried to keep their product alive until money changed hands. In 1802, a Maryland farmer called Thomas Moore created a cabinet with an icebox to keep his butter cool on the way to market. Moore called his innovation a 'refrigeratory' for a while, before dropping the 'y' in his patent application the following year to give us the word we know today. 'Every housekeeper', he shouted hopefully in a pamphlet, 'may have one in his cellar, in which, by the daily use of a few pounds of ice, fresh provisions may be preserved . . . at any temperature.'

Despite such promotional claims, it was probably Frederic Tudor who made the domestic market viable. His innovations with Nathaniel Wyeth, in both the cutting and the insulating, made good-quality ice available to more people from the mid-1820s onwards. The second factor in the rise of iced transport was the population explosion in the cities of the East Coast, full of sedentary people for whom their forebears' heavy, monotonous diet of salted and smoked fare was both unpalatable and unsuitable. Increasing numbers of people were affluent enough to pay for fresher and more varied food.

By the 1840s, a refrigerator was present in many well-kept urban American homes, a wooden box insulated with cork or zinc with an ice compartment at the top designed to fit the standardised blocks delivered by the city's ice men. And the view from *that* side of the Atlantic was that the Old World was backward: 'Ice is an American institution – the use of it an American luxury – the abuse of it an American failing,' asserted an (American) magazine writer in 1855, adding that, while domestic refrigeration was widespread in the US, in Europe it was 'confined to the wine cellars of the rich, and the cooling pantries of first class confectioners'.

'First class' may well be the salient words here: given the social context and the famous strictures of the class system, my hunch is that the idea to use ice for preservation rather than jollification in Britain must have been introduced by the staff. On country estates, ice houses were in some instances the responsibility of the gardeners (if at a remove from the house) and, in others, the domestics (if close).⁵ Some country ice houses are situated en route from the kitchen garden to the kitchen, making them natural receptacles for produce. And some of those same gardeners, cooks and maids might also have had suppliers, relatives or acquaintances in the fishing business. After all, many big houses,

⁵ One of the most curious uses of ice was in forcing the vegetation of ornamental plants – presumably banked around the unfortunate plant to trick it into thinking summer was late that year.

including the Windhams' Felbrigg Hall in north Norfolk, are not far from important fishing ports.

But the caricatured American view of stuck-up Brits, at least ice-wise, does seem to be broadly true. Notwithstanding ice's relative availability to households in London and other big cities, and the booming street trade in 'penny licks', elsewhere it was more restricted, divided between industry and high society.[6] The truth was that the forces driving change in America were so much more consequential. As with many things, Americans did food preservation bigger and, for a long while, better. The USA had climate extremes – both the cold to create the product and heat to create demand – as well as explosive population growth, millions of immigrants who both brought with them European food traditions, including perhaps a predilection for ice, and constituted a fast-expanding market for more and better food. And the vast distances that opened up as European settlers pushed west demanded grand logistical solutions. None of these, in this particular story of nineteenth-century American modernity, were more important than 'that amazing iron net which now covers . . . all the civilised portions of the Earth': the railroad.

Refrigerated transport by rail was an idea that had multiple fathers, and they were all American. It originated on the East Coast, which seems, given the concentration of money, people and cold there, only natural.[7] By the 1840s ice was being used on the railroads around Boston to keep butter and cheese cool – again, hardly surprising, given that in this neck of the woods any carpenter would have been able to learn enough from the storage compartments on Frederic Tudor's ships to build something railworthy. There was also an Albany-to-Buffalo oyster express as well as salmon trains inland from Maine. By 1852 Boston cod and haddock were being sold in Chicago.

---

[6] Elizabeth David, however, states that any ice destined for fisheries came in tax free – which probably led to a black market in fishery ice for domestic use.

[7] The UK was simply too small – and ice too scarce – to make figuring out how to chill and insulate railway cars worthwhile. Instead, meat was packed in hampers, which were unwieldy for those loading them, and did little to protect the cargo. Insulated ice-cooled railway cars began appearing on the continent around the turn of the twentieth century.

Farmers of other fresh foodstuffs then began to create viable ways of icing up their goods for transport to faraway markets by rail – producers like Samuel Rumph growing peaches in Georgia, Edwin Tobias Earl producing Californian oranges and Parker Earle with his strawberry plantations in Illinois. So ice helped to create regional specialities and a widely distributed consumer economy: there was no point in marketing a Georgia peach, an Oregon apple or a Florida grapefruit if it was rotten when it was unloaded from the freight train. Local character was great as long as you could sell it.

Maybe that last line is just sour grapes, a glance in the rear-view mirror from a world in which chilled foods travel from continent to continent, creating monocultures and destroying seasonality. Ours is a privileged place where good things to eat can be found on every street corner, but our relationship and attitudes to food are complicated. At the time these technological marvels were often seen as liberating, and vital: the huddled masses needed to eat. Ralph Waldo Emerson expressed this New World optimism in a lecture entitled 'The Young American' that he gave in Boston in 1844: 'the locomotive and the steamboat, like enormous shuttles, shoot every day across the thousand various threads of national descent and employment, and bind them fast in one web,' he said. 'An unlooked for consequence of the railroad, is the increased acquaintance it has given the American people with the boundless resources of their own soil.' Note the association with that other great engine of the Industrial Revolution, the steam-powered weaving loom.

More than any of these fruit, however, the real prize in these grand geographical imbalances of supply and demand lay in mastering the transportation of meat. During the first years of the nineteenth century, cattle and sheep might be driven as far as 500 miles from the states of Kentucky and Ohio to Philadelphia or Baltimore, on their way to the hungry mouths that awaited.[8] But

---

[8] And by driven I mean herded on foot. Pigs were more rarely driven, since they fared less well on the road and they lost more weight, and are in any case more tasty salted or smoked than are cattle or sheep.

being driven such large distances led to significant weight loss and poorer-quality meat. And this was only an option for medium-range meat – some states were just too far away. Ice would bridge the gap between the vast herds of the Great Plains and Texas, the slaughterhouses of the Midwest and consumers on the Atlantic coast. Achieving the final technological link in this supply chain is often attributed to a businessman called Gustavus Swift.

Swift, born in Massachusetts in 1839, was first a butcher, then a livestock buyer and then a prime mover in meatpacking, an industry whose rapid growth depended on ice. He moved west as his business grew and in 1875 finally settled in Chicago, where a major confluence of railway lines consolidated livestock trains from the West. A decade earlier, a consortium of railroad companies had built the Union Stockyards, a vast facility for processing live animals destined for sale, onward travel or slaughter, attracting businessmen like Swift like wasps to a picnic. But after the stockyards came the tricky bit: how to get the animals in prime condition to the tables of the East Coast without resorting – low-value product klaxon! – to salting or smoking the meat? From Chicago to New York was another four days' journey, and a significant number always died en route. Also, given that roughly 50 per cent of a cow or a pig is inedible, transporting the whole beast was simply inefficient.[9] Before the railroads, Chicago had a poor supply of ice, which was mainly used in brewing beer; with the arrival of the railroads, plentiful ice could roll in from Wisconsin, and then roll back out again with the meat – extending the meatpacking business into a year-round trade.

It remained only to work out how to arrange this best. Early attempts to keep Chicago-slain carcasses from spoiling in transit had been no more sophisticated than leaving the boxcar doors open so the cargo was cooled by the wind (this worked in cool weather); and it was found that packing meat *in* ice affected the

---

[9] In most histories it is mainly cattle that are talked about, possibly because this fits more easily into the country-defining myth of the Wild West and the great American cowboy. Texan sheep and the millions of hogs produced in states like Iowa, Illinois and Minnesota are somewhat less romantic.

taste and made it discolour. Various efforts were made to separate ice and meat, but early refrigerated boxcar designs placed the meat above the ice, resulting in a top-heavy load: when a speeding train entered a corner, the carcasses would swing on their hooks, which could cause derailments. In the late 1870s, several patents were issued for improved versions, and in 1878, Swift hired an engineer, Andrew Chase, who cracked the conundrum. In their design, the ice was placed in a ceiling cavity connected by adjustable vents to the meatpacking space below. This had the virtue of conforming to basic laws of physics on two counts: first, the cool air descended, regulating the temperature more evenly; second, with the carcasses placed low down, the boxcar had a lower centre of gravity. A stable car that kept its contents at a stable temperature.

The wider railroad industry, however, was reluctant to buy into this new refrigerated technology: since the birth of the Union Stockyards it had invested far too much in livestock cars, feedlots and pens for live transports to willingly make them obsolete – so Swift put his railroad cars into production himself and took delivery of rolling stock in 1880.

Keeping the boxcars cool also required ice stations to be set up every 250 miles or so to replenish the cold, with each car of refrigerated beef needing 880 lb (400 kg) of ice and 660 lb (300 kg) of salt at each one.[10] But it was worth it: in 1882 Swift had around 200 cars and, in total, 2,683 tons of dressed beef reached New York that year; by 1886 it was nigh on 70,000 tons, and the tonnage of live cattle had fallen by around 20 per cent.

Seventy thousand tons of beef, 'dressed' and packaged to be sold (and also graded and traded on futures markets); as much as the railroads were weaving the country together, they were also severing the links between the food consumers bought and the people, animals and plants that provided it. In 1842, one of the earliest attempts at creating a refrigerator car promised to convert 'the whole country into a garden for our great cities'. In the 1880s, the industry was making good on that promise. Or, at least, making it all pasture for cows, sheep and pigs.

---

[10] There'll be more about the role of salt in freezing things in Chapter 9.

By delaying the processes of decay, ice froze time. And freezing time collapsed space: it enabled a supply chain to span a nation so large it did not yet know its own edges, with Chicago's 'disassembly-line' slaughterhouses at its heart, just as it enabled salmon to leap from one end of Britain to the other. Fresh stuff could get from where it was (a Scottish stream, Dogger Bank, the Texan plains) to where it was needed (Chicago) or at least desired (Felbrigg Hall, New York, London).

Refrigerated transportation was not just aggressive in a business sense. It possessed a colonising force. The connection between the spread of railroads across North America and the dispossession of its native peoples, the gunfights, the forced requisition of land and its turning over to cattle, its enclosure in vast ranches, is well known. By carrying carcasses one way, ice funnelled dollars the other and helped to secure the economic viability of the new cowboy settlements, playing a role in 'civilising' the Wild West.

It also supplied other wars more directly. An army marches on its stomach. Chicago's rise to prominence in the meat trade had been boosted during the American Civil War (1860–5), even though cold supply was still experimental, at best, thanks to large orders from the US government destined for the front lines. Thirty years later, during the Spanish–American War of 1898, the links in the cold chain were still sometimes no more reliable. That war, which began as a dispute over Spain's influence in the Caribbean, lasted a matter of months, but long enough for one of the commanding generals to accuse the government of providing up to 337 tons of condemned meat to his men in Cuba. A subsequent inquiry held on President William McKinley's orders found that poor hygiene, slow delivery and a lack of ice in transport and cold storage facilities in Cuba were instead to blame.

Even the might of the government – however hard it worked and however much ice could be harvested in the north-eastern states – could not guarantee there was enough cold in the right places.

\*\*\*

As a consequence of the Spanish–American War, the Americans took control of Spain's possessions in the South Pacific. When they arrived in Manila in 1900, one of the first things they did was build a giant ice plant. Once fully up and running, this manufactured about 1,200 tons of ice per month. In addition, it provided cold storage at 1 °C for perishables including dairy and fruit, and rooms at −14 °C for meat.

The technology to manufacture ice was, at this point, around half a century old, yet it had ancient roots. As we saw in the previous chapter, an all-natural version of icemaking had been practised in Persia probably for thousands of years, and employed in India too. In Europe, icemaking had been a preoccupation at least since the seventeenth century. In 1624, no less a figure than Francis Bacon wrote: 'The Producing of Cold is a thing very worthy the Inquisition. For heat and cold are Nature's two hands, by which we chiefly worketh; and Heat we have in readiness; but for Cold we must stay 'til it cometh.' If we could readily control the manufacture of ice, suggested Bacon, then all sorts of possibilities might await.

The mechanisms behind ice's modern manufacture are in part based upon what the Persians and Indians intuitively knew when they built their shallow pools: that when a substance changes phase from solid to liquid or liquid to gas – like water evaporating under a clear desert sky – it draws heat from its surroundings. The second vital principle is derived from the laws governing a gas's pressure, volume and temperature, which began to be formulated by Robert Boyle. Essentially, the combined gas law (which unifies Boyle's Law with the work of other scientists that followed him) decrees that if you pressurise a fixed amount of gas it heats up. Decompress it and it will abstract heat, make things cold.

The first person to create artificial cold mechanically was a Scotsman called William Cullen, who in 1741 put some diethyl ether in a partial vacuum. As the liquid ether depressurised and became a gas, it lowered the surrounding temperature, even creating some ice, but Cullen did not explore the practical possibilities of his achievement. In 1828, Richard Trevithick – a more practical man, the Cornish inventor of the first working locomotive – heard about the reputed £100,000-a-year ice trade from Norway to the UK and wondered if there might not be a better form of supply. 'A thought struck me at the moment that artificial cold may be made very cheap by the power of steam engines,' he wrote. He was right: technology was finally catching up with the desire to make ice, and the next thirty or forty years saw experimentation with steam-powered refrigeration systems across Europe and in the US.

As with refrigerated boxcars, several people came up with systems to manufacture ice at around the same time, although they flipped Cullen's modus operandi around in various ways. Several different refrigerants were used early on – ether, ammonia, ethanol (alcohol) and even air itself – but the 'vapour compression' system, first patented in 1834, eventually proved to be the most thermodynamically efficient. Most air-conditioning units, modern refrigerated transport and commercial and domestic refrigeration work in this way. To take the kitchen fridge as an exemplar, the thin pipes at the back are full of pressurised liquid refrigerant. When this is passed via an expansion valve into the wider pipes within the insulated compartment, it depressurises, evaporates and absorbs heat from that space, cooling the contents down. As the refrigerant leaves the compartment, it is compressed, and condenses and heats up, then runs through the external pipes again, cooling all the while, and goes for another ride. This, in its own quiet way, is miraculous: by making heat move from a cold place (the refrigerated compartment) to a warmer one (the outside), it thwarts the second law of thermodynamics. Bacon had not believed producing cold was possible; it only took 200 or so years to prove him wrong.

One of the first to develop a viable method of mechanical cooling in the USA was a doctor called John Gorrie. In the 1840s, it was commonly thought that diseases such as yellow fever and malaria, which regularly swept through the southern US states, were caused by miasma (not viruses carried by insects: *mala aria* is Italian for 'bad air'), and that this bad air was made worse by heat. In the house in the Floridian port town of Apalachicola where he had set up business, Gorrie hung buckets of ice in the infirmary above his feverish patients, with a complicated series of pipes spanning several floors to try to ensure air movement and ventilation, and to remove the humidity from the warm air. This had some tangible cooling effect, but ice was very difficult to come by.

Hearing of early experiments with refrigeration, Gorrie threw himself into developing his own icemaker, using compressed air as a refrigerant. A similar system was patented in the UK well before his, but Gorrie was astute enough to know that healthcare was not the only application, and he set about publicising his invention. In 1847, on Bastille Day, he invited the French consul, Monsieur Rosan, to serve champagne flutes nestled in ice to a select gathering. 'On Bastille Day, France gave her citizens what they wanted; and Rosan gives his guests what they want – cool wines!' the consul is reported to have said.

J. GORRIE.
ICE MACHINE.

No. 8,080.                    Patented May 6, 1851.

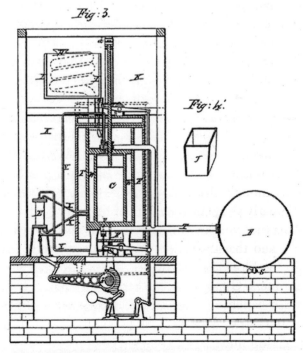

*A page from Dr John Gorrie's US patent.*

Gorrie's path to success was not smooth. Although he received a UK patent in 1850, followed by a US one in 1851, he met opposition, vilification and ridicule. Sir John F. W. Herschel of the British Royal Society claimed that in 1848 *he* had invented the idea of producing ice using compressed air (Herschel had manufactured nothing, and Gorrie had credited him for his thinking). There was also a backlash against the very idea of manufactured ice on those age-old grounds of it being somehow against nature and sacrilegious; Gorrie was a 'crank' who 'thinks he can make ice by his machine as good as God Almighty', according to a journalist for the *New York Globe*.

This was all, he suspected, a smear campaign by Frederic Tudor, then at the height of his wealth and fame. 'Moral causes . . . have been brought into play to prevent [the machine's] use,' Gorrie wrote, though he did not name names. It would be entirely reasonable to think that Tudor, with his established supply routes to southern cities like Savannah, Charleston and New Orleans, *did* feel threatened. Perhaps God *was* against Gorrie, or perhaps Gorrie was simply paranoid and unlucky; in the 1850s, a business partner died, leaving him without money, and he was reduced to writing advertorials for his discovery under pen names ('This discovery must be *of immense value to all living South* . . . contains full instructions for making ice and ice creams, cooling water, and other useful matters, will be forwarded to readers for Two Dollars, by addressing Dr. James R. Wilmington.') – the pseudonyms, it has been suggested, to protect him from criticism. There were also other inventors sniffing around: an engineer called William Siemens, a naturalised Brit born in Germany, took an interest in the machine and filed some patents of his own.

Gorrie ran out of steam before realising his icy vision. Unlike Siemens, whose name lives on through his connection to the home appliances brand, he died in poverty, all but forgotten, in 1874.

From a modern vantage point it seems strange that Gorrie and other pioneers did not succeed. The fundamental processes were understood and the basic technology existed; their challenge was rather to prove there was a commercial application for machines that created ice. But to change industrial practices and ingrained habits takes time. That change was coming. What followed the arrival of commercially viable icemakers was a kind of battle for the soul of ice.

Even when God's supposed opposition to the machines was overcome, there were plenty who did not like manufactured ice and refused to use it. Manufactured ice lacked life, according to some, who doubted it would conserve food in the same way lake ice did. It also tended to be cloudy, thanks to tiny air bubbles trapped within during the rapid artificial cooling process, whereas the best slow-frozen lake ice was crystal clear. Lake-ice purveyors vaunted its purity, even though many of the Massachusetts lakes where the industry had been born were increasingly polluted (in the late nineteenth century, Maine would take over from Massachusetts as the US's prime supplier). It may seem bizarre now, but natural ice companies also advertised their harvest as more reliably available, since early mechanical systems were prone to breaking down.[11] Queen Victoria – and many others – stayed faithful to their daily delivered Wenham Lake ice for many years after manufactured ice went on sale.

In the US, the tipping point from natural to artificial came with the American Civil War, which cut the South off from the northern lake ice. This was bad for the Confederate war effort, and also for those who liked fresh produce, meat and fish, iced tea, juleps and all the other indispensables and daily luxuries to which people had become accustomed. This spurred the investment in artificial-ice production; by 1865, New Orleans had three factories producing ice.

Around two decades later, Mark Twain took a trip along the Mississippi and, reaching the city of Natchez, found cause for reflection in how the establishment of an ice plant had transformed one of the river's most venerable towns: 'like Vicksburg and New

[11] This might have been true in the US, with plentiful supplies and ice houses with sophisticated insulation, but the UK had very poor natural supplies and was at the mercy of the climate, both at home and abroad. For example, on Valentine's Day 1846, the *Berwick Examiner*, which kept a close eye on the salmon trade, reported that 'The winter has thus far proceeded and not a single load of ice has been procured. In fact the pools which are kept for its production have never so much as been once coated.'

Orleans, [Natchez] has her ice-factory; she makes thirty tons of ice a day. In Vicksburg and Natchez, in my time, ice was jewelry; none but the rich could wear it. But anybody and everybody can have it now.'

Twain visited an ice factory in New Orleans, 'to see what the polar regions might look like when lugged into the edge of the tropics', but he was disappointed. All he saw instead was 'a spacious house with some innocent steam machinery', plus row upon row of tin boxes full of water, pipes to bring the refrigerant, men stirring the water as it cooled to liberate the air bubbles, and frozen blocks being dunked in a vat of boiling water so they could be removed from their tin jackets. This ice was incredibly cheap and was supplied by cart to New Orleans, to saloons, restaurants, homes and even barbershops and other premises, which would place ice in their windows to cool the room.

What had begun as a harvest was now an industrial process almost like any other.

\*\*\*

I've used 'cold chain' a couple of times in this chapter, a term that describes the series of subzero environments linking the farm or the slaughterhouse to the point of sale and the consumer, wherever they may be. Today, we have reached its apotheosis and logical endpoint: no more steam engines and carts loaded with blocks of ice wrapped in cloths, but freezer factories, refrigerated air cargo, shipping containers and HGVs, chiller cabinets and home freezers, a series of unbroken links so normal and so hidden from view behind the branded, packaged product that we don't give them a second thought.

This endpoint is of course a daily reality only in the privileged parts of the world, and, while logical, it was not preordained. To get here took a grand vision. This is, after all, a story of scale increasing exponentially. But who could think bigger than the Americans? Inevitably, it seems, that means delving once again into the history of the British Empire, to people who desired to span not only a continent but the whole world.

Thomas Sutcliffe Mort was born in Bolton in Lancashire in 1816, and had been fascinated by freezing since childhood, when he had first learned about woolly mammoths appearing miraculously intact from the Siberian permafrost. It might seem surprising, then, that after receiving a general education in commerce and working as a clerk, he emigrated to Australia, where he duly became involved in the wool trade. In a spirit of cheerful settler idealism, he branched out into mining, dry docking, manufacturing and farming as he prospered. Although he made a lot of money, he spent almost as much on community-minded schemes in loose affiliation with businessmen, thinkers and those with dirt beneath their fingernails, and when his old obsession with freezing came back into play, he drew on these contacts – including a French-born engineer called Eugène Dominique Nicolle, who was experimenting with refrigerant technology, and a Scotsman, James Harrison, who in 1851 opened Australia's first commercial ice plant at Rocky Point in New South Wales.

Mort's challenge, initially, was to get the butter produced on his farm to market in better condition, but from modest beginnings grew a campaign combining his love of ice with his hatred of waste. Australia does not have much in the way of natural ice resources, but it did have increasing amounts of products, including Mort's butter, that would benefit from refrigeration. Which brings us back to the sheep.

It is a truism that certain countries have more sheep than people, none more so than Australia in the nineteenth century: in 1874, figures for New South Wales, Victoria, Queensland and South Australia record 1,760,865 people and 47,824,299 sheep.[12] Most Australian sheep were primarily kept for wool, and tallow was a secondary product, but there was a wild excess of meat. Mort quoted these numbers in a speech to an agricultural body in 1875 and, even allowing, as he did, for 350 pounds (about 160 kilos) of lamb per person for local consumption annually (350 pounds!),

---

[12] Also 5,648,709 cattle.

Australia could, in his opinion, still afford to export 300,000 tons a year. Indeed, it couldn't afford not to.

Meanwhile, Britain, at the centre of the Empire, badly needed more food to support burgeoning numbers of urban, industrial workers who weren't producing it themselves.[13] Mort believed passionately that these complementary though very distant wants and needs should be connected, but the voyage was far too long and the cargo too delicate for Frederic Tudor-style ice-powered cooling to be viable. For a shipment to survive the journey across the equator, there would have to be an on-ship refrigeration plant, but, in terms of maintenance, safety and numerous other factors, this would be a much more difficult proposition than a land-based plant. Mort spent years canvassing for subscriptions for an experimental sailing. He also bankrolled Nicolle's work researching freezing technologies for over a decade, latterly at the Fresh Food & Ice Company on Darling Harbour, spending at his own estimation about $100,000.

His zeal, while commercial in intent, seems genuine. On 2 September 1875, he held an inauguration ceremony for his newly built slaughterhouse and iceworks near a town called Lithgow. For this, he organised a train from Sydney with more than 300 notables and members of the press aboard. There he served a picnic of beef, pigeon pie and a quince pie with ice cream for desert and made a stirring speech, in which the human mastery of ice is presented not as heresy, presumption or impudence – attitudes that we've seen repeatedly throughout this history – but as jubilant, optimistic:

> I now feel that the time is not far distant, when the various portions of the Earth will each give forth their products for the

[13] For those who think that Great Britain used to be self-sufficient in food production, in the industrial era that's never been the case. Live animal imports started in the 1850s and by 1882 the UK was importing 654,000 tons of livestock from Europe and the US. Dead meat was not imported into the UK in significant quantities until the mid-1860s, when an outbreak of cattle plague, which had probably come into the country in Russian cattle via an Estonian shipment, finally convinced authorities to limit live animal imports. This presented business opportunities for those wishing to import carcasses, and ports began to be equipped with more advanced cold storage facilities.

use of each and of all; that the overabundance of one country will make up for the deficiency of another; the superabundance of the year of plenty serving for the scant harvest of its successor; for cold arrests all change . . . Climate, seasons, plenty, scarcity, distance, all will shake hands, and out of the commingling will come enough for all.

Mort continued by explaining to his guests some of the difficulties behind refrigeration. Then as a *coup de grâce* he revealed that the beef and the pigeon they'd just eaten had been killed more than a year previously. Whether this stunt impressed anyone enough to sign up to his cause the newspapers do not record.

As with Gorrie, Mort's path to success was not smooth. In 1875, a shipment of ice-cooled Texan beef successfully reached London, both proving Mort's point and threatening to take over his market. The Atlantic voyage was short enough for Frederic Tudor-style ice chilling to be effective (and it would turn out that chilled rather than frozen beef was a better product). In the years that followed, ice-cooled meat shipments across the Atlantic would become common. And in 1877, on the morning Mort's first experimental shipment was supposed to sail, there was an ammonia leak and all the carcasses had to be offloaded. Also that year, the Australians and the British were beaten by the French in the quest to send meat from the southern to the northern hemisphere: in May 1878, the SS *Paraguay* docked in Le Havre laden with 5,500 sheep carcasses. Due to a crash, it had taken more than seven months to travel from Buenos Aires, but the soundly frozen meat was still good. However, it seems that a subsequent trip by the *Paraguay* for a much larger quantity of meat never set sail.

Mort in fact did not live to see his dream realised. After his death in 1878, experiments continued, and continued to fail, sometimes leading to whole cargoes of spoiled carcasses being thrown overboard mid ocean. Finally, on 6 December 1879, the SS *Strathleven*, a steamer that a group of entrepreneurial Queenslanders had borrowed from its usual Atlantic route, left

Melbourne packed with sheep and beef carcasses, plus some kegs of butter. It docked on 2 February 1880 in London, and the meat was reportedly excellent. Mort's dream of connecting Australasia to the UK was realised.

Some later shipments, however, fared less well. The meat may have arrived in good condition, but it was reported that the resulting cuts – perhaps because they were rather crudely frozen and not just chilled – were not to the Brits' tastes. There were also worries about the effects of the freezing process on the palatability and the nutritiousness of the flesh. In response to this 'alimentary truculence', as an academic, Rebecca J. H. Woods, put it, the Antipodeans could only do one thing: slash prices, inaugurating the uneasy dynamic we still live with today – domestic producers fearing for their livelihoods because their products are undercut by inferior, cheaper imports. But, overall, the arrangement worked for the British, providing cheap protein for mouths at home. Shipping meat strengthened Australasia's ties to the UK and sent much-needed money south, thereby reinforcing its colonial project. Again, ice was not innocent in this dynamic. As Woods also writes elsewhere: 'The ability to control, produce and claim ownership over cold was a matter of imperial economics and the politics of colonialism.'

It might seem a funny thing to say against this background of imperial transit, but I grew to like Mort as I tracked him through old books, newspapers and academic journals. Although his cryo-schemes were all forged within the politics of Empire, of all the Victorian gentlemen one meets in such travels, with their often dubious world-improvement schemes, there was something about his humanism that rang true. I think Mort was fighting against decay: food rots, people grow old, cities crumble and societies fall, everything decays eventually; not even ice can stop it. And he realised that ice meant lamb, butter and fresh greens on the table – nutrition, money and simply a cool place to sit on a summer's day free from the rigours of life in a hot and boundless land.

In Greek mythology, Prometheus stole fire from the gods and gave it to humankind, bestowing upon them civilisation. But if fire did civilise us, it only did half the job. Maybe the true Promethean moment happened when we mastered ice.

And here, on the cusp of large-scale production and consumption of cold, is where this chapter draws to a close. Because even though the story of the cold chain was only just beginning, ice quickly ceased to play a major part. Making ice was never really the endgame, you see: the endgame was making things cold, and ice was a middleman to be cut out as soon as was technologically possible. Cold became the product, not ice, and so from here on refrigeration will continue its journey without us.

There's just one more name to mention from this twilight period in ice's life as a preserver of food, and that's Birdseye. Not Captain, but Clarence. Clarence Birdseye was born in 1886 in Brooklyn, New York, and was an oddball child with a strong feeling for the natural world. As a young man he worked for the US Biological Survey, first in the Southwest, then Montana, where he removed thousands of ticks from wild mammals, helping to identify them as a cause of Rocky Mountain spotted fever. In 1912, he went to Labrador, then part of Newfoundland. There he spent some years farming fur, and, trying to keep his young family well fed, became interested in freezing food.[14] Whereas commercially available frozen food was generally mushy and unappetising (recall Robert Boyle's 'insipid' beef), Labrador-frozen food was almost indistinguishable from fresh. 'That first winter I saw natives catching fish in fifty below zero weather which froze stiff as soon as they were taken out of the water,' wrote Birdseye in an article for the *Beaver* magazine. 'Months later, when they were thawed out, some of the fish were so fresh that they were still alive!' (In this he was being literal: Arctic fish can survive being frozen, and revive when they are thawed in seawater.)

Birdseye began a process of experimentation that would lead him to conclude that flash freezing produces much smaller ice

---

[14] Bizarrely, both Birdseye's son and brother were called Kellogg.

crystals, thus damaging the flesh of the frozen foodstuff less. In the same article he admitted that when he was starting out he 'knew nothing of the virtues of quick freezing . . . and couldn't, in fact, have told a refrigeration compressor from a condenser'. His path to success was not smooth, but, as we all know, Birdseye, unlike Gorrie, succeeded.[15]

However, we should leave him there, as a young man with his long journey to ubiquity all before him. In his future, the complexities of the cold chain. Its transformation into the 'coldscape'.[16] The as yet unimagined and subtle complexities of the perfect fish finger. Here, in front of a hole cut in the ice on a frozen lake in Labrador, ringed by trees garlanded and muffled by snow, we are returned full circle to the start of all this: the wonder of a frozen fish.

[15] 'Captain' Birdseye, the marketing mascot, did not appear until 1967, nine years after Clarence's death, by which point the Birdseye brand was owned by the General Food Corporation. Clarence had sold his refrigeration company and patents in 1929 for the eye-watering sum of $22 million.

[16] Coined by writer Nicola Twilley in 2012, 'coldscape' has been defined as 'a constellation of social and technical systems that stabilize otherwise ephemeral and dynamic materials such that they can circulate, producing nutrition, comfort, health and knowledge, albeit unevenly across the globe'.

# 7

# The Tourists

## *The Mer de Glace: men and women in the upper ice world*

*The ice is near, the solitude is terrible – but how peacefully all things lie in the light. How freely one breathes! How much one feels beneath one! Philosophy, as I have understood it so far, is a voluntary living in regions of ice and high mountains – the seeking out of everything strange and questionable in existence, everything which hitherto morality has forbidden.*
Friedrich Nietzsche, *Ecce Homo* (1908)

*Strong as iron, carvable as cheese: what genius could have conceived so delicious a union of opposites if, by some disaster, glaciers had not been made?*
C. E. Montague, *Action* (1928)

*Well, then, now I am reduced to these white pages which I am to blot with dark imagery.*
Mary Shelley, journal, 2 October 1822

June 1741 and we're back to where we started, with William Windham as he quits the comfortable salons and theatrical pursuits of Geneva, and with seven friends and five servants makes his way to Chamonix, where he will discover ice.

Specifically, the Mer de Glace. He cannot have any inkling of it, but with this journey he is inaugurating an astonishing tradition of visitors to this frozen river (not sea!) in the shadow of Mont Blanc. In no small part because of Windham, over the course of the next century European intellects turned towards the mountains, elevating the Mer de Glace to a unique spot in our cultural imagination. On the Mer de Glace – site of scientific discoveries, literary inspiration and gateway to physical endeavour in the 'upper ice world'[1] – romanticism, scientism and athleticism became intimately intertwined. It is these three strands that I shall try to unpick, following them over the course of the eighteenth and nineteenth centuries as each one comes to the fore.

BW,[2] superstition reigned. Glaciers had been noted and described as early as Roman times by travellers in the mountains, travellers who, like Windham, may not have quite possessed the vocabulary to name what they were seeing, but who nevertheless recognised the danger and the desolation. Strabo (63–23 CE) correctly surmised that these great masses of ice were formed of layer upon layer of snow. Over the course of millennia this knowledge seems to have been lost. Leonardo da Vinci, for example, thought glaciers were formed by 'unmelted hail accumulating through the summer'.

For a very long time it was a common conjecture that ice was mountains, and mountains were, in some important way, ice. The most obvious sign of this was the crystal that could be found when you dug beneath the surface. Crystal was, wrote Pliny the Elder, in his *Natural History*, 'a substance which assumes a concrete form from excessive congelation . . . Crystal is only to be found in places where the winter snow freezes with the greatest intensity; and it is from the certainty that it is a kind of ice, that it

---

[1] A popular turn of phrase, possibly coined in *Peaks, Passes and Glaciers*, an early publication of the Alpine Club. It is also found in the title of a pioneering set of watercolours of Mont Blanc painted by Edmund T. Coleman in the 1850s and released as a set of prints in 1859, two years after the Alpine Club was founded.
[2] So large was Windham's impact that I am tempted to divide our ice/mountain timeline into Before and After Windham.

has received the name which it bears in Greek.'³ Later, the Arab philosopher and polymath Avicenna (c. 980–1037) speculated, in his treatise *De Congelatione et Conglutinatione Lapidum* ('On the Freezing and Cementing of Stones'): 'As regards the stony kinds of naturally occurring substances, the material of which they are made is also aqueous, but they have not been congealed by cold alone,' meaning, I think, that rocks were a product of a kind of ultra-freezing process, another phase change, if you like.

The ghost of this thought – that mountains, and rock more generally, owe their existence to ice – haunted humankind for centuries. In 1250, Albertus Magnus wrote that the high mountains make the ice so hard it becomes 'crystal'. By 1550, Agricola was only able to report that crystals may not be ice but 'juice thickened by cold'. And something similar was still so widely believed in the mid-seventeenth century that Thomas Browne saw fit to write in his *Pseudodoxia Epidemica*, his great catalogue of errors: 'the common Opinion hath been, and still remaineth amongst us, that Crystal is nothing else but Ice or Snow concreted, and by duration of time, congealed beyond liquation.'

Mont Blanc, whose year-round whiteness dominates the Mer de Glace and the whole of the western Alps, is indeed rich in crystal grottoes, which the French call *fours* – 'ovens' – as if this ice were baked into the rock. In 1673, it was reported to the English Royal Society that a Capuchin monk had found a mountain 'all of ice and crystal' near Geneva. But my favourite mention of Mont Blanc comes courtesy of a poet called René Le Pays who, in 1669, finding his amorous advances rebuffed, wrote a wounded letter to his would-be lover from Chamonix: 'Here, Madame, I see five mountains that are just like you. Five mountains, Madame, which are pure ice from head to feet, but an ice one might call perpetual. Tradition here says that they have been ice since the creation of the world.'

BW, then, misapprehension and false beliefs about mountains and ice shaded into irrationality and fear. An alternative name for

---

³ The English word 'crystal' is derived from the Ancient Greek κρύσταλλος (*krústallos*), which carries a dual meaning of both 'ice' and 'rock crystal'.

Mont Blanc was *la montagne maudite*, the 'cursed mountain', and across the Alps there are local tales of dragons, hauntings, demons and headless priests, as if proximity to ice infects both the air and the mind. 'As in all countries of ignorance people are extremely superstitious, they told us many strange stories of witches, etc., who came to play their pranks upon the *glacières*, and dance to the sound of instruments,' Windham wrote in his pamphlet.

These superstitions are substantiated by reports in the seventeenth century from Chamonix and its environs, whose inhabitants several times called on church officials in Geneva to perform Christian rites upon the Glacier des Bois (this was the name for the Mer de Glace where it debouched into the valley containing the town).[4] In the early 1600s, it had begun to advance upon them at speed, devouring two villages and much land. 'Whenever the bishop would make his visits to these areas, the people would petition him to go and exorcise and bless these mountains of ice,' writes a seventeenth-century source. In 1642, the Glacier des Bois was, according to an arbitration report, advancing by a 'musket shot' every day, swallowing fields and threatening houses.[5] In 1644, some 300 locals, fearful that they were being divinely punished for some vague and unspecified sins, followed the coadjutor bishop of Geneva to the Glacier des Bois for a blessing. The next day, the church official gave the nearby Argentière and Bossons glaciers the holy treatment. Literally miraculously, it worked. The glaciers went into abeyance until 1663, though the land they had covered remained stubbornly ice-burned and barren.[6]

---

[4] After the ice flow retreated from the valley floor in 1905 this double naming became obsolete.

[5] Arbitration because glaciers posed an economic and bureaucratic problem as well as a spiritual one, since lost land affected the payment of tithes.

[6] Given that glaciers respond to sustained changes in climate with a time lag measured in decades, these surges in the Chamonix valley fit fairly neatly with the start of the second phase of the Little Ice Age. The Little Ice Age caused consternation across the Alps. In the Schnals valley in the South Tyrol – Ötzi's valley – the inhabitants 'witnessed the extinction of the forests from high up down towards the valley', according to a writer and theologian in the early nineteenth century. 'They saw it as the gradual extinction of the World, and to them it seemed that even now the light was becoming dimmer.'

A curious thing: later retellings of these stories confused – perhaps on purpose – the rites being performed upon the glaciers, and turned exorcisms into excommunications. In Catholic doctrine an excommunication excludes its target from the communion: it is 'the most severe sanction or punishment within the ecclesiastical jurisdiction'; animals could be excommunicated, and frequently were, but mere things could not. An exorcism, meanwhile, is a recitation to cast out the devil, who has never been, nor could ever be, part of the church.

Were these glaciers inanimate objects diabolically possessed or creatures to be chastised? Never-living (if not quite inanimate) or impossibly alive?[7]

\*\*\*

After Windham had put the Mer de Glace on the map, others soon followed. In the first year AW of 1742 Pierre Martel, an engineer and mathematician living in Geneva and the eventual co-author of Windham's pamphlet, brought real observational rigour to his expedition, as well as many scientific instruments. Martel quickly debunked the crystal myth, and also took the first measurement of the height of the 'cursed mountain' that he would rename: at 2,076 *toises* – 4,046 metres – he was not far out.[8]

Then, in 1760, came a nineteen-year-old Genevan called Horace Bénédict de Saussure, who was inspired to visit the Mer de Glace after reading a privately printed copy of Windham and Martel's letters. This first trip was the start of a long love affair with the mountains: he would become famous, laying the groundwork for naturalists, glaciologists and mountaineers to come. Before he left Chamonix he offered a reward to the first person to reach the summit of Mont Blanc. (This would be achieved in 1786, with de Saussure himself making the third successful attempt in 1787.)

[7] In certain northern Native American traditions, glaciers are thought to be sentient. They 'take action and respond to their surroundings. They are sensitive to smells and they listen. They make moral judgements and they punish infractions.' According to John Tyndall, Franz Josef Hugi, a respected Swiss scientist, hypothesised that from the noises they made glaciers might possibly be alive.

[8] We know now that it's around 4,808 metres tall, and losing about thirteen centimetres annually.

In 1779, Goethe visited Montanvert, and Chateaubriand in 1808. Joséphine de Beauharnais, the newly divorced ex-Mrs Napoleon Bonaparte, employing sixty-eight guides and eight porters, made it up the hill in 1810. And in 1814, Marie-Louise of Austria, Bonaparte's second wife, visited, travelling light with only eighteen guides – as if it were a competition – while the Nightmare of Europe served his exile on the island of Elba.

In 1816, it was the turn of Mary Wollstonecraft Godwin.[9] For her, the Mer de Glace provided the inspiration she needed to bring *Frankenstein* to life.

As a child, like so many, I was captivated by Frankenstein's monster, all looming terror, vast forehead and heavy brow, with those terrific bolts protruding from his neck. More recently, when I actually picked up the unread Penguin Classics paperback I'd carried from home to home since university or even earlier, it became abundantly clear that it was not Mary's book I had in mind at all (she barely describes the monster physically apart from its awfulness and prodigious size) but more probably *The Munsters* or *The Addams Family*, both of which are a kind of juvenile echo of Boris Karloff, the definitive screen monster, in James Whale's film of 1931. Like Frankenstein's creature, the book now enjoys a monstrous afterlife of its own quite independent of its creator, lumbering from adaptation to bastardisation and never finding rest.

When I finally read *Frankenstein; or, the Modern Prometheus* around the time of its bicentenary in 2018, what struck me was not the old familiar tale but rather its icy geographies. Mary Shelley's fable has been interpreted in many ways but it is, before anything else, an icebound story that begins and ends in the Arctic. In choosing this setting, Mary was paying tribute to a venerable maritime obsession, the search for a northern passage

---

[9] Mary and Percy Shelley eloped in 1814, but were only married on 30 December 1816, after they returned from Chamonix and two or three weeks after Shelley's first wife, Harriet, drowned herself in the Serpentine in Hyde Park. Harriet was twenty-one years old. From here on I'll call M. Godwin/Shelley 'Mary', to avoid confusion.

to the Orient, whose origins we looked at in Chapter 4 and which was slowly drawing to a close.

The letters that open *Frankenstein* are initially full of these follies. Their author, Captain Robert Walton, is aboard a ship heading for the north-east passage somewhere above Arkhangelsk; he positively glows with naive faith in the prospect of breaking through into the Open Polar Sea. 'I try in vain to be persuaded that the pole is the seat of frost and desolation,' he writes; 'it ever presents itself to my imagination as the region of beauty and delight. There . . . snow and frost are banished; and, sailing over a calm sea, we may be wafted to a land surpassing in wonders and in beauty every region hitherto discovered on the habitable globe.' Yet as they approach the extreme north the ship's progress slows, and it is as Walton's hopes begin to founder on the implacable barrier of the polar ice that Victor Frankenstein appears, chasing his monster across the disintegrating pack ice, on a path to self-annihilation.

When Frankenstein is rescued and persuaded to tell his tale, the chase for the monster decamps to the Alps, and a key encounter takes place on the Mer de Glace. Though it conforms perfectly to Mary's Romantic sensibility, by using it as a backdrop she is paying homage, perhaps, to the glacier's emerging scientific importance, as well as stealing the scenery of the birth of mountaineering.

The tale of *Frankenstein*'s genesis is worth repeating. In 1816, Mary travelled with Percy Shelley to Geneva, where they met Lord Byron and friends including Claire Clairmont, Mary's stepsister and Byron's lover. Byron took a villa on the lake, but their stay would not be the Romantic idyll that the eighteen-year-old Mary was hoping for.

In April of 1815, Mount Tambora in Indonesia had erupted, ejecting around a hundred cubic kilometres of rock into the air, and dust and gas as high as the stratosphere. It was the largest and most devastating volcanic eruption in recorded history. The following year came to be known as the 'year without a summer'. People around the world experienced weak suns, dry fogs and vivid sunrises and sunsets, and rain and bad weather confined Mary's party to the villa, where they 'often sat up in conversation till the morning light'. One evening in mid-June, Byron challenged them all to write a ghost story, but Mary struggled for inspiration until the central revivification idea came to her in a ghastly waking dream late one night.

But what palette, materials and substances might give this nocturnal vision life? On 20 July 1816, while still in the early stages of writing, Mary and others travelled from Lake Geneva to Chamonix; on the 23rd, with Claire Clairmont, she visited the terminus of the Glacier des Bois; and on the 24th they tried to climb to Montanvert, that same viewpoint over the Mer de Glace that William Windham had visited, but they turned back because of the rain. That evening, Mary's journal mentions her 'story' for the first time; the following day, she set off by mule and foot anew. This time she reached Montanvert and beheld the glacier.

'This is the most desolate place in the world,' Mary wrote in her journal that night in 1816. 'Iced mountains surround it – no sign of vegetation appears except on the place from which [we] view the scene – we went on the ice. It is traversed by irregular crevices whose sides of ice appear blue while the surface is of a dirty white . . . We arrive at the inn at six fatigued by our day's journey but pleased and astonish[ed] by the world of ice that was opened up to our view.'

The brooding, creeping Glacier des Bois/Mer de Glace – this thing-that-lives-but-cannot-be – was almost immediately recycled into her draft. It is as if Mary preternaturally and instantly absorbed everything that has been thought or felt about glaciers to this point – the science and the superstition, the danger and ruin, the sublime and peculiar beauty and the physical challenge – and compressed it into her book. It is described thus by Victor Frankenstein:

> The abrupt sides of vast mountains were before me; the icy wall of the glacier overhung me; a few shattered pines were scattered around; and the solemn silence of this glorious presence-chamber of imperial Nature was broken only by the brawling waves, or the fall of some vast fragment, the thunder sound of the avalanche, or the cracking reverberated along the

mountains of the accumulated ice, which, through the silent working of immutable laws, was ever and anon rent and torn. These sublime and magnificent scenes afforded me the greatest consolation that I was capable of receiving.

Later, Victor climbs to Montanvert, where he confronts his creation: 'I suddenly beheld the figure of a man, at some distance, advancing towards me with superhuman speed. He bounded over the crevices in the ice, among which I had walked with caution.'

Mary was not the only one to be affected by the ice. Percy Bysshe Shelley, when he visited Montanvert, also saw chaos and death. 'These glaciers flow perpetually into the valley, ravaging in their slow but irresistible progress the pastures & the forests which surround them, & performing the work of desolation in ages which a river of lava might accomplish in an hour, but far more irretrievably,' he wrote to his friend Thomas Love Peacock. He continued:

We walked some distance on the surface, – the waves are elevated about 12 or 15 feet from the surface of the mass which is intersected with long gaps of unfathomable depth, the ice of whose sides is more beautifully azure than the sky. In these regions every thing changes & is in motion. This vast mass of ice has one progress which ceases neither day or night. It breaks & rises forever; its undulations sink while others rise. From the precipices which surround it the echo of rocks which fall from their aerial summits, or of the ice and snow, scarcely ceases for one moment. One would think that Mont Blanc was a living being & that frozen blood forever circulated thro' his stony veins.

The experience inspired and filled him with despair in equal measure, and, reflecting on the glacier's progress down the valley – it was advancing at around a foot a day – and the seemingly perpetual snows atop the mountain which fed it, he predicted gloomily, following the French naturalist the Comte de Buffon, 'that this Earth which we inhabit will at some future period be changed into a mass of frost'.[10]

A glacier up close is a profoundly disquieting presence. At its terminus the saturated dirt can be spongy and untrustworthy, uncompacted and more like mousse, cookie dough or even wet cement than mud; as if it has just been laid down (it has) and has not yet been fully reassimilated into its Mother Earth after its voyage in the ice (it hasn't). Surrounding you is glacial moraine that again has been lightly deposited: gravel and shingle, pebbles and rocks and boulders of tremendous size strewn higgledy-piggledy, loosely poised in illogical attitudes that, iceless and subject to gravity and the shifting, melting materials below them, seem absurd and barely tenable. Perhaps the precarity of the scarce-balancing shapes alerts something primal within you, but even on a fine and sunny day with no wind, with only the gurgling of meltwater and the odd pebble clattering down as it becomes dislodged, you are nevertheless on high alert. It is unsettling because it is unsettled. Everything is uncertain and strange, topsy-turvy and insubstantial, and the water is the most solid thing around.

*Every thing changes & is in motion*, wrote Shelley.

Further up a glacier, away from the terminus, even on broad, serene, snow-covered expanses – no looming seracs or tumbling rocks – there is always the thought of what lies beneath, waiting to claim the unwary wanderer. If a glacier lives, it lives at a geological speed: its processes, pressure and time, are measured at an inhuman scale; but perhaps that is all it will take – pressure and time – for you to make a misstep and for a deep blue crevasse to open up under your feet.

---

[10] The factors governing a glacier's growth and the mechanics of its movement were not at this time understood; so people looked at the 'eternal snows' that seemed to accumulate constantly atop Mont Blanc and feared the worst. Robert Macfarlane went as far as calling the low-level threat of annihilation posed by a new ice age the era's 'nuclear winter'. The Mer de Glace reached its maximum modern extent in 1821 (probably helped along by Mount Tambora); it has been receding for the majority of the years since. All Alpine glaciers have been mostly in retreat since the mid-nineteenth century.

But these, perhaps, were exactly the kind of sensations that Mary and Percy had come looking for – an admixture of awe and terror characteristic of the sublime, that exalted yet troubling feeling when confronted by the insurmountable grandeur of nature, very much in vogue among the Romantics after Edmund Burke's *A Philosophical Enquiry into the Origin of Our Ideas of the Sublime and Beautiful* in 1757. The lovers were early proselytisers for the delicious, shivery appeal of the upper ice world.

*Frankenstein* and Shelley's 'Mont Blanc: Lines Written in the Vale of Chamouni', as well as Byron's *Manfred* and part of his *Childe Harold*, resulted from this trip. As one modern critic puts it: 'Of all the landscapes in nature, those that are frozen are perhaps the most sublime. The reason: the blankness of ice.'

\*\*\*

Aside from Mary and Percy, glacier tourism prospered over the course of the nineteenth century. Victor Hugo, Franz Liszt, Madame de Staël, John Ruskin, Alexandre Dumas, J. M. W. Turner, George Sand (who scandalised the valley with her men's clothes and cigar smoking) and Charles Dickens all visited Montanvert. Every time someone important came, the path to the glacier became literally and metaphorically wider. In 1820, Marie Couttet, a local notable and guide, excavated and dynamited the mule track to improve access; in 1840, a small stone refuge was built, which in 1880 was replaced by a large and luxurious hotel.

*We went on the ice*, wrote Mary, and this changed her experience qualitatively from detached Romantic contemplation to physical engagement. By the late nineteenth century, as innumerable photographs and postcards attest, men and women both had colonised the Mer de Glace, prodding it with their alpenstocks like a sleeping beast, their curiosity making of its erstwhile terrors the pastime of an afternoon. Driven by the celebrities, by the views captured by Turner and Ruskin, by Thomas Cook, who began selling package holidays to the Alps, and by new and affordable railway lines across Europe, glacier tourism became fashionable, even widespread.

The Chamonix valley's popularity was given a further boost when, in 1851, Albert Smith, an Englishman, brought the chill of the upper ice world to central London, in a show at the Egyptian Hall in Piccadilly that dramatised his ascent of Mont Blanc. Within, the proscenium arch was transformed into the gables of a Swiss chalet, the stage featured boulders and there was a mini lake stocked with fish. During the interval St Bernard dogs distributed chocolates among the children in the audience. Smith's show ran for six years and more than 2,000 performances, in which time sixty-four ascents of the real 'ice mountain' were made – more than doubling the total number of the previous sixty-four years. Charles Dickens, a friend, said of Smith: 'Only one of those [Alpine] travellers, however, has been enabled to bring Mont Blanc to Piccadilly, and, by his own ability and good humour, to thaw its eternal ice and snow, so that the most timid ladies may ascend it twice a day "during the holidays" without the smallest danger or fatigue.'

Though Chamonix was a centre, glacier tourism spread across the Alps. At Grindelwald, under the Eiger, one could, in the 1820s be 'carried on to a glacier to eat wild strawberries whilst a bearded man blew on an Alpine horn'. In the Swiss Valais region the Rhonegletscher (the glacier from which the River Rhone springs – no Côtes du Rhône without ice) became an early star attraction thanks to its proximity to important mountain roads. In 1882, a hotel, the Belvédère, was built on the Furka Pass road overlooking the glacier, and in 1894 an ice grotto was bored into the glacier's flank opposite, permitting visitors to walk a hundred metres or more deep into the shimmering blue guts of the beast. (Ice grottoes were also built at the Mer de Glace, the Aletsch, Bossons, Morteratsch and numerous other glaciers for ice-curious tourists.) In 1890, the Hôtel Belvédère was extended and remodelled, and again, in 1904, in a Belle Époque-cum-army barracks style straight out of a Wes Anderson film. It was the site of many parties, as well as, in 1964, a visit by James Bond in *Goldfinger*.

Unfortunately for its proprietors, road improvements and the shrinking of the glacier progressively weighed against the

An auroch on the walls of Lascaux, south-western France, painted *c.* 17 Ka. The four dots on its flank may form part of a revolutionary Ice Age 'proto-writing' system.

Fabled mountaineers Reinhold Messner and Hans Kammerlander with Ötzi the Iceman, Ötztal Alps, 21 September 1991.

Hendrick Avercamp, *Winter Landscape with Skaters* (c. 1608).

Thomas Wyke, *Frost Fair on the River Thames near the Temple Stairs* (1683-4).

Christiaan Julius Lodewyck, *Death of Willem Barents, 20 June 1597* (1836).

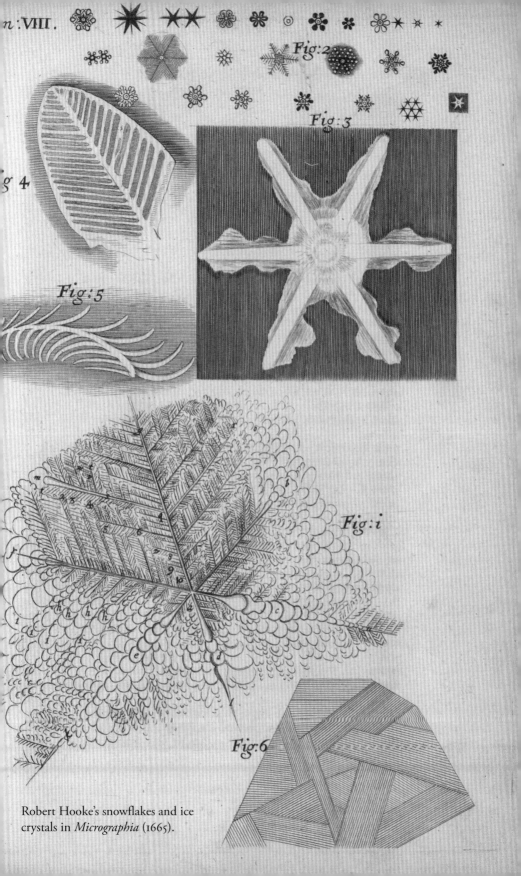

Fig: 2

Fig: 3

Fig: 4

Fig: 5

Fig: i

Fig: 6

Robert Hooke's snowflakes and ice
crystals in *Micrographia* (1665).

The ice house at William Windham's Felbrigg Hall, Norfolk, constructed in the late eighteenth or early nineteenth centuries.

Yakhchāl, Yazd province, Iran. Some of these structures are hundreds of years old, and there is strong evidence that yakhchāls were being used in antiquity.

Harvesting ice on a lake in Massachusetts in the nineteenth century.

J. J. 544 *Traversée de la Mer de Glace à Chamonix*

*We went on the ice:* glacier tourists on the Mer de Glace, probably in the early 1900s.

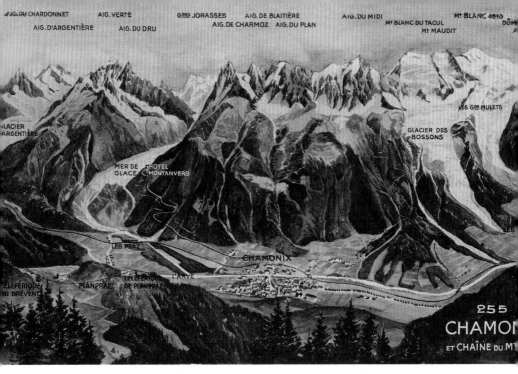

Chamonix and its glaciers in the early twentieth century, after the Mer de Glace had retreated from the valley floor.

Old Man Rhône glacier in a lithograph from 1898. The Hôtel Belvédère is on the hairpin turn closest to his nose.

The Hôtel Belvédère and the diminishing Rhône glacier seen (above) in the 1900s and (below) in the early 1970s. Today the glacier barely extends below the hotel.

Lizzie Le Blond protects herself from the glare of the upper ice world. Self-portrait on Durmaalstind, Norway, *c.* 1900.

A nineteenth-century engraving depicting the Adams mammoth's discovery.

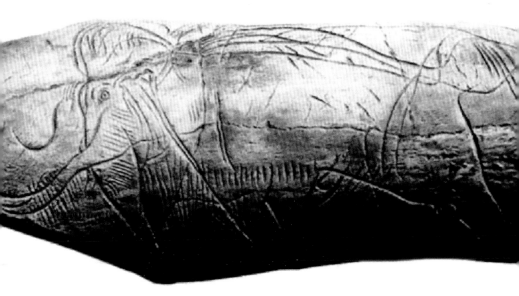

Indisputable proof that humans co-existed with mammoths, found by Édouard Lartet at the La Madeleine cave in south-western France and revealed to the world in 1864.

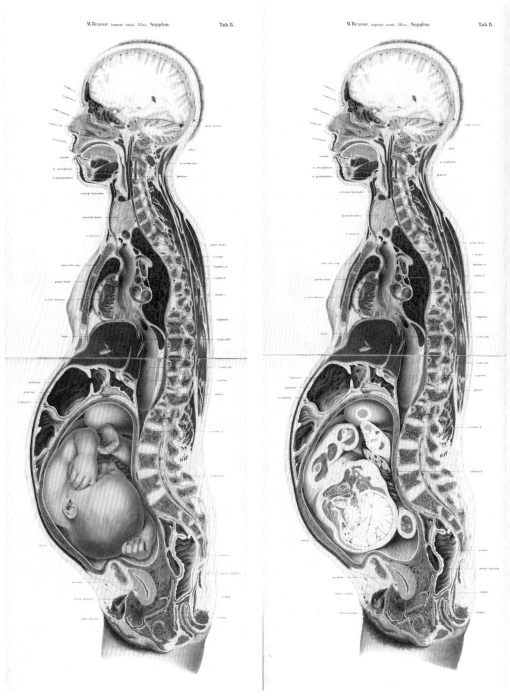

Wilhelm Braune's frozen sectioning: one woman and her unborn baby, from 1872. The two images of the baby in utero are puzzling – until you read Braune's method.

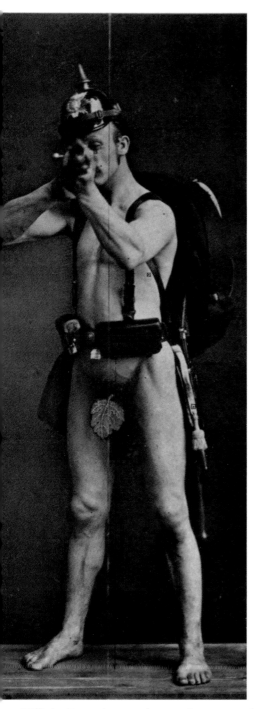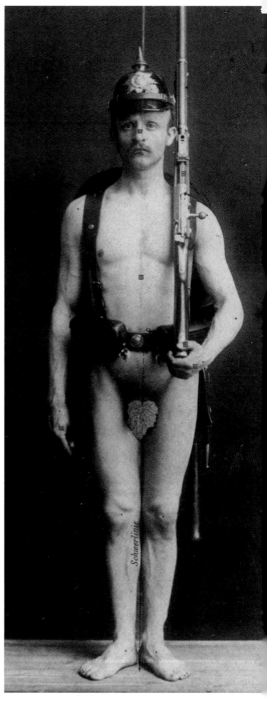

Wilhelm Braune's researches into human gait for the Royal Saxon Army used ice to determine the centre of gravity of body parts. These soldiers, photographed in 1889, also somehow played their part.

A photo by Austro-Hungarian engineer Leo Handl of a bridge over a crevasse in the *Eisstadt*, in the Marmolada glacier, *c.* 1917.

Irving Langmuir (left), Bernard Vonnegut and Vincent Schaefer (bottom) seeding a snow cloud in the laboratory 'cold box' at the GE Research Lab in the 1940s.

One of the three cannons abandoned on the Cima Ghiacciata in 1918, and the Cevedale glacier behind.

An iceberg being towed away from an oil rig.

Belvédère. Once the Furka Pass could be accomplished in a day trip rather than involving a journey that required an overnight stop, the number of prospective guests declined. Things that once stopped people awestruck in their tracks they now passed at speed, hair streaming from the omnibus window into the sunlit air. Photos, artworks and particularly picture postcards chart the glacier's marked retreat over the years, the birth of glacier tourism and the changing nature of our attention to the Rhonegletscher: first, etchings and watercolours filled with sublime melodrama; then tinted photos of horses and carriages; and finally postcards bustling with motorcars, people and full-on sixties Alpenkitsch. *Every thing changes & is in motion.* That the increase in motorcars on the Furka Pass road directly hastened the demise of the natural phenomenon their occupants flocked to see is an irony that shall not be ignored.

In a bric-à-brac shop in a nameless Swiss town I once found a postcard, a delicate lithograph from 1898, depicting the glacier as a corpulent, grumbling old man squatting upon the valley hundreds of vertical metres below the hotel. He watches, perhaps belligerent, perhaps just fearful about the future, while an angelic figure waves from the first splashings of the Rhône river as she begins her journey to water the grapes of the south of France more than 600 kilometres distant. Of all natural features, the preternaturally restless glacier is among the most likely to be anthropomorphised or animated (as I have done repeatedly in the preceding paragraphs); but perhaps this is not so weird, because are we not, like the Romantics, projecting our emotions on to the landscape, externalising our secret terror or shame?

Now the glacier languishes, girdled within a small rock amphitheatre nowhere near the precipitous drop to the valley below, meekly dipping its nose into a glacial lake cloudy with ground-up rock, and you must walk several hundred metres from the hotel (though it is boarded up, having definitively closed its doors in 2015) along cement walkways and sun-baked planks to enter the ice grotto.

\*\*\*

As we saw earlier, scientific enquiry arrived on the Mer de Glace with Pierre Martel, and became established with de Saussure. After him, rare was the expedition to the glacier, or higher on the slopes of Mont Blanc, that did not carry scientific instruments and proceed with some sort of didactic zeal. Science became the excuse to climb higher and, by the mid-nineteenth century, glacial rationalism had definitively banished the witches, spirits and demons from the ice with barometric, meteorological and geodesic instruments, leaving it to be enjoyed by the tourists ferried by mule up to the Montanvert Hotel.

*We went on the ice.* The upper ice world seemed to offer to scientists the opportunity for experimentation in a place of purity, somewhere that the fundamental truths of nature, and of the cosmos above, might clearly be seen. Louis Pasteur visited the Mer de Glace in 1859 while undertaking research to disprove the theory of the spontaneous generation of life.[11] And Louis Agassiz, who we shall hear much more of in the next chapter, made a career out of bringing his observations from the glaciers of the Alps – mainly in Switzerland – down to the learned societies below. However, the major scientific figures associated with the Mer de Glace are James David Forbes and John Tyndall.

Forbes, a Scotsman born in 1809, started his glacial researches with Agassiz. Then, on research trips to Montanvert in the 1840s, measuring and tracking the frozen waves on the Mer de Glace, he became convinced that glaciers moved in a semi-viscous flow, like lava. Or honey: John Ruskin, a prominent supporter of Forbes, handily simplified Forbes's ideas using his breakfast materials, while staying in the Chamonix valley:

> Pouring a little of its candied contents out upon my plate,
> by various tilting of which I could obtain any rate of motion

---

[11] Pasteur sterilised beef stock in a swan-necked flask, which prevented microbes from entering it and multiplying inside. Yet if you broke the neck and allowed air to flow in, microbes arrived. A flask of beef broth opened in Paris would quickly become very cloudy with microscopic organisms; in the purer air of the glacier, much less so. This was the death knell for the long-held idea of spontaneous generation.

I wished to observe in the viscous stream; and encumbering the sides and centre of the said stream with magnificent moraines composed of crumbs of toast, I was able, looking alternately to table and window, to compare the visible motion of the mellifluous glacier, and its transported toast, with a less traceable, but equally constant, motion of the glacier of Bionnassay, and its transported granite.

Tyndall, an Irishman who took up the study of glaciers a little after Forbes, argued against this, believing (wrongly) that glaciers moved thanks to a repeated process of cleavage, refreezing and cleavage once more – which he, after Michael Faraday, called 'regelation'.

The relationship between these two students of the solid form of water was sometimes acrimonious. Both agreed, however, that their mountaineering was essential to their work. Take Forbes: 'People who visit a glacier and return to the civilised world at night think they get a good idea of it, but it is only a protracted residence amongst the Icy Solitudes which imbues one truly with their spirit [and] enables one to reason confidently concerning things so widely rumoured from common experience.' Or Tyndall: 'You cannot contract a closer relationship with the landscape than through a solo traverse of a glacier.'

Theirs was a muscular science dependent on physical toil, on things that were observed directly, walked upon, felt with one's whole body. Ice's affront to the nineteenth-century mind was irresistible, but so was its challenge to the flesh. The two pursuits combined and complimented each other: the ice was a test bed not only of ideas, but of men.

Tyndall's *The Glaciers of the Alps* (published in 1860), in particular, reads like a kind of Indiana Jones-esque science/ adventure hybrid. In the opening pages – his first ever steps on a glacier – he witnesses an avalanche and dodges wild storms, then walks to a hut atop the Unteraar glacier built by Agassiz, noting the famous names carved above the door. The symbolism could hardly be more Hollywood. On later trips, in his researches and his climbing, he would surpass these predecessors. He was boldly going where no man had gone before.[12]

The literal high point and metaphorical low point of the ice science taking place around Chamonix came in the 1890s, when Pierre Janssen, president of the French Academy of Science, proposed erecting an observatory upon Mont Blanc's summit – which is not a rocky promontory but an unfathomable mass of snow-covered ice. It was a vainglorious and hubristic thing to attempt. Janssen hired Gustave Eiffel to build this observatory, and the famous engineer picked a site only fifteen metres from the top, but, after tunnelling twenty-nine metres into the mountain and not hitting rock, gave up without erecting anything. Janssen ordered that the work continue, and kept on boring into the ice with no more success than Eiffel. Eventually, his workers mutinied, and he made do with an iron-and-wood structure without foundations, which quickly sank into the snow and was lost. For the eternal snows of altitude are perpetually feeding the voracious glaciers beneath; even Percy Shelley knew that.

\*\*\*

From the 1850s onwards, the ice that captivated Forbes and Tyndall began also to attract a new kind of tourist: the mountaineer. Often British, and often middle or upper class, they appreciated the aesthetic and cerebral aspects of the experience, but came mainly for the physical challenge – an approach legitimated by the formation of the Alpine Club, the world's first mountaineering association, in 1857. Matthew Arnold and Michael Faraday became members, as did John Ruskin; and Leslie Stephen, father of Virginia Woolf and Vanessa Bell, was president from 1865 to 1868. In 1871, Stephen published *The Playground of Europe*, one of the most important early Alpine climbing narratives.

Although Mont Blanc had been summited in 1786, it then for many years stood alone among the highest peaks in being

---

[12] There is definitely something about the combination of boy's own adventure and scientific endeavour that resembles classic sci-fi. An equivalent target to Mont Blanc in the twentieth century might have been the moonshot.

conquered. But, between 1854 and 1880, English climbers claimed the summits of seventeen of the remaining twenty highest mountains in the Alps. Why was this achieved by Brits and not others? In part, I suspect, down to Britain's Romantic leanings, and scientific prowess, as well as a kind of territorial acquisitiveness linked to the heyday of Empire. In all, a collection of peculiarly Victorian sentiments: 'a desire to exert oneself against formidable odds; to cast one's character in the light of ennobling ideals; to sojourn among exotic things; to make collections and erect monuments'.[13]

These new mountaineers of what came to be known as the 'Golden Age' of alpinism did not completely set aside the scientific tradition. (Tyndall, for one, is listed among the Age's luminaries, with a notable first ascent to his name of the 4,506-metre Weisshorn in 1861.) And when they returned to civilisation, they read papers about their exploits – often detailing their claim to priority in achieving a peak or discovering a new route – to the Alpine Club, much like scientists reporting their discoveries to learned institutions such as the Royal Society.

The later, increasingly athletic alpinists also became interested in physiology and the sciences of the extremes – altitude and diet, the limits of exhaustion and what happened when digits and limbs froze. Their exploits pushed against the limits of the body and of the human condition, an increasingly hypermasculine vigour that evokes a dark counterpart, Frankenstein's monster on the Mer de Glace – 'the figure of a man, at some distance, advancing towards me with superhuman speed ... bound[ing] over the crevices in the ice, among which I had walked with caution'.[14]

Because – and this goes without saying – it all came with a high level of risk. As people explored further and climbed higher,

[13] Let's also remember that they were almost invariably guided, by locals, who received no credit.

[14] John Ruskin devoted a volume of his *Modern Painters* to 'mountain beauty', and, though a handy walker, definitely preferred looking to touching. He was scathing about this new breed of Alpine visitor, describing athletic mountaineering as akin to 'soaped poles in a bear-garden, which you ... climb and slide down again'.

what had begun in a spirit of awe, genteel optimism and a zest for discovery started to become a lethal passion.

The first truly significant accident was that which befell Dr Hamel's three guides, who were, as we saw in Chapter 2, swept away in an avalanche. The tragedy left the tightly knit population of the valley in turmoil, and increased the volume of criticism – already loud enough – of those who climbed into the upper ice world. But Dr Hamel, however unlucky or foolhardy he had been, belonged to the generation who climbed for the sake of science. As the emphasis shifted towards adventure, the dangers increased. Even though they were generally scrupulously prepared and gratefully reliant on talented local guides, the eagerness shown by the English to take on the Alps heralded a new attitude to risk.[15] There are several ways of viewing this reckless impulse for adventure. Some have suggested that life in the increasingly regulated and safe Victorian Britain created a frustrated, macho desire for danger, which had to be found elsewhere; others that, in a fast-changing society, with rapidly evolving structures and mores and an increasing emphasis on the individual, perilous mountain escapades were a way of acting out and mastering anxieties about an unprecedented future. *Every thing changes & is in motion.*

Ice became a protagonist in many of these narratives of risk, an active adversary of the hero's upward progress. John Tyndall, to take one example, describes the ice during his first ascent of Mont Blanc in terrifying terms:

> On the heights to our right, loose ice crags seemed to totter, and we passed two tracks over which the frozen blocks had passed some short time previously. We were glad to get out of the range of these terrible projectiles, and still more so to escape the vicinity of that ugly crevasse. To be killed in the open air

[15] England being a country where not a single mountain attains the altitude even of Chamonix village, itself some 3,750 metres (2.3 miles) below the peak of Mont Blanc.

would be a luxury, compared with having the life squeezed out
of one in the horrible gloom of these chasms.

However, given this is Tyndall writing later, looking back on his
adventures, we the readers know these chasms have been safely
overcome. The danger is contained, safe: a delicious frisson before
the crowning capture of the peak.

Not everyone was lucky enough to live out this heroic journey
narrative. The worst and most famous accident of all came in
July 1865, when four men died climbing the Matterhorn with the
writer and photographer Edward Whymper. Whymper had been
engaged for years in a desperate race with John Tyndall to be the
first to summit the imposing 4,478-metre peak above Zermatt.
On his eighth attempt, Whymper succeeded, but on the triumphal
return, descending a section of mixed rock and ice, an Englishman,
Douglas Robert Hadow, slipped, dragging two other Englishmen
and a Chamoniard guide over the edge of the mountain. All four
fell more than a kilometre on to the Matterhorn Glacier below.
Only because one of the ropes joining the climbing party together
snapped did Whymper and the three other climbers avoid being
taken with them into the abyss.

It was a tragic accident that resulted in bitter, lengthy
recriminations. A Fall that marked an end of innocence, if there
ever had been one, for the boys romping in the mountains of the
Golden Age. The Alps might have been the playground of Europe,
but many who went there were undoubtedly playing with their
lives. The upper ice world was irresistible, but also deadly.

*Excelsior* is a Latin word meaning 'ever upward'. It became
a common mountaineering motto, and provided the title to
a celebrated and somewhat sentimental poem about a young
traveller who ignores warnings to stop for the night, written in
1841 by the American Henry Wadsworth Longfellow. As it ends
it becomes an anthem for doomed youth:[16]

---

[16] The icy obsession with going harder, faster, better, stronger exemplified here would
lead Europeans, with Robert Falcon Scott, Ernest Shackleton, George Mallory and other
Anglo-Saxons prominent among them, literally to the ends of the earth and the top of

At break of day, as heavenward
The pious monks of Saint Bernard
Uttered the oft-repeated prayer,
A voice cried through the startled air,
     Excelsior!

A traveller, by the faithful hound,
Half-buried in the snow was found,
Still grasping in his hand of ice
That banner with the strange device,
     Excelsior!

*\*\**

There is something quintessentially macho in this 'get high or die trying' attitude, and it will not have escaped your notice that all of the above adventures were decidedly male affairs. From the very start, the metageography of the ice mountains was defined by masculine heroism. This was reinforced in the written reports and policed by the institutions governing and promoting alpinism worldwide. Alpine climbing was to a very large extent a boys' club, and many would have liked to keep it that way.[17] There were rebels, but they knew they were pushing against intractable prejudice. 'The masculine mind ... is, with rare exceptions, imbued with the idea that woman is not a fit comrade for steep ice or precipitous rock,' wrote the accomplished woman mountaineer May Mummery in 1895.

This bigotry existed both in unspoken form and explicitly in writing. Here's Dickens again. He's worth quoting at length:

The fact is – and it cannot be too strongly insisted on – that there really exist three distinct Switzerlands, suspended one over the other at different altitudes. The first – the Switzerland

---

the world – often heroically, sometimes foolishly, sometimes fatally – into the most inhospitable environments imaginable.
[17] While there was a Ladies' Alpine Club from 1907 onwards, the Alpine Club itself did not admit women until 1976. The Royal Geographic Society began accepting female members in 1913.

of ladies, children, elderly gentlemen and ordinary folk in general, includes all the valleys and lakes traversed by railways, highway roads, and steamers . . . The second region, sometimes dovetailing with the first, sometimes soaring above it, takes in the localities which cannot be reached in carriages, but to which prudent lads and lassies may roam on foot or on horseback, with proper precautions . . . Our third and uppermost Switzerland supplies the Alpine Club with spots where human foot has never trod, or where the number of its footprints may be counted. It furnishes peaks ascended only by scientific men and human donkeys.

It wasn't only Dickens expressing such ideas. Leslie Stephen also classified tourists by altitude, like flora and fauna, to show the immutable nature of these zones:

Travellers, like plants, may be divided according to the zones which they reach. In the highest region, the English climber . . . Lower down comes a region where he is mixed with industrious Germans, and a few sporadic examples of adventurous ladies and determined sight-seers. Below this is the luxuriant growth of the domestic tourist in all his amazing and intricate varieties.

Thus, with a few strokes of their pens, Dickens and Stephen – one of the most influential men of his age, and an ex-Alpine Club president writing the classic guidebook of the era – relegate all but the most adventurous of ladies to the status of tourists, and claim the upper ice world for men. It is *explicitly gendered as male*. Mary Godwin may not have been alone among her sex to go upon the ice in 1816, but even fifty years later the gatekeepers would still have her excluded from its higher reaches.

Even before considering these 'rules' of the new alpinism, wider social prejudices were already militating against nineteenth-century women climbers: to begin with, they would have had far less freedom than men to determine the course of their own lives, to travel or even to pick their pastimes, if indeed they were allowed much leisure. For women of the era, strength, fitness and technical expertise were considered indecorous; those that did climb risked damage to their 'reputations' and were pressured into wearing clothing that was often inappropriate, heavy and constricting. Bogus science was also marshalled against them, which warned of altitude's particular dangers to health, of excessive fatigue to the feminine constitution and of damage to their reproductive systems.

In *Victorians in the Mountains: Sinking the Sublime*, Anne C. Colley presents the experience of Mary Taylor, a close friend of Charlotte Brontë, who, climbing with four other women in 1874, was refused a lead on a certain route by a guide because it was, in his view, unsuitable for ladies. Taylor recorded in her diary that night that she felt as if the guide 'had just struck away the snow and shown us a deep crevasse right before us'. As a metaphor for the gender gap in opportunity, this seems perfect.[18]

Despite these prevailing attitudes, women mountaineers were quite numerous, and many were celebrated by their male peers. In 1808, Marie Paradis, from Chamonix, made the first female ascent of Mont Blanc, and Henriette d'Angeville, a French countess, repeated the feat in 1838. Following d'Angeville, the second half of the nineteenth century was also a gilded age of women's alpinism, spearheaded by Anglophone women. Sometimes they climbed with women, sometimes with their husbands or other men, or sometimes, just like the men, alone with male guides. However, we know their stories less well than the men's, since women were given far fewer opportunities to publish their narratives, and therefore received less recognition from other climbers or the general public. Where they do exist, however, their stories are remarkably free from hyperbole and bravado, very different in tone from some of the men's.

There is, for example, Frederica Plunket, an Irishwoman, who calmly recounted falling into an icy crevasse in 1875: 'It is a queer sensation . . .' she wrote.

---

[18] This very same trip, Taylor and her friends became the first all-female party to climb Mont Blanc – but presumably with a different (male) guide.

Suddenly you sink in much deeper than usual and find, to your surprise, that you have nothing under one foot . . . you become aware that you are on a snow bridge, and that if it gives way, you will soon be hanging suspended by the rope over one of those gigantic cracks that sometimes reach to the bottom of the glacier. Of course there is no danger if the rope is strong enough.

The queen of understatement, however, must be Margaret Jackson, who achieved seven first ascents of peaks over 4,000 metres – the yardstick in the Alps – of which three were also first ascents for either sex. Her account of a winter crossing of the Jungfrau in the Bernese Alps in 1888 starts by marvelling at the beauty of the environment. 'It was a keen, frosty morning, without a breath of wind, the whole glacier glistening in the moonlight as if strewn with countless diamonds,' she writes. 'It was just a fairy ballroom, and I much wonder whether we rough mortals had any right to trespass there.'

After reaching the 4,158-metre Jungfrau (the name translates to 'Maiden'), the party was benighted on the descent and sought shelter in an ice cavern on the mountain. Again, to Jackson, this was a wonderful, almost spiritual experience: 'Icicles of all shapes and sizes hung from the roof and sides, and the whole place glistened in the light of our faithful lantern,' she wrote. What she does not mention at all is the frostbite she suffered during that night in the ice cave, which meant she never could climb seriously again.

At a time when few men were engaged in it, women like Jackson seemed both adept at and constitutionally suited to the rigours of winter climbing, and they are comparatively well represented in the records. Isabella Straton, from Sussex, was in the first party to summit Mont Blanc in winter, in 1876. And Meta Brevoort, an American, was also partial to a winter ascent – even more so than her famous nephew, the historian W. A. B. Coolidge, with whom she summited many notable Alpine peaks. Brevoort was, however, beaten to the Eiger (in 1864) and the Matterhorn (in 1871) by Lucy Walker, a Liverpool-born climber, about whom, on that latter success, the following ditty was composed:

No glacier can baffle, no precipice balk her,
No peak rise above her however sublime,
Give three times three cheers for intrepid Miss Walker.

And finally, because the list could go on, in 1888 Lizzie Le Blond made the first winter ascent by a woman of the Aiguille du Midi, a famous 'needle' on Mont Blanc's flank directly above Chamonix.[19] Le Blond, an Irishwoman from an aristocratic family, had travelled to the town in 1881 on a travel cure for lung problems and quickly found health in the mountains. Her first mountain 'walk' took her two-thirds of the way up Mont Blanc. She decided to stay in the Alps and the final third did not remain unclimbed for long.

As May Mummery made clear, ice was just one aspect of alpinism the patriarchy thought was unsuitably dangerous for women, but Le Blond found a liberation in the upper ice world that was difficult for her (even as a woman of independent means, as most of the early women climbers were) to possess in the lower worlds. She disdained dresses and pinafores for her climbing, and would often change into her bloomers when out of sight. Consequently, in her accounts, descending into civilisation sometimes seems like a literal comedown, and a return to unwanted pressures.

Once, in Switzerland, having discarded her skirt on the way up, Le Blond found on the descent it had blown away, and her climbing partner was obliged to go to their hotel to fetch her a replacement. This tale she recounted in 1932, by then a doyenne of the Ladies' Alpine Club, which she had helped establish in 1907: 'To my horror, he appeared after a long interval with my best evening dress over his arm!' she wrote. 'There was nothing for it but to slink in when he gave the word that all was clear, and dash up to my room hoping I should meet no one on the stairs.'

Elsewhere, she wrote, 'I owe a supreme debt of gratitude to the mountains for knocking from me the shackles of

---

[19] Elizabeth, née Hawkins-Whitshed, married three times and published under several surnames, but she was often referred to by her climbing friends as Lizzie Le Blond, so for the sake of consistency I'll use that here.

conventionality, but I had to struggle hard for my freedom.'
Perhaps winter climbing was an extra jolt of liberty, a kind of
supplementary two-fingered salute at the parts of the patriarchy
that did not want to see women exerting themselves on the
glaciers and among the high peaks in summer, let alone during
the cold season.

***

Since 1909, Montanvert has been accessible via a pillar-box-red
train that runs on a rack-and-pinion track as sinuous as the Mer
de Glace itself, making the 871-vertical-metre climb easy, even
banal. And since 1955, the Aiguille du Midi has been served by
a cable car from Chamonix, which takes passengers to a Bond
villain-esque glass-and-steel visitor centre wrapped around and
bored into the very top of the 3,842-metre peak. Step out on to
the gantry and there, right before you, are laid out in panorama
a good number of the famous summits, ridges, glaciers and
snowfields of the range; and this bird's-eye view, combined with
the exertion-free ascent in the cable car and the falsification of
distance and perspective caused by dry mountain air, softens for
a moment the impact of the dazzling white, makes everything
look surprisingly close, tantalisingly possible.

At least this is what I thought, before the lung-busting climb
up the short staircase to the next viewing platform reminded me
how thin the air was up there and that I was, even in a visitor
centre, barely in my comfort zone. And I wondered all the more
at the efforts of all the pioneers who left their mark on the icy
peaks and rocky faces all around.

Far below you lies the domesticated valley; above that, the
lower mountain slopes tamed by woodcutters, frequented by
cowherds and then rationalised by naturalists, botanists and
scientists; above that, the snowline, the glaciers and the summits,
where the scientists and the adventurers penetrated but which they
never quite humanised nor rendered safe. The upper ice world: a
space which has over the years held many contradictory activities
and credos – methodical experimentation and ineffable sentiment,
noble striving, extravagant risk-taking, superstition, patriarchy

and rebellion, liberty, pain and death – if not in synthesis then at least in a productive tension.

It was, for Mary Godwin, a place in which the terrible sublime could coexist with the latest scientific theories, as the darkness on the north side of the ridge does with the south side's blinding light. In some ways it still is. But, since then, we have made of these desolate and threatening spaces a source of life and happiness, turned these Alps into 'the playground of Europe'. And, though it is soiled and cheapened by tourism, weakened and diminished by industry, thanks to all those who passed before – but especially to Mary, to Tyndall and to Jackson and her peers – this seat of frost and desolation ever presents itself to my imagination as the region of beauty and delight.

# 8

# The Pachyderm

## Palaeontology and geology; or, ice kills Adam and Eve

*Large are the treasures of oblivion . . . much more is buried in silence than recorded.*
Sir Thomas Browne, *Pseudodoxia Epidemica* (1646)

*Ice is only another form of terrestrial love. I am astonished to hear you speak so unbelievingly of God's glorious crystal glaciers.*
John Muir, letter of 11 December 1871

*There are more things in heaven and earth, Horatio, than are dreamt of in your philosophy.*
William Shakespeare, *Hamlet*, I, v

In 1799, a new creature came into the world. It was discovered on the edges of the Frozen Sea – quite dead – by Ossip Schumachov, a nomadic tribesman of the Yakutia region in Siberia. That first year it protruded only slightly out of subterranean ice in the Lena River delta on the Laptev Sea, but the ice did not give up its treasure easily and the creature's (re)birth was slow. Returning to the spot the following year, Schumachov distinguished two feet. A year later there was a flank and a tusk, and a year after that he returned to procure and sell the tusks. But in vain: 'the summer being colder and more windy than usual kept the mammoth' – you'd guessed that, right? – 'sunk in the ice, which scarcely melted at all that season. At last, about the end of the fifth year afterwards, the ardent desires of Schumachov were happily accomplished: the ice which inclosed the mammoth having partly melted, the level became sloped, and this enormous mass, pushed forward by its own weight, fell over upon its side on a sand-bank.'

This was March 1803. Mikhail Adams, an adjunct in zoology at the St Petersburg Academy of Sciences, who wrote the above words, was alerted to the mammoth's presence when in Yakutsk three years later. It took him a month to get to a settlement called Kumak Surka, where he met Schumachov, and a little longer for the winds to change, but finally, after three days' further journey, he was led to the vast carcass.[1] By the time he arrived it was almost picked clean: locals had been ripping off chunks of meat to feed their dogs (as if this ancient meat had just been taken out of an enormous freezer which, in a way, it had)[2] and polar bears, wolves, wolverines and Arctic foxes had scavenged the remains, but the skeleton was, save for the tusks and a missing forefoot, complete. It also retained some ligaments and connective tissues, the sole of one foot, the remnants of both eyes, the brain and three-quarters of its skin. It was about

---

[1] As Adams describes it, the mammoth was found in pure ice, which had been buried and preserved under a layer of soil. He describes it as 'clear . . . but of a nauseous taste'. This very much interested later glacial and permafrost researchers, since, if it were ice and not permafrost, it would necessarily have been a remnant from the last Ice Age. Such subsurface relic ice is sometimes called 'fossil ice'. But Adams's is the sole account of the find, so this was impossible to verify, even by a research party in the 1840s.

[2] It was once claimed that in 1951 the Explorers Club served 250,000-year-old mammoth meat at its annual dinner. The club, which lists as members the first men ever to reach the North Pole, South Pole and the summit of Everest, is famous for serving weird meats at the event, including polar bear, lion and tarantula. The mammoth was said to have come from the Aleutian islands, Alaska, and was served on place settings fashioned from Arctic vegetation and with cocktails cooled by glacier ice – a tribute both to Arctic climes and to the cold chain that transported the iced goods there. Remarkably, a piece of the meat was kept by a guest and put into a museum. When investigated by Yale researchers in 2016, it was found to be labelled not *Mammuthus* but *Megatherium* (giant sloth). Less remarkably, when it was DNA-tested, it turned out to be neither, but rather green sea turtle.

3 metres high by 4.5 metres long. The head alone weighed 200 kilograms and the tusks, when Adams bought them back in Yakutsk, were in themselves about 2.8 metres long and ninety kilograms in weight.[3]

While Adams inventoried and arranged the bones, it took ten people to lift the hide and take it to be floated away. Adams also dug around and collected over eighteen kilograms of thick bristly hair. Then, after boiling the bones and packing his prize, he headed slowly back to St Petersburg, a total journey of around 11,000 kilometres, triumphantly in possession of something nobody had ever seen before.

What he had extracted from the ice would help humanity begin to approach the fundamental truths behind the chaos of creation. It would cause fault lines to appear in the cultural and social orthodoxies of the day and it would change the way people thought. Rather than the story of a Fall, this is how a few mammoths, some glaciers and some strangely shaped rocks killed Adam and Eve.

The genus *Mammuthus*, though now completely extinct, was an incredibly successful branch of the mammalian family tree, evolving in Africa 5 million years ago before spreading into Europe and Asia and across the Beringia land bridge into North America. These proboscideans, characterised by their large size and very long noses, adapted to different habitats and climates over millions of years yet essentially maintained the instantly recognisable silhouette shared by elephant species today. There is strong evidence that populations of this deep time traveller survived until around 2000 BCE on an isolated island in the Chuchki Sea off Siberia, thus bridging from prehistory into historical time. The woolly mammoth, which is what Adams's was, was one of the last in the genus and was our companion in the Ice Age across Eurasia. At around the same size as an African elephant, it was by no means the biggest mammoth species, but with its long coat, sloped back and very large, curved tusks it

---

[3] He claimed to have bought back the originals, but was actually swindled and sold a smaller pair by the very ivory merchant who had alerted him to the carcass.

is the classic mammoth you're probably picturing in your head right now.[4]

'According to several writers, the term "Mammoth" is of Tatar origin, and is derived from *mama*, which signifies the earth,' wrote Wilhelm Tilesius, the man who put Adams's bones back together again. 'According to others it is derived from *behemoth* mentioned in the Book of Job, or *mehemoth* an epithet which the Arabs commonly add to the word "Elephant" to designate one which is very large.'

Since prehistoric times, mammoth ivory has been used in Siberia and across the steppes as a durable material for building dwellings, as well as making fittings and implements. It is also probable that prehistoric Siberians hunted mammoths using spears and arrows fashioned from mammoth ivory – it was easy to work and very available. Thanks to the permafrost, a very large quantity of very large mammoth tusks and other remains were preserved that subsequently, when dug out of the ground, became articles for use and trade.

The ancient Chinese used mammoth ivory for ornamentation and in medicine. Tusks and teeth are mentioned as far back as the fourth century BCE in Chinese ceremonial books, though it was not all that clear to the Chinese what exactly the bones were from. One official serving the early Han Dynasty emperor Wu (140–87 BCE) wrote: 'In the regions of the north, where ice is piled up over a stretch of country ten thousand miles long and reaches a thickness of a thousand feet, there is a rodent, called *k'i shu*, living beneath the ice in the interior of the earth. In shape it is like a rodent, and subsists on herbs and trees. Its flesh weighs a thousand pounds and may be used as dried meat for food.'[5]

Mammoth bones were also well known in Ancient Greece and by the tenth century tusks had found their way into southern Europe and central Asia. From that time on, the trade in ivory

---

[4] We think of mammoths as creatures of frozen climes because ice is such a good preserver – another example of the preservation bias we saw in Chapter 1.
[5] Given the circumstances it is not that strange that the Chinese compared it to a burrowing creature like a rodent. Some Siberians also thought the mammoth was a creature that lived underground, like a giant mole, making the earth shake with its comings and goings.

to China and further afield only grew, although the mammoth tusks, cleaned up and often chopped down to a manageable size, were later frequently mixed in with walrus tusks, becoming just a fungible ivory product. The first published reports of Siberian mammoth remains appeared in Europe in the 1690s and zoological papers followed, speculating on the finds. By the middle of the eighteenth century the Kunstkamera in St Petersburg contained at least one mammoth skull; it was recognised that this came from something like an elephant, though nobody knew quite what. Tusks were dug out of the tundra in increasingly large quantities and by the end of the eighteenth century there was a thriving trade flowing towards western Europe. According to one source, about 16.3 tons of mammoth ivory were sold at Yakutsk alone every year during the first half of the nineteenth century, and in some years twice that amount. Even considering that one tusk can weigh ninety kilograms, there was a lot of it.

So it wasn't that mammoth parts were unknown before Adams – far from it. Simply that people could not, or did not want to, comprehend the size and shape of the animal to which these parts once belonged. In medieval times and during the Renaissance, when the odd mammoth bone was found in Europe – in Lucerne, Gloucester, Krems in Austria, the Dauphiné in France and other places – if they weren't recognised as elephantine and attributed to Hannibal and his armies, they were often thought to belong to giant humans. Such bones were usually very poorly preserved. Before Adams, when it had only been tusks arriving from the East, their awkward presence could be ignored, dismissed or reduced to a curiosity. These were isolated anomalies, talking points mounted on a palace wall.

The problem of strange relics being dug out of the ground had already arisen in the form of ancient and strange seashells, which people kept finding in rocks on the top of mountains. However, seashells were less of a problem because they were really very small, and the oceans really very deep and mysterious – the seas might still contain all sorts of strange living creatures hitherto unknown to humankind.

The Adams mammoth, though, was a first: the first full mammoth skeleton (and assorted extras) that had survived the long journey from Siberian ice to a museum. In St Petersburg it was reassembled like a jigsaw puzzle, using for reference an Indian elephant skeleton that had belonged to Peter the Great, and it was exhibited to great acclaim in 1808. This was much bigger and more difficult to reason away than seashells. Its existence raised a number of difficult questions. What was this new creature? Or rather, how old was this *old* creature? Why was this almost-elephant found in the frozen north and not in the tropics? And if they were *not quite* elephants (which they visibly weren't), why were there no live ones still to be found?

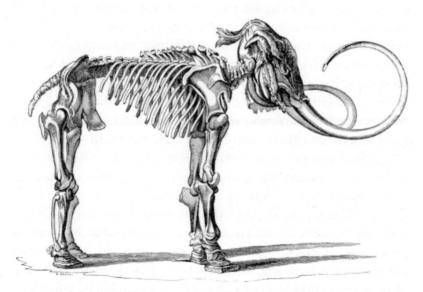

*Wilhelm Gottlieb Tilesius's etching of the Adams mammoth skeleton.*

These were deeply problematic issues, since 'prehistory' literally did not exist before the mid-nineteenth century: the Oxford Dictionary's first recorded use of the word was in 1836, and it was only popularised in 1865, by John Lubbock's bestselling *Pre-Historic Times as Illustrated by Ancient Remains*. Previously, the concept was hardly necessary: the Bible had everything covered. The world, its contents, its history and time itself had been glorious in their plenitude. In traditional Christian thought the earth was created in six days (plus a rest), which process had begun, according to one rather precise estimate, at 6 p.m. on 23 October 4004 BCE.[6]

It was also believed that animal species were stable and unchanging. Everything that had disembarked from Noah's Ark was still here. Things simply did not just go extinct. Now fractures and doubts were creeping in. The elephant in the room was, in fact, an elephant in a room. Ice had provided humankind with some kind of enigmatic revelation. Nobody was sure quite what it meant, and most did not want to believe it. How to explain the mammoth without shattering the established ideas of the earth's origins and our place within it? These difficult questions only had awkward answers.

One way of shoehorning the mammoth into the traditional Christian narrative was to hypothesise a kind of series of creations. In this version of events, the bones being uncovered belonged to creatures from a previous version of the earth, one that God scrapped before starting again, at the accepted time, with Adam and Eve and then Noah and all that. Earth 2.0, if you like.

Thus history was made to make sense again.

Another explanation for mammoths was that they had been part of our creation but had been simply too big to fit into the Ark and so had died in the Flood. These were not good animals and they hadn't made the cut. Or, some claimed, they had survived on the Ark but then, being simply too heavy, had sunk into the mud upon disembarking and died. Another contention was that the antediluvian world had been warmer, which explained why these kind-of-elephants were found at unexpected latitudes. The Flood had been mighty enough to scatter their carcasses, which had

---

[6] This date and time were calculated by James Ussher, Archbishop of Armagh and Primate of all Ireland between 1625 and 1656. His *Annals of the World* was a work of great scholarship, gathering together as it did swathes of information about the furthest possible reaches of history. The precise timing was not universally believed, and competing theories abounded, but a chronology starting around 4,000 years before the birth of Christ was accepted by many.

then fallen into crevices and frozen in the newly austere climate of Earth 2.0.

Thus everything was back in a box and all was well with the world. Right?

As for Adams himself, he was alive to the dizzying possibilities suggested by his mammoth but sensitive to the problems it posed. He was also clear about his position: from examining the skeleton, plus the mane and other evidence, he was sure that his creature was not an elephant. In this he sided with the great French naturalist and pioneer of palaeontology Georges Cuvier. In 1796, Cuvier had, from the very few bones available to him for study, persuasively highlighted many anatomical differences.

Adams also stated that he believed the mammoths had been killed in a flood and washed north, but confessed that the large amount of hair he had collected did not suit an animal from the tropics. He was troubled by the implications of his discovery. 'I shall merely add', he wrote, 'that it appears incontestable to me that there has existed a world of a very antient date.'

What he found in the ice had changed his conception of time, as it later would shape ours. He had assisted at the birth of modern palaeontology and of the very idea of prehistory itself.

As the nineteenth century wore on, more and more ex-mammoths headed west, to be displayed in St Petersburg, Brussels, Stuttgart and other major cities, as well as in the USA – though, of course, the Americans had mammoths of their own. It was increasingly difficult to stick one's head in the sand and ignore what was emerging out of the ice. And, in the early 1830s, a young man named Charles Robert Darwin began to think about taking a boat trip.

\*\*\*

Emerging ideas in geology were also turning biblical wisdom on its head. James Hutton's revolutionary *The Theory of the Earth*, which first appeared as a paper read to the Royal Society of Edinburgh in 1785, proposed that the rocks under our feet were produced by heat from the earth's core; it also suggested that the layers of strata, which might sometimes be seen where rocks protruded out of the ground, were formed by processes of erosion and deposition operating over unimaginably long periods – exactly the same processes that were still ongoing in the present day.[7] Those strata furthest underground – if the layers had not been disturbed – were necessarily older than those above, but Hutton also theorised that rocks that had been at the bottom of ancient seas could, over innumerable years, be thrust upwards by subterranean forces and become tall mountain tops – to be eroded, carried away and deposited below in their turn.

Hutton's theory came to be known as uniformitarianism, and it was later adopted and advanced by Charles Lyell, perhaps the most important geologist of the nineteenth century. This new geology was above all an empirical exercise in which one took deep notice of one's surroundings – its goal, to establish a timeline for all the world's rocks.

Fossil remains were being found in strata at remarkable depths, which indicated their incredible age and, once defined and widely recognised, some fossils could be used as 'index fossils', time markers that could fix the period a layer was laid down over many sites. If for example a shale layer in Oxfordshire and a gravel layer in Derbyshire contained a certain identical fossil species, then they could be dated similarly. Thus the foundations of a universal chronology were being established. If one took the accumulating evidence of this perpetual change seriously, the implication was that the slow building up and wearing down had been taking place over millions and millions of years: the record in the rocks was inconceivably older than Genesis allowed.

One could, of course, choose not to understand Genesis literally, and geology's distinct periods might even be thought of allegorically as the 'days' during which God had done the housework and made the world ready. But there was no sign that at some point – that seventh day – the creation of the world

---

[7] Much of the prevailing opinion before and after Hutton attributed the strata to – you guessed it – the work of great deluges.

had just stopped, and every sign that Hutton's uniformitarianism was right.

As the fossil record of dinosaurs and prehistoric megafauna grew larger and better known, the Creationists' intellectual contortions became ever more tortuous.

And here glaciers joined the geological attack. As we saw in the previous chapter, the inhabitants of Alpine valleys had long been used to the glaciers around them ebbing and flowing. Their transportive power was equally well understood, but the idea that past glaciers were far more extensive that those of the present day had not seriously been entertained. Hutton was one of the first to suggest this possibility, and from his time onwards more and more evidence to support it was being found. Glacial moraine was being identified a long way from existing glaciers, and erratics of Mont Blanc granite on the flanks of the Jura mountains, or Norwegian rocks in the Netherlands.

These were accounted for by some, clinging to the idea of a great and catastrophic flood, as having been carried by icebergs riding the deluge. And one explanation for the fine, unstratified glacial till (sediment) that covers large swathes of England proposed that a volcano had erupted under the sea to the north and west of the UK, washing the land with water. But searchers across the globe continued to find all the features of glacial landscapes – striated and shaped bedrock in the lowlands, high and distant trimlines in the mountains, arêtes and cirques and glacial lakes – in places where it was impossible to conceive of ice.

Although he did not coin the term 'Ice Age', Louis Agassiz, a Swiss zoologist and geologist, was the first to propose an Ice Age theory unifying these phenomena. His reading of the landscapes of the Alps (and some judicious reading of the work of acquaintances and contemporaries) led him to believe that there had been a series of Ice Ages during which glaciers had spread across vast portions of the world's surface and then receded, drastically shaping landscapes far from the current bounds of the ice. These periods of intense climatic change also plausibly explained the extinction of ancient creatures, including the mammoth.

Agassiz's paper introducing these ideas to the Swiss Society of Natural Sciences in 1837 caused consternation and was scorned. Undaunted, Agassiz spent the next three summers engaged in field work and in 1840 published the landmark *Études sur les Glaciers* (*Studies on Glaciers*).

That same year he toured the British Isles to look for traces of glacial activity in these lands without permanent ice. He also promoted 'his' glacial theory, and on 4 November gave a paper to the Geological Society of London. This lecture was recorded in the society's annual published *Proceedings*, which stated: 'If the analogy of the facts which [Agassiz] has observed in Scotland, Ireland, and the north of England, with those in Switzerland, be correct, then it must be admitted . . . that not only glaciers once existed in the British Islands, but that large sheets (*nappes*) of ice covered all the surface.' And Agassiz went even further: 'Great sheets of ice, resembling those now existing in Greenland, once covered all the countries in which unstratified gravel is found.'

William Buckland, a keen follower of Agassiz and president of the Geological Society, endorsed these conclusions wholeheartedly. The glacial theory was undoubtedly gaining some traction, and Agassiz was pleased with his progress. In a letter to Alexander von Humboldt dated 27 December 1840 he wrote: 'I have accumulated so much proof that nobody in England now doubts that glaciers existed here.'

Unfortunately, this was completely untrue.

The critical backlash to his challenging theories had been fierce and immediate, and it was again recorded in the Geological Society's *Proceedings*. Immediately after Agassiz's reading, George Greenough, the Society's founding president, questioned whether he really believed that Lake Geneva had once been under 3,000 feet of ice, to which Agassiz replied: 'At least!' Then Sir Roderick Murchison, a two-time president and one-time director general, stood up: 'The day will come when Highgate Hill will be regarded as the seat of a glacier, and Hyde Park and Belgrave Square will be the scene of its influence!' he barked. And these were self-described geologists, scientists who implicitly believed in the idea of deep time in the first place. Others must have found Agassiz's ideas even less tolerable.

The criticisms were also surprisingly long lived. Murchison's outburst was still being quoted approvingly in 1896, by a certain Rev. H. N. Hutchinson in a book entitled *Prehistoric Man and Beast*.[8] Hutchinson did not completely disagree with the glacial theory (and it is true that Agassiz overstated his case, claiming that the ice sheet had stretched all the way to the Mediterranean), but he was sceptical that ice could have done all the work Agassiz claimed for it. In a chapter entitled 'The Myth of the Great Ice Sheet', he writes:

> The idea of what they are pleased to call a 'Great Ice Sheet' has possessed them like a demon . . . In some unaccountable manner ice became a kind of select scientific cult – a new religion in fact. The glacier and the ice-sheet were objects of worship, endowed with mysterious and awe-inspiring powers before which geologists must prostrate not their bodies but their minds.

Other Christian believers in this post-Darwinian era also did not hold back. The charge was led by Sir Henry Hoyle Howorth, a reactionary and sometime Conservative MP in the north of England, who took issue with the scope of Agassiz's vision and wrote several now obviously wrong-headed screeds marshalling religious, meteorological, astronomical and other evidence to support his opinions. These included: 1887's *The Mammoth and the Flood*, which argued against uniformitarianism and stated that mammoths had lived before a catastrophic flood; 1893's *The Glacial Nightmare*, against the Ice Age theory; and 1905's *Ice or Water*, which contended that great floods might easily have

---

[8] This was far longer than Murchison himself held on to his resistance to the proposed Ice Age: letters show that by 1842 he was warming to the idea and by the 1860s he had recanted, writing to Agassiz: 'I have had the sincerest pleasure in avowing that I was wrong in opposing as I did your grand and original idea of my native mountains. Yes! I am now convinced that glaciers did descend from the mountains to the plains as they do now in Greenland.'

caused the landforms and geological features attributed to glacial action.

Five years into the twentieth century seems very late in the day to be giving such ideas credence. In reality, these creationists, climate deniers, culture warriors, call them what you will, were philosophical dead men walking long before that.

***

As far back as 1797 there had been undeniable proof that human beings had inhabited the deep past – that we were present during the last Ice Age, or even perhaps before. In that year, an East Anglian landowner called John Frere was alerted to a variety of finds at a brickmaker's workings near the village of Hoxne in Suffolk, including knapped-flint hand axes removed from a layer of gravelly soil at a depth of around 3.5 metres. These clearly ancient stone tools were not in themselves remarkable; what was remarkable was that in layers *above* the hand axes there were fossilised seashells, and even the bones of some giant creature, the like of which was no longer seen. 'The situation in which these weapons were found may tempt us to refer them to a very remote period indeed, even beyond that of the present world,' Frere wrote, in a report of the finds to the Antiquarian Society.

Evidence of human activity so long ago was yet another front in the attack on received ideas; Frere's finds were numerous, their stratigraphy unambiguous. They definitely undermined the traditional chronology of life on earth – or at least they would have, had anyone been paying attention.[9] The world of 1797 was not ready for Frere.[10] He received a letter of thanks from the Antiquarian Society and published an article in its journal, but his hand axes did not make a splash.

---

[9] We know now that these hand axes are around 400,000 years old, so were made by a previous *Homo* species – they are around ten times older than *Homo sapiens*' presence in Europe.

[10] A. Bowdoin Van Riper, author of *Men Among the Mammoths: Victorian Science and the Discovery of Human Prehistory*, cites the youth of all these disciplines and their informality – the lack of institutions and the amount of information circulating only in private – as well as simply the paucity of knowledge for this oversight. Hand axes are also much smaller than mammoths and, frankly, less sexy.

It would take another sixty years or so for the Christian conception of human antiquity to be totally discredited. After Frere, there were many other discoveries of human-made stone tools commingling with the remains of primitive creatures, but British geologists in particular seemed keen to deny the empirical evidence they would – ironically – in other circumstances have championed. On one cave dig in 1820, for example, William Buckland refused to recognise human remains found next to mammoth bones as being from the same era, on the grounds that the site may have been disturbed; on another dig, he told the cave's discoverer that the flints he had found must have been dropped into oven pits dug into the prehistoric floor, thus appearing to be from an earlier strata.

Geologists on the continent were also finding evidence of humans and prehistoric animals together, in the south of France at Bize and Montpellier, in Belgium and at Saint-Acheul, near Abbeville in the Somme. Some of these individuals were more open to the radical new ideas, but their digs and their discoveries were not widely seen by outsiders. Evidence like Frere's in England, or Jacques Boucher de Perthes's in Abbeville, really had to be seen to be believed. Word did not spread far and, where it did, it encountered strong resistance.

Critical mass was reached in 1859. The previous year, knapped flints and animal bones – mammoths, aurochs, hyena – had been discovered in an undisturbed cave in Brixham, Devon, which had then been rigorously excavated and catalogued. Several of those who worked on the site – including an archaeologist called John Evans and a geologist, Joseph Prestwich – then toured a number of European sites seeking to independently document the discoveries there. At the Saint-Acheul quarry they discovered a hand axe still embedded in the rock face, under other prehistoric fossils, and took a photograph of it still in place. Evans and Prestwich then chanced upon Frere's hand axes, whose importance they recognised, since they were very similar to those they'd seen in France.

The weight of evidence, including the French photograph, was compelling. A coordinated salvo of papers were given at the

Geological Society, Royal Society and Society of Antiquaries. And at that September's meeting of the British Association for the Advancement of Science in Aberdeen, in front of more than 2,500 people, Charles Lyell laid out the new theories – stone tools were synchronous with prehistoric beasts, men had lived among mammoths – and gave them his support. The tide of opinion among the cognoscenti turned.

It was, of course, a year pregnant with revolutionary ideas. Also in 1859, Charles Darwin's landmark work *On the Origin of Species* stated the case for natural selection as the driver of evolution. Darwin had for years been right at the heart of the debates about natural history and the beginnings of human life, and was sensitive to the way different currents of thought ebbed and flowed in London's illustrious meeting chambers. In 1840, just after he'd published his *Journals and Letters* (a.k.a. *The Voyage of the Beagle*),[11] he had attended, as secretary of the Geological Society, Agassiz's controversial reading on glacial theory – a paper that disagreed with some of Darwin's recently published ideas on Scottish geology. What the controversial and bestselling *On the Origin of the Species* did was thrust into the mainstream many of these ideas that had previously only been discussed behind the closed doors of gentlemen's societies, in clubs and select meetings and via private correspondence.

No longer did it seem so impossible that species might change or that – as implied by the famous dictum of 'the survival of the fittest'[12] – they might even die out completely. Indeed, the mammoth's obvious familial resemblance and antecedence to the elephant might have seemed a powerful empirical proof of the probability of Darwin's conjectures.

---

[11] Darwin was, at the outset of the voyage, more of a geologist than a naturalist, though that obviously would change. 'I have just got scent of some fossil bones of a Mammoth, what they may be I do not know, but if gold or galloping will get them, they shall be mine,' he wrote in a letter from Valparaíso, Chile, in 1834.

[12] This phrase did not appear in Darwin's work until its fifth edition in 1869; although it perfectly sums up one aspect of Darwin's evolutionary theory, it was coined by Herbert Spencer.

In 1863, Lyell published *Geological Evidences of the Antiquity of Man*, which accessibly presented the new evidence and powerfully summarised his change of thinking: 'Lyell's book brought the case for the "men among the mammoths" to the educated public and gave it the stamp of scientific orthodoxy,' a modern palaeoanthropologist wrote.

Finally, in 1864, Édouard Lartet, an archaeologist at a now famous rock shelter at La Madeleine in south-west France, uncovered an image of a mammoth etched on to a piece of mammoth ivory. A more perfect and self-referential smoking gun could not have been found. The case was closed.

\*\*\*

The above is, I know, a whistlestop tour. But imagine how it felt at the time. Here's a little thought experiment: it's 1797, you are five years old and you live in London. You've just learned about Adam and Eve, apprised of their existence by your mother or father, or by a minister in a church, people who absolutely believe in the couple's existence circa 4,000 BCE. Then about the Fall and their banishment, and Noah and the Flood and all the rest. Unbeknown to you, as you play on the muddy banks of the River Thames, a brickmaker in Suffolk is at that very moment examining flints he has found in some gravel, and a giant jawbone and some teeth. A couple of years later as you reach the age of seven or eight, a new century is dawning and Adams's mammoth is poking out of the ice.

The ramifications of these two events within the bounds of your allotted three-score-and-ten will be metaphysically and culturally earth shattering. By the time you reach your deathbed everything that you – an average person – thought you knew about the existence and continuation of life on earth, about how the earth itself came into being and about how humankind fitted into nature will have been blown away. What's more, these new theories will be, perhaps for the first time in history, both intelligible and available to you – if you are interested and have learned to read. Even given the pace of change throughout the twentieth and the twenty-first centuries, I'm not sure that any more genuinely disruptive (an overused word) or momentous events have ever happened in the course of a single human life.[13]

But there you are, lying on your deathbed in the 1860s, metaphorically floored by it all. What happens next? Well, you may still be destined for heaven (or hell). The new perspectives offered by geology and evolutionary biology did not preclude a belief in God – or, at least, not at first. Many people, of course, had never believed that the Bible was literally true, deriving moral guidance from a looser, allegorical interpretation of its stories. Billions still lean on the Bible and the holy books of other religions in this way. In the nineteenth century there was a whole school of thought, natural theology, that adduced arguments for the existence of God based on reasoning and observing natural phenomena. It *was* possible to believe that mammoths were no less God's creatures than any other (even if they didn't make the cut for the Ark); and equally possible to view glaciers as part of God's plan.

When Louis Agassiz, for example, went to America for the first time, on a speaking engagement in 1846, he saw the continent as a vast canvas for his theories. But, as he made clear in an article for the *Atlantic Monthly*, God was the ultimate artist:

> One naturally asks, What was the use of this great engine set at work ages ago to grind, furrow, and knead over, as it were, the surface of the earth? We have our answer in the fertile soil which spreads over the temperate regions of the globe. The glacier was God's great plough; and when the ice vanished from the face of the land, it left it prepared for the hand of the husbandman ... I think we may believe that God did not shroud the world He had made in snow and ice without a purpose, and that this, like many other operations of His Providence, seemingly destructive and chaotic in its first effects, is nevertheless a work of beneficence and order.

[13] You'd have to be very long lived to have been there before motorcars and have made it through powered flight and TV to the internet.

In this he was foreshadowing another great naturalist, John Muir (born 1838), the Scottish-American known as the 'father' of America's national parks and one of the forefathers of the modern ecological movement. In his wanderings, Muir, a confirmed but unconventional Christian, developed a spiritual, transcendental attachment to landscape and nature.

Muir's observations, particularly of his beloved Yosemite Valley in California and of parts of Alaska, were instrumental in promoting glacial theory in the USA. In a letter, he named ice-created landforms 'glacier ghosts', and saw glaciers, above all, as part of God's plan, a divine tool for shaping the earth into its predestined shapes. And he expressed this in exalted prose, as with this passage describing Glacier Bay in Alaska: 'Though the storm-beaten ground it is growing on is nearly half a mile high, the glacier centuries ago flowed over it as a river flows over a boulder; but out of all the cold darkness and glacial crushing and grinding comes this warm, abounding beauty and life to teach us that what we in our faithless ignorance and fear call destruction is creation finer and finer.'

To delve into this nineteenth-century intellectual history is to be immersed in a great thirst for knowledge on issues of the most profound import and reach, but also plunged into great turbulence. Reading the arguments and the counterarguments, the tumult rises palpably off the page and the excitement and confusion are visceral. Living in that time of flux, watching reference points shift, be torn away, discredited, reinstated, anointed – living in a whirlwind of opinions in which science, for some, was merely a belief, and with no clear arbiter of truth – must have been vertiginous. And exciting.

It's easy to see with the benefit of hindsight who was right and who was wrong. Things seem clear-cut now that we know what indeed we know. Mistakes and missteps were numerous, and many of these thinkers were wrong about as many things as they were right about. Charles Lyell very quickly endorsed and then drew back from Agassiz's glacial theory, and despite being great friends with Darwin struggled to reconcile his religious beliefs with the idea of natural selection. Louis Agassiz was pro-Ice Age but anti-Darwinism, and held what we now would call abhorrent, scientifically racist beliefs. The Rev. H. N. Hutchinson maintained his Christianity while agreeing with some of Darwin and repudiating Ice Age theories, whereas John Muir absolutely believed that his Christian views were compatible with the forces that had shaped the Yosemite landscape. Charles Darwin took a while to come around to Agassiz's ice-sheet idea, and later described a marine (rather than glacial) theory he had formulated as 'one long gigantic blunder'. *On the Origin of Species* evinces a strain of natural theology; in fact, after the first edition, Darwin added words and sentences here and there to emphasise its congruence with Christian thinking. However, Darwin, who had a non-conformist background and almost entered the Anglican clergy, by the end of his life defined himself as an agnostic.

So much going on. And it might seem, from the course of the past few pages, that this hasn't been much about ice at all, or only tenuously. But I would argue that ice was intimately tied up in everything that was at stake during this period in the distinct and yet deeply intertwined fields of palaeontology, archaeology and geology. As Elizabeth Cary Agassiz wrote, concerning her husband Louis: 'To him his work had but one meaning. It was never disconnected in his thought, and therefore he turned from his glaciers to his fossils, and from the fossil to the living world, with the feeling that he was always dealing with kindred problems, bound together by the same laws.'

Or, as John Muir more poetically put it: 'When we try to pick out anything by itself, we find it hitched to everything else in the universe.'

Ice was revelatory, proving the past to be far stranger than anyone had ever imagined. It was a contested object in the geological arguments, and also a provider of clarity, supplying evidence that killed off Creationism and changed our conception of history. Mammoth bones taken from the ice were tools – first blunt but then increasingly sophisticated – that chipped away at the foundations of wrong-headed beliefs about human antiquity.

Glacial geology was also a weapon in this concerted and multidisciplinary attack on long-standing ideas about the past.

These ideas, as elucidated by ice, forever changed our relationship with the Bible, and the Bible's with reality; and they definitively severed religion's claim to authority on the biggest questions of existence.

*Engraving of Yosemite, nineteenth century.*

# 9

## Dr Sawbones

### *Ice, medicine and the body*

*Mortui vivos docent ('The dead teach the living')*
Anatomists' adage

*Knowledge spins where once larva was formed.*
Michel Foucault, *The Birth of the Clinic*
(trans. 1974)

If *Frankenstein* was born from an encounter between Mary Shelley and the upper ice world, the human and the non-human, it can also be interpreted as a parable of uneasiness about new technologies and scientific methods. In his voracious thirst for knowledge, the young student Victor Frankenstein is captivated by the idea of the elixir of life, the fabled potion that granted eternal life or eternal youth, which was the highest pursuit of the branch of natural philosophy known as alchemy. Soon Frankenstein turns away from alchemy's ancient follies and concentrates on the most modern aspects of chemistry. Enlightened people know that alchemy is hocus pocus – so the logic of the book's anxiety runs – but *what might science do*? And what Frankenstein achieves – 'bestowing animation upon lifeless matter' – upsets not only his world but the balance of nature itself.

Although Frankenstein's secret is never revealed, the monster's birth involves galvanism, a modish late eighteenth-century theory that electricity can give life to the inanimate or restore life to the dead. It is also explicitly tied to ice: we see the monster first – he is in fact *born for us* – in the framing narrative of Walton's voyage to find the north-east passage.[1]

Thus ice gives life. But what else might ice do? In Shelley's tale it is a radically disruptive substance, straddling the border between the natural and unnatural, beauty and horror. And the more I looked into the history of ice and the body, the more this seemed to be carried over into reality. Ice as a medical technology weaves together sickness, health, life and death, in unexpected and often gruesome ways. It also opens the lid on a Pandora's box of profound ethical questions.

Above all, what we see, from antiquity onwards, is a complete lack of consensus about whether ice was beneficial or harmful. While some extolled the health-giving effects of ice-cooled drinks and food, others were worrying about their damaging effects on the body. Galen was broadly against them, and Hippocrates warned that eating ice or snow could cause chest colds – which feels like homespun wisdom akin to parents warning children not to go out with wet hair. The idea that an external chill causes illness echoes across the centuries.

Following completely the opposite line of reasoning, the *frigidarium* – the cold room at the Roman baths, often cooled with liberal amounts of snow – was greatly reputed for its medical properties after the Emperor Augustus had been cured of a dangerous disease by his physician using a regime of *frigidarium* visits and cold compresses; yet it equally quickly fell out of favour again after Augustus's nephew Marcellus fell ill with the same disease and died, despite icy treatments, that same year.

Yet other sources, meanwhile, record ice's use in Roman times to treat fevers, colic, kidney problems, gangrene and other ailments. Frozen water, at the intersection of medicine, biology and the natural world, was becoming a way of working on and healing the body.

---

[1] The galvanic force behind the monster's birth is often represented as a lightning bolt (though not by Mary Shelley). Curiously, the electric charge that becomes a stroke of lightning is in fact produced by ice particles colliding with each other in a thundercloud.

Fast forward more than a thousand years and, as ice use became widespread across Europe once again, familiar doubts about its deleterious effects resurfaced. One such worry was specifically that the temperature gradient between a chilled drink and a hot Mediterranean summer's day was harmful to the body. Following Hippocrates, many doctors and rulers counselled against ingesting ice-cooled substances, stating that they could provoke colic, convulsions, paralysis, blindness, madness and/or sudden death, among other things. On the other hand, many advocated for it strongly, for the treatment of fevers, cholera, quinsy, 'trembling of the heart' and other complaints.[2]

In 1584, a Sevillan physician, Nicolás Monardes, appealed to his home city's council to facilitate the ice trade on public health grounds, while a contemporary of his in Italy stated that the introduction of a reliable snow and ice supply to Naples saved thousands of lives during a torrid summer season of fevers. A couple of centuries later, in 1775, a Neapolitan physician, Filippo Baldini, published a whole book detailing the health benefits of different flavours of ice cream, a course of treatment I can definitely get behind. Cinnamon, he believed, was one of the most effective. And, in 1779, a certain Dubuisson, a Parisian distiller, published *The Art of the Distiller and Liqueurs Merchant, Considered as Medical Foodstuffs*, which cited the conviction of a doctor named Mazarini that contagious diseases spread more quickly through Italy in years when less snow had been collected because of a warm winter. The seasonality of some viruses is of course now well known. Somewhere among the ignorant, the fearful and the quacks, a medical science was emerging.

As I dug deeper the thing that began to fascinate me was not the ingesting of the ice; it was ice's development as a tool – ice as

---

[2] Note the crossover between the ancient lists and the later ones. It is characteristic of a poorly understood substance that myriad contradictory and competing claims ('miracle' and 'dangerous') can be held to be true at the same time. And the doubters about ice persisted. Peruse the catalogue of the Wellcome Collection Library in London, and even into the nineteenth century treatises such as *On the Treatment of Pneumonia by the Ice-Bag* (1889) and *Crushed Ice and Lard in the Treatment of Burns and Scalds* (1884) are counterbalanced by ones like *An Account of Two Cases of Gout, which Terminated in Death, in Consequence of the External Use of Ice and Cold Water* (1804).

an aid to surgery and, eventually, a lens that opened new vistas on the body itself.

But to tell this tale I need to take you back to ninth-century China, where alchemists (who, like Frankenstein, were looking for the elixir of life) discovered a miraculous substance that could produce violent, uncontrollable heat and also dramatically increase our power to create cold.

*\*\**

The story starts with a bang. There is a Taoist recipe from around 850 CE that contains a dire warning: 'Some have heated together sulphur, realgar [arsenic disulphide] and saltpetre with honey. Smoke and flames result, so that their hands and faces have been burned, and even the whole house where they were working burned down.' It seems very likely that Chinese alchemists searching for eternal youth accidentally discovered gunpowder.

Gunpowder was initially used for medicinal purposes – its Chinese name translates to 'fire medicine' – and it is recognised as one of ancient China's most significant contributions to global technology (paper and printing being two others). However, the parallel development of one of gunpowder's ingredients, saltpetre, as an artificial coolant has in the long run been almost as significant and yet is comparatively overlooked.

Saltpetre is properly called potassium nitrate, but we know it by its Roman name, more or less – our word being derived from the Latin *sal petrae*, meaning 'salt of stone'. But while the Romans were dabbling with saltpetre in Europe, the Chinese were harvesting the stuff from around the first century CE. By the Tang Dynasty (618–907 CE) – or so claim several Chinese sources I have found difficult to corroborate – they were using it to create ice. How does this work?

When common soluble salts are dissolved in water an endothermic reaction occurs: that is, as the solid salt crystals decompose into their constituent ions the chemical reaction draws energy from its surroundings, thereby cooling them. And the ions present in the resulting salt solution then interrupt the hydrogen-bonding, lattice-making activity of the water molecules. This depresses the freezing point below that of pure water.[3] And the more salt you add – up to a point – the lower the freezing point gets. A saltpetre-only solution stays liquid to about −18 °C, but a mixture of salts can push this lower. Now place a vessel of pure water in a very cold salt solution: it freezes!

As knowledge of the substance spread west, it became known as 'China snow' by the Persians and 'China salt' in Arabic. It was recorded in use in the *History of Medicine* by Ibn abī-Uṣaybi'a in 1242, in which the Damascan noted the ability to make ice using water and salt, but the cooling powers of saltpetre seem to have been introduced to Renaissance Europe via India.[4] By the mid-sixteenth century, there was saltpetre experimentation in Padua, Bologna, Rome and Antwerp. In 1589, the Neapolitan Giambattista della Porta included experiments with saltpetre in his enlarged edition of *Magia Naturalis* (*Natural Magic*), in which he describes freezing wine so that 'you cannot drink it but by sucking and drawing in of your breath.'

In 1620, a notable experiment in artificial cooling took place in the Great Hall of Westminster Palace. On a hot summer's day, Cornelis Drebbel, a Dutch-born natural philosopher working in England under the patronage of King James I, demonstrated what seems to have been an early air-conditioning device. When the king and his courtiers processed into the hall, the chill was so great that it apparently caused them to flee shivering. Drebbel, who was playing to the king's interest in 'daemonologie' by dressing as a magician, did not publicly disclose his method, but Francis

[3] This is why we spread salt on roads. First the salt dissolves in any liquid water present – there is a very thin film of liquid water on the surface of any ice, or it's often sprayed in a briny solution, to kick-start the cooling process – and this causes a little more of the ice to melt, and more of the salt to dissolve, and so on.

[4] Saltpetre rarely occurs in most parts of Europe but it is abundant in India. *The Institutions of Akbar*, commissioned by the Mughal emperor Akbar the Great and completed around 1590, details the long-established court procedures for cooling drinking water. 'Saltpetre,' writes the chronicler, 'which in gunpowder produces explosive heat, is used by his majesty as a means for cooling water, and is thus a source of joy for great and small.' Saltpetre is one reason among many why India was important to the British Empire, though for gunpowder rather than for cold drinks.

Bacon took note of the experiment and later that year stated that he believed that 'the late experiment of artificiall freezing' had used saltpetre (which he called 'nitre').

As a counterpoint to the exciting advances by these early scientists, from other quarters came apprehension and disapproval. These added a spiritual dimension to the oft-repeated concerns about the decadence of eating ices and supping on cooled wines – that 'degenerate custom of turning the seasons upside down'. Essentially, people worried that the scientists were tampering with God's work. Not a surprising conclusion, perhaps, if you consider that saltpetre is a principal ingredient in two revolutionary and antagonistic processes, one producing explosive heat and the other producing ice.[5]

*\*\**

Saltpetre brought ice out of the realm of foodstuff and took it into a completely different realm. What set me on the path to uncovering a more visceral and more morally complex relationship between ice and the body was the archaeologists' report on William Leftwich's newly rediscovered ice well near Regent's Park in London. As well as summarising the now familiar story of London's international ice trade, there was a line about some of the ice being sold to dentists in nearby Harley Street to be used as crude anaesthesia.

As I tumbled down this new rabbit hole, I read that the anaesthetic properties of ice had been well known at least since the seventeenth century, when surgeons like the famous Marco Aurelio Severino in Naples would apply ice to the skin in narrow parallel lines to produce surface numbness before operating.[6] After fifteen minutes of gentle pressure, he could remove the ice

---

[5] In fact, it is said that by around 1750 the Russians were using gunpowder to lob cannonballs of ice out of ice-hewn mortars, so, in a certain fashion at least, the two seemingly antipathetic sides of saltpetre can be reconciled.

[6] Naples is an ice hub we keep returning to. It benefited from a local volcano for snow collection, from scorching summers to induce ice fever and, as the most important city of the Spanish Empire in the eastern Mediterranean, from not only culture and learning but also a huge military presence – guaranteeing gunpowder and its constituent saltpetre.

and cut without pain. (The parallel lines of ice reduced the risk of gangrene in the incision.)

In the 1790s, a Scottish surgeon called John Hunter anaesthetised a rabbit's ear, the muscles in a frog's legs, a bullock's neck and the skin of a sheep, as well as treating his own wasp stings with ice. By 1807, it was possible, according to Napoleon's chief surgeon, Baron Dominique Jean Larrey, to amputate limbs on the icy battlefields of the Polish campaign, if the soldiers in possession of said limbs were frozen enough. Time was passing, and surgeons were pushing the boundaries of their art.

In the nineteenth century came general anaesthesia. After the first successful operation on a fully blotto patient, performed by a Japanese doctor in 1804, chloroform and ether began to be used, at first slowly then more regularly, to put patients under, but the inhalation of gases was fraught with danger and a number of patients drifted off never to return. Believing that number to be unacceptably high, a Scottish doctor, James Arnott, waged a long campaign against gas, as well as experimenting with better ways of employing ice than either the two-parallel-lines or frozen-battlefield scenarios, as he explained in *On Cold as a means of producing Local Insensibility* (1848):

In applying cold . . . I have taken care to avoid reaction – by reducing the temperature very gradually. To benumb a small portion of skin a very simple apparatus is required. A small pig's bladder, some pounded ice, and a little salt. The bladder containing tepid water is placed so as to cover the portion of skin to be rendered insensible; the ice is then gradually dropped in and last of all the salt so as to bring the temperature considerably below freezing point . . . when all sensation has ceased, which I have generally found to be the case after fifteen to twenty minutes, the operation should be proceeded with.

Thus patients with a dodgy wisdom tooth were faced with the choice of unadulterated pain, gassy oblivion or resting their cheek on a freezing pig's bladder while someone not far removed from a barber – for a long time the go-to for minor surgery and dental problems – delved into their mouth with a large pair of pliers.

Arnott claimed he had found a mixture of salts that could 'in dissolving, reduce the temperature to below zero of Fahrenheit's thermometer, or more than thirty degrees lower than any temperature hitherto employed in medicine'. He believed that such extreme cold had completely different physiological and remedial effects on the patient to those produced using cold water or ice, just as there is a big difference between the effect on the body of a hot poultice, steam treatment or a red-hot iron (which was in those times used as an escharotic, to destroy diseased tissues). Salt-cooled ice was opening up new avenues in medical treatment.

From 1846, under Arnott's supervision, the Brighton Infirmary, which sat above the new developments of Kemp Town to the east of the seaside resort, became a centre of frigorific experimentation. Here he explored using ice to treat cancer (analgesically) as well as ulcers and various skin conditions and unwanted protuberances. Not only did congelation numb pain, he found, when used as an anaesthetic in surgery it prevented catastrophic bleeding. Surgeons had to take care, however, to adapt their scalpel technique. 'The skin does not cut as crisp as natural when frozen, but like tough soap,' one wrote. Arnott was a keen proselytiser of his methods, and there are reports of congelation being used on a lipoma, on a strangulated hernia and in various knee operations. One contemporary, it was recorded, removed a large crop of venereal warts 'with but little pain or haemorrhage . . . Some were the size of a fig.'

\*\*\*

Anaesthesia was interesting, and not a little gruesome. But it was, somewhat . . . expected? I had an intuition, given the beguiling powers of ice, and the recurrent worries about its effect upon the body (not to mention the undertow of moral panic in *Frankenstein*, which I have to say coloured just a little my perceptions of early science and medicine), that there must be something more. Something ambiguous, something that crossed the line. Something hidden. And then I found something. Or rather someone: Wilhelm Braune, the nineteenth century's foremost practitioner of anatomical frozen sectioning.

Biographical details about Christian Wilhelm Braune are hard to come by. He was born in Leipzig, Germany, in 1831 and studied at Göttingen and Würzburg. After this, and before his death in 1892, he had a first career as a military surgeon before taking up the chair of professor of topographical anatomy at the University of Leipzig.

Perhaps because of his time soldiering, Braune's anatomical practice emphasised movement, stressing that form followed function and that biological development was guided by mechanical principles. Historically, anatomy had tended to focus on particular organs or systems; topographical anatomy instead viewed the body in concrete unity, looking at the spatial and relational aspects of different internal parts, treating our insides like unknown landscapes or dark regions to be mapped. It was, in a sense, the human eye invading the body and colonising it with knowledge.

Rather than following tissues as they crept obscurely from place to place, topographical anatomy prioritised the section – a slice of the body through whatever was there, showing the positions of each constituent part. But there was a problem: human beings are quite squashy. And once the dead tissues and organs were deformed or displaced, the endeavour lost all value to surgeons. Given that they operated upon the living, if the section did not accurately represent what they would find as they cut into live flesh, it was useless. Before Braune, anatomists had enveloped bodies in gypsum or soaked them in strong alcohol to try to prepare them to withstand the long two-handed saws that were used to cut them apart. It was not enough:

These methods are still insufficient to give to the organs the rigidity necessary to keep the parts from becoming disturbed in preparing them. It is by freezing cadavers that we can preserve the organs, their respective relations and exact form. This method permits making sections of various parts of the body and at levels perfectly determined. The examination of these plane sections gives the most exact appreciation of the situation, of the form, and of the relations of the organs.

This is not Braune writing, but a slightly earlier French contemporary, Docteur Eugène Quintien Le Gendre. For Braune did not invent frozen sectioning;[7] what he did was perfect it and make the medical establishment take notice, inaugurating what was even at the time referred to as the 'Ice Age' of anatomy and obstetrics.

In 1872, Braune produced an 'atlas' of topographical anatomy, with all the grandeur of scale, exactness of delineation and nuances of colour which that word implies. Three dimensions turned into two. A map of the body as big as the body itself.[8]

I wanted to see more, so I booked a visit to the Rare Materials Room of the Wellcome Collection, a London museum and library specialising in medicine and human sciences, where there is an original copy – of the English translation at least. Although it did not reproduce the Indian ink of the lithographs in colour or at full size, the forty-six woodcuts were still impressive. How to describe seeing them in the flesh? I am tempted to call them delicate, but they are not; they still possess a corporeal solidity under the fine lines, as does the relief of a mountain range on a map. The divided bodies are so beautiful that they do not look incomplete. Fulfilled by their own truth, they possess a kind of radiant wholeness. Perhaps I had expected that the sectioning might have frozen the trauma of its preparation into its subjects? If so, it was repressed below the lithographs' calm and untroubled surface. Think too hard about their provenance, however, about the humans beneath the illustrations, and they are profoundly disquieting.

[7] It seems to have been developed at least twice: once by Pieter de Reimer, a Dutchman, in the early nineteenth century, and later by Nikoläi Pirogov, a Russian, who believed he had invented the technique himself: 'Nobody before me, as far as I know, has ever proposed or employed a method by which the human body could be so solidified by freezing that it could be cut like wood into thin sections,' he wrote in the 1850s. Pirogov was envied by Braune, since his laboratory in Moscow was naturally incredibly cold in the winter and, in the Moskva river, he had a ready supply of ice.

[8] I have not seen the original German 'large atlas', as Braune calls it, but in his introduction to the English translation he writes, 'they are the size of nature.'

The most striking sections are those that Braune published in an appendix to the *Atlas*, of two women who killed themselves: one in the final month of pregnancy; the other, a 35-year-old working woman who drowned herself as she went into labour. In each, Braune has taken a full mid-sagittal section (right along the midline, between the eyes and down), revealing in each lithograph a baby *in utero*: one a boy, one a girl. The girl cradles the umbilical cord, which lies against her like a twist of rope, and each appears tranquil, sleeping. The images are disturbing, exquisite, intrusive, captivating. I imagine that to see them in colour and life size would be overwhelming. Each one contains a person – two people, in fact – transcribed and transposed on to paper, in the most intimate detail, exposed like nobody ever had been before.

How did Braune do it? It is not fully explained, only hinted at, in the *Atlas* itself. He likes to note that a body is 'prepared in the usual manner' – as if there is anything 'usual' about it – which leads me to think it was perhaps something of a trade secret. But the generalities are easy to reconstruct. Having procured a fresh cadaver – mostly those of people who had committed suicide – Braune would first arrange it depending on the plane he wanted to cut, for symmetry or ease of access. One body he left exposed in the cool Leipzig air for fourteen days before freezing; in other cases, he notes that he injected the arteries with paint. Once prepared, the corpse would be placed into a watertight metal box, and that box submerged in an ice bath with a special salt mixture of Braune's formulation.

In the appendix with the two pregnant women, he gives a fuller description:

Though it was the month of March when the body was brought into the dissecting room, yet the weather being warmer than is usual in this season, it was judged advisable to employ an artificial freezing mixture composed of salt and ice, and in this mixture the body was kept for 6 days during which time the ice and salt were repeatedly renewed, the temperature being maintained at — 10 °R.[9] So long a time was considered advisable in order to ensure the thorough congelation of all parts within the abdominal and pelvic cavities. And on sawing through the body it was actually found that the freezing had succeeded as well as could be desired.

In order to make accurate tracings of both halves of the body and correctly represent what was shown in the preparation, the work was carried on in a cool cellar. Each day before the body began to thaw, the drawing was discontinued and the parts were again put into the freezing mixture in which they remained during the night. During this time the parts were left in the same unaltered position and the drawings correctly executed.

Cutting took place in a cold room, with a chilled saw: sagittal, coronal (across the body widthways from top to bottom), transverse or sometimes obliquely across a body part – across the head at the level of the eyes, to reveal their connections to the brain, for example. Sometimes the sawn section would not quite hit the exact line of a particular part of interest – say, the brain, or the urethra – so there might be a little fettling with a razor to get the details of the plane just so. Even the finest saw and the most skilful operatives would tear and blur the best-frozen flesh, so the section would afterwards be brushed and washed. (A later anatomist would polish them with a rapidly revolving wooden wheel, wet and covered in finely powdered pumice stone.) Then it would be plunged into alcohol, which would harden it. Sections could be cut cleanly at thicknesses of about an inch, if they were peripheral or transverse; if mid-sagittal or coronal, sections had to be considerably thicker.

In the case of the two pregnant women there was one final twist. Braune again: 'The parts into which the foetus had been divided in sawing through the maternal body were at the last reunited, so

---

[9] This would appear to be given in Rankines, a unit denoting the absolute temperature scale related to Fahrenheit, established in 1859 by William John Macquorn Rankine, a Scottish engineer and physicist. If so, the temperature appears to be nonsensical: somewhere close to or actually below absolute zero. It may be a translator's error, and I have left it as is.

that a view of the original position of the child within the body of the mother could be obtained.'

Look at the illustration again (it's in the plate section), and now you see it: a perfectly lifelike, three-dimensional baby disrupting the two-dimensional space.

Later, many anatomists would specialise in particularly thin slicing, presenting multiple, evolving views of the internal organs from slice to slice. Braune's preferred method of presenting only key sections of interest was, by contrast, curiously orthodox; his most important innovation lay in devising a way to make incredibly exact drawings: he would take the hardened section and freeze a thin layer of water over it, then place a transparent sheet of paper upon the ice and trace the details directly from 'life', before passing the drawings on to a lithographer. 'I place special emphasis upon careful details of anatomical drawings . . . When the drawings concern such an elaborate mechanism as the human body, every line must be true to nature and copied with the greatest care,' he wrote.

Some anatomists would photograph their work for presentation, but photography at that time could not capture the details or the nuance as an artist could. It is ironic that the most accurate and objective depictions demanded a high degree of artifice. There was something of the showman in Braune, it seems to me – witness the baby in the womb – but the atlases were intended as a teaching aid, to help students familiarise themselves with the contours of a strange subterranean country and learn to navigate around it. In this, his methods were meticulous – even, for example, injecting water into the knee cavity so that it froze, stopping the cavity collapsing when the body was placed into the salt solution and chilled.

Ice was a tool to defer death's decay. It made things visible that were not visible before. Braune's obsession, it seems to me, was to see things clearly, and ice helped him do that. The clarity of his frozen gaze, the beautiful and terrifying vision afforded by ice, was astonishing. No more deft fumbling with blind fingers. What had once been unseen – unseeable even – was now revealed and could be wrapped up in words and learned.[10] But at what price?

[10] Michel Foucault's *The Birth of the Clinic* (trans. 1974) charts the privileging of the gaze in the treatment of human diseases and ills. 'Doctors described what for centuries

Anatomy is a noble discipline. Dissection traces its roots back to the Ancient Greek city of Alexandria in the third century BCE, and it flourished and was modernised during the Renaissance. When Leonardo da Vinci took anatomy up to perfect his understanding of musculature and bone structure, his interest grew more profound and he dissected at least thirty bodies. Rembrandt recorded seventeenth-century anatomy lessons in two paintings, one of which, *The Anatomy Lesson of Dr Nicolaes Tulp* (1632), survives as one of the pinnacles of Dutch art. 'He who neglects anatomy will wrong and kill his patients,' wrote Abulcasis, a tenth-century Andalusian Arab physician who is known as the father of modern surgery.[11] But despite its usefulness anatomy was, during long moments in its history, neglected and even shunned. And dissection was also either proscribed or very tightly regulated by the church and other authorities.

One major obstacle to its attaining respectability was that helping the living required the already dead. This provoked a moral squeamishness. Delving into a corpse, even in the spirit of understanding, offended religious sensibilities, which saw it as tampering with God's design. In the eighteenth and early nineteenth centuries, dissection in Europe passed through a particularly dark era. The number of medical schools multiplied and the demand for cadavers – always larger than supply – shot up. Decaying bodies were stolen from gallows and murders committed to supply suitable candidates. Grave robbing and bodysnatching became rife. In eighteenth-century England, the men responsible for illicit night-time exhumations were known as 'resurrectionists'; sometimes these resurrectionists, after being sentenced to death, ended up on the anatomy table themselves. Stories abound of dying people being hastened along

had remained below the threshold of the visible and the expressible,' he wrote. 'A new alliance was forged between words and things, enabling one to see and to say.' Although Foucault was writing about pathology – disease – in the early nineteenth century, and Braune's anatomy came a little later, I have the sense that Braune provides the moment that vindicates Foucault.

[11] This was paraphrased by Sir Astley Cooper, a prominent nineteenth-century surgeon-anatomist: 'He must mangle the living if he has not operated on the dead.'

and anatomists, who only had a short operating window before decomposition set in, opening up still-living bodies.

Since being dissected rendered a body unrecognisable and precluded a traditional Christian burial, capital punishment was the major source of legitimate medical cadavers, and, in the eighteenth century, in some parts of Europe, new offences punishable by death were introduced simply to increase the supply of corpses. The dishonour of being dissected became almost synonymous with, and almost as powerful a deterrent as, being hanged.

Some countries responded to the shortage by making new laws to allow the unclaimed bodies of paupers, criminals and those in mental institutions to be used in anatomy demonstrations. In the UK, change took longer, fuelling the bodysnatching trade, but even when the legislation was eased in 1832 supply could not meet demand. From 1858, doctors were required to complete two full years of anatomical training, dramatically adding to the body burden, in effect turning their professors into shills for the corpses (or even amputated parts) their students desperately required.

Hospitals could usually procure bodies from local slums, but universities had to look further afield. Cambridge University went as far as organising a twice-weekly, high-speed 'dead train' that travelled overnight from Doncaster, delivering bodies from as far away as Hull. The freight carriages at the rear were unloaded after the passengers had disembarked, and even the most strong-stomached anatomists then had only a few days at most before the putrefaction became overwhelming. Undoubtedly, the increasing use of ice would have alleviated their discomfort somewhat.[12] This is the backdrop to the frozen sectioning of the latter half of

---

[12] The practice of preserving the dead in ice has been known since Ancient China. A book from the late Eastern Chou dynasty (770–256 BCE) describes the palace 'ice service' of ninety-four staff, who chilled everything from wine to corpses. A new public morgue opened in Paris in 1804 ('morgue' seems to come from the archaic French verb *morguer*, which means 'to look solemnly') had display cases for public viewing but no ice supply, so relied on a constant drip of cold water to keep them cool. As for dead trains, the Yankees during the American Civil War had a similar aroma problem when transporting home the bodies of fallen soldiers. Their solution: embalming.

the nineteenth century: the alternatives that any trainee doctor or an anatomist would have had to consider.

What did the frozen sectioners themselves feel about their work? The pervasive stench of death, the manipulation, the sawing? Did one have to have a frozen heart to cut in two a frozen heart?

Dicing with death to improve life blurs fundamental ethical boundaries. It reeks of the Faustian. Ice helped Braune to see his subjects clearly, but did this entail a moral slippage? In a surviving photo, Braune is inscrutable, quite the respectable gent of his time: grey-bearded, with a military bearing, a full dark jacket and crisp white shirt. And from his writings you would have to conclude he slept easily at night. They are masterworks in the nineteenth-century art of containing horror within a neutral, didactic tone, smoothing over difficulties like ice on a freshly sawn section. Nowhere did I see any recognition that these organs were once living and moving, parts of actual people: I searched hard for names, anything to restore the humanity to Braune's subject-objects, but in vain, finding only scant descriptors of age, height and provenance. Perhaps that was the way it had to be.

Nowhere in the writings of these anatomists was it easy to discern any doubts or hesitations about their methods. The closest I found was in the writings of an American, Thomas Dwight, who in his 1881 work *Frozen Sections of a Child* (yes, quite) wrote: 'Believing, as I do, that frozen sections will play an important part in the anatomical teaching of the future, I shall say nothing of their advantages, which speak for themselves.' This rebuttal to unexpressed criticisms seems to indicate a defensive position fraught with repressed anxieties.

The awkward truth about medical advances in any age is that they frequently come with a high price tag, one that is hidden from their beneficiaries or that society prefers not to acknowledge. Braune's frozen sections undoubtedly helped to advance the spread of anatomical knowledge and alleviate pain and suffering. And childbirth in Braune's time was fraught with mortal danger; how many doctors and midwives benefited from the lithographs of the two pregnant women, how many mothers' and babies' lives were improved or saved? Can that be weighed against the body being lowered into the ice?

Even if one is on a humanist crusade, feels morally justified, spotless, an uncomfortable apposition of ends and means is never far away.

In the medical profession, frozen sectioning had plentiful detractors: its opponents were reluctant to make the hand subservient to the eye and argued that as a teaching aid it was inferior to actual time spent with a scalpel in a body. It could never replace skilled fingers schooled by surgical experience. Perhaps the most serious objection was that, according to some, frozen organs did not retain the bulk and the disposition they had when full of hot blood, so the topography would be badly drawn and the map would not resemble the territory.

In the decades immediately after Braune's magnum opus, frozen sectioning spread to Britain, the USA and beyond, but Braune's eerie, unprecedentedly accurate lithographs remained the reference, the set text for students of anatomy, surgery and obstetrics, for many, many years. His work was solidly useful and ephemerally beautiful, and in many senses unimprovable.

At the intersection of life and death, visual pleasure and body horror, the highest ideals and the lowest methods, science and science fiction, it seems to me to sum up perfectly a nineteenth-century moment – one in which it was possible to fill a steel tank with ice, put a corpse in it and then saw it up and be lauded for your efforts. To be a Frankenstein, almost.

\*\*\*

Later in his career Braune's focus turned back towards the military, but he continued to search for ways to make the unseen seen. As befitted someone deeply involved in the mechanical and physiological aspects of anatomy, he was fascinated by motion and gait. Human (and animal and insect) locomotion was a subject of great curiosity during the nineteenth century, because its constituent parts – feet landing upon and leaving the ground, a dragonfly's wings beating – happen too fast and too minutely for the eye to comprehend. They were invisible.

His quest to understand the flow of a body through time and space brought him into proximity with pioneers in another field: photography. Perhaps the best known was Eadweard Muybridge, who in 1872 produced a celebrated series of photographs of a horse in motion. This was at the behest of Leland Stanford, a former US state governor and railway tycoon, who was desperate, in the way that only very rich people can be about seemingly trivial abstractions, to know whether horses in a trot ever lifted all their hooves from the ground at once. I could not unearth what Braune did or did not know about Muybridge's work, but he was certainly inspired by Étienne-Jules Marey, a French physiologist and photographer who in fact proved Stanford's trotting conjecture before Muybridge did, in that same year of 1872. Marey's proof was in diagrammatic form rather than photographs, via feedback from four pressure sensors mounted on a horse's hooves. Unlike Marey and Muybridge, Braune characteristically expressed his fascination, at least in part, by enveloping things in ice.

In the 1880s, Braune began a colossal study of human motion, which would culminate in *Der Gang des Menschen* (*The Human Gait*), published after his death, between 1895 and 1907. The final experiments for determining how a man walked involved rigging Geissler tubes (electric-light-filled tubes that worked on similar principles to today's neon lights) on all the significant moving parts of a heavily insulated human subject and, in the dead of night (to ensure darkness), taking photographs of him walking, so the lights left a precise spatial map of where he had been, not unlike some of Marey's diagrams.[13] The uncanny echoes of galvanism – animation through electricity – in the picture still extant of this process make this perhaps the most Frankenstein-esque thing Braune did.

It was in the preparatory phases to these final experiments that ice came in handy. Disentangling some of the thorny questions

---

[13] It took six to eight hours to dress the subject. The authors admitted they had possibly gone overboard with the rubber insulation, but had the subject been scared of being electrocuted it might have affected the way he walked.

of biomechanics required a good knowledge of the centre of gravity of different bits of body, and Braune and Fischer had done years of research on this, subsidised by the Royal Saxon Army, even publishing a book, *On the Centre of Gravity of the Human Body as Related to the Equipment of the German Infantry Soldier.*[14]

Before Braune, the existing method was essentially hanging a corpse by a rope from different points and using a plumbline to work out where the centre of gravity fell. But Braune believed dealing with a rope led to inaccuracies. So he set to it scientifically in the way he knew best: 'We used rigidly frozen cadavers in order to avoid errors resulting from the softness of the material,' he wrote. 'Using an artificial freezing mixture we froze the cadavers so hard that they remained completely rigid until the end of the investigation, both as whole cadavers and as the segments into which they were later divided.'

Once a cadaver was frozen 'in the usual manner', Braune and Fischer then hammered a steel rod through it and hung the body up from the rod. After a series of calculations with two plumblines and some chalk, they repeated the operation, with the steel rod along a different axis. After the third time they could triangulate the point; then, by sawing the body transversely and using thread to trace where the lines on the skin intersected internally, they pinpointed the precise centre of gravity. Once the whole body had been measured, it was jointed and the calculations made for each major region (foot, calf, thigh, torso . . .) separately.

Thus, by freezing the body, Braune began to understand how it moved.[15] Though the methods were crude, the work was rigorous and it is still considered valuable. In fact, the book blurb for the English translation (not published until 1985) states: 'Although they date from the end of the last century, Braune and Fischer's

[14] Marey was doing similar work for the French military: how infantry operated under heavy loads and how they became fatigued in action were questions crucial to an effective army.
[15] And is this not what Muybridge did too – for what is photography except freezing moments in time? In her book on Muybridge, *River of Shadows*, Rebecca Solnit calls photography 'the freezing eye'.

results have hardly been questioned . . . They remain the most accurate data on the subject to date.'

Towards the end, *On the Centre of Gravity* takes a bizarre turn. Suddenly there are photos of soldiers in various poses: at ease, standing to attention, presenting and shouldering a rifle . . . so far so normal. However, save for the regulation equipment – knapsack, cartridge pouch, bayonet and spade, water gourd and *Pickelhelm* (spiked helmet), the subject is completely and always naked, with only a literal fig leaf covering his embarrassment at turning up for battle so underprepared. After reading pages and pages detailing brutality meted out on to human lollipops or full of dense mathematical equations, the light relief was welcome, although I confess I could never fathom entirely why the cosplay was necessary. Try as I might, I could not see how they fitted into Braune's *Weltanschauung*. He had spent his life opening windows on to the body; bodies were his subject but his medium was ice.

***

Frozen sectioning's first life at the forefront of anatomical techniques was short. By the 1890s, the chemical formalin had emerged as a rival for hardening cadavers for research and display. However, in the 1990s – another fin-de-siècle moment – the spirit of Braune's work was revived. First came the Visible Human project at the University of Colorado, which began to create an archive of digital images of cryosections of the human body. After scanning a male and female who had donated their bodies to medical research (completed in 1994 and 1995 respectively), the director of Colorado's Center for Human Simulation, Dr Victor M. Spitzer, agreed to take the body of a woman called Susan Potter after she died – after much petitioning from Potter herself. When they met in 2000, Potter (who coincidentally was born in Leipzig) had undergone twenty-six operations and been diagnosed with melanoma, breast cancer and diabetes. She was also using a wheelchair after a car accident and wasn't expected to live long. In the fifteen years that followed, until she died of pneumonia in 2015, Spitzer became her firm friend. Then he froze her body, cut it into four pieces and photographed it 27,000 times, in sections of around 63 µm (millionths of a metre) thick.

The 1990s also saw the rise to prominence of Gunther von Hagen, a German showman-anatomist whose proprietary plastination technique allowed him to display, in his *Body Worlds* exhibitions, dead people, dogs, horses and even a giraffe in various states of subdermal undress – with their bones, organs, arteries and veins and other systems converted into plastic and displayed to the world. Von Hagen's work was not without controversy – questions of consent, propriety and taste never go away – but he insisted that the exhibits were for educational purposes. He was also reportedly working on a new technique to make wafer-thin frozen sections. In 2011 von Hagen announced that he had Parkinson's disease and that, when he died, his body would be plastinated and displayed.

Braune's body, or what remains of it, is still, as far as I know, where it was left, in a Leipzig cemetery in 1892. However, as Thomas Dwight insisted in 1881, frozen sectioning has proved of lasting usefulness and Braune's icy obsession has had an afterlife that neither he nor the subjects of his experiments could ever have envisaged.

# The Fighters

## *Ice in war, war in ice*

*Oropolitics, n.* – Mountaineering with a political goal

*It is not only this country but the whole world which, as compared with knowledge of other natural phenomena, lacks knowledge of snow and ice. This is fortunate, for whoever gets there first may get a great advantage.*

Max Perutz, scientist, UK government
memorandum (1942)

'Last Sunday a boy was saved just in time from certain death by drowning. The boy stepped on to newly formed ice on the Inn below the garrison hospital and broke through. Luckily he was saved by his courageous comrades.'

Three sentences, the entirety of a story that appeared in the *Donau-Zeitung*, a newspaper covering the border town of Passau, Bavaria, on 9 January 1894. In substance completely unremarkable, the stuff of news-in-brief sections everywhere, what local papers were invented for; yet this incident might have changed the course of the twentieth century.

It is rescued from the dustbin of obscurity by another historical footnote: in 1892 an Austrian customs officer received a promotion and posting to Passau, and moved his wife and young children to an apartment owned by a local family, the

Kühbergers, only fifty metres from the river. That man was born Alois Schicklgrüber, but several years previously he had sought to have his stepfather, Johann Heidler, recognised as his biological father, and the authorities, when recording the change of surname, noted it down wrong and renamed him Alois Hitler. An unusual name, unfortunately not a one-off.

It had long been town tradition that Johann Kühberger, the son of the Hitlers' landlord, did once pull a young Adolf from the river. Johann Kühberger himself, who became an organist and choir conductor, confessed it to his successor at Passau's Catholic cathedral, and he is said to have regretted his act of mercy-turned-mortal-sin to his dying day; however, only when the newspaper fragment came to light in 2012 did anything like corroboration exist.

Hitler, as is well known, never did learn to swim. In later life he avoided Passau, for fear that his ignoble origins be exposed – instead he had a castle nearby – but the river dunking appears not to have marked him. Had those young comrades not been so Christian or so brave, a whole world of counterfactuals opens up.

We've seen in many previous chapters how ice has been a formidable obstacle throughout history, one that has defined the boundaries of our world. But it is also a geopolitical fact that wars often take place over – and sometimes *at* – boundaries. Before the twentieth century, for attackers to attack and attackees to defend they had to be pretty close together. War demanded proximity – proximity to where people lived and to where power lay. Catapults and cannon do not fire far.

Grand icy spaces, therefore, were long a natural coolant to hotheaded urges. In 1812, Napoleon found this out to his detriment after the sack of Moscow, when he delayed his return march west. Winter closed in and his armies retreated in temperatures as low as −37 °C. Horses fell and broke their legs as they were not shod to walk on ice, and men died of dehydration as there was no liquid water to drink.

Proximity to power – or lack of it – is why the USA and Russia have been able to exist side by side where Siberia almost touches Alaska. There is simply nothing to attack there, not enough people to do the attacking and no way to keep them alive there if there were.[1]

But at the start of the twentieth century, more or less, that changed. Modern industrialised warfare does not need proximity. No longer do we need to be near our enemy to hurt them. Grand icy spaces consequently acquired a new strategic value for some Western powers, one that had nothing to do with what they might contain or where they led to. War dragged people into terrain they would not otherwise have visited. Instead of proximity to each other, some fighters were forced into proximity with ice, and so ice became a factor like never before – it became a shelter, a competitive advantage, a hazard, even an enemy in itself.

*\*\**

When the Archduke Franz Ferdinand was assassinated in Sarajevo in June 1914, precipitating the beginning of the First World War, Italy remained, at first, aloof. In 1882, it had formed the Triple Alliance with Germany and Austria-Hungary, but its relationship with the Habsburg Empire was nonetheless fraught. On Italy's northern frontier the Empire straddled the Alps; and in its far eastern corner the border ran uneasily across the Friulian plains and into the foothills of the Julian Alps, leaving Venice and the Veneto region, in Italian eyes, dangerously vulnerable.

In 1915, Italy reneged on the Triple Alliance and entered the war on the side of the Allies, tempted to switch allegiance, in part, by the prospect of seizing lands that many thought were rightfully 'Italian' – principally Trento and the Trentino–Alto Adige region (what the Austrians called the Südtirol) and Trieste. Italy also hoped to gain territory around the Adriatic and extend its influence even into Albania. All in all, its generals envisaged a quick and easy campaign that would lead them, victorious, to Vienna by Christmas.

They could not have been more wrong.

---

[1] It is also why China and India, two huge, ancient civilisations that meet at the Himalayas, for most of recorded history have had a relatively peaceable relationship – or, at least, one that is as notable for Buddhism as for tension.

Immediately, where the terrain was flatter in the east, the Italian Army encountered fierce resistance from the Austrians, who had had plenty of time to prepare for them. Hundreds of thousands were killed and millions wounded during the battles of the Isonzo (now the Soča river in Slovenia), between June 1915 and November 1917. Ernest Hemingway, who was an ambulance driver in the Piave region, would later describe the Italian Front as the 'most colossal, murderous, mismanaged butchery'; yet in some senses the young, would-be journalist missed the story. As the border between Austria and Italy runs from east to west, the Dolomites, the Adamello–Presanella and the Ortles–Cevedale mountain ranges rear up, almost 4,000 metres high. This is one of the least known corners of the First World War, less deadly by far than the conflicts in the lowlands, but in its own way more spectacular and more pointlessly inhuman. Here, the Italians and Austro-Hungarians engaged in a desperate, otherworldly stand-off known as the *Guerra Bianca*.

'The White War': by the time the Italians had mobilised on this Alpine Front, the Austrians had drawn back from their low-lying forts and dug in, placing their weapons and men on strategic points on high ridges above sheer cliffs and on the mountain peaks. It was, in the words of Gunther Langes, a Tyrolean soldier, mountaineer and writer, a 'front among rocks and ice'.

Since the attacking attentions of both sides were elsewhere – Isonzo for the Italians, Trentino for the Austrians – neither was well resourced in these mountains, and keeping positions supplied and manned was a huge challenge. Every gun, every shell, every plank to build with and log to burn, every tin of food, every litre of water and bottle of schnapps, had to be carried up there somehow. The Austrian incumbents, often local Tyrolean hunters who were literally at home there and well practised with a rifle, had the dramatic topography as their ally. The Italians had greater strength in numbers, but that made little difference on this terrain. Neither were motor vehicles any use. The Italian orders were to push forward but, unprepared for mountain warfare, they made elementary mistakes: there was, for example, a lack of white camouflage gear at the beginning of hostilities, which led to soldiers in standard grey-green uniforms being easily picked off as they crossed glaciers or snowfields below Austrian positions.

It was a war of contrasts: of distant shelling and dynamite, and of close combat between small groups. Two forces stretched thin across perilous jagged ground, often living more than 3,000 metres up in the air; handfuls of men in crude shacks or even caves, perched on rock pinnacles in charge of precious artillery, a searchlight, a telegraph. These were not battles, but long moments of exhaustion and extremity punctuated by short bursts of laborious, deadly activity. The Italians were unable to advance meaningfully; the Austrians unable to do more than hold steady. Sometimes one side took a ridge or a peak; sometimes a raid took it back. Neither gained or lost much, and an uneasy impasse was reached.

Perhaps the situation was novel at first, the privations noble, the views on fine days a consolation, but it became absurd. An example: when the Austrians learned that the Italians were plotting to occupy the 3,851-metre Königspitze (now known as Gran Zebrù), they scrambled to do the same, resulting in the two armies facing off and then camping out only 150 metres apart, over 3.5 kilometres above sea level.

Königspitze, in the Ortler Alps, was the highest permanently occupied point of the war. And as the winter of 1915 approached it became clear that both sides would have their work cut out fighting a third enemy: nature itself. Snow and ice and howling storms hit the isolated peaks. Cold and malnutrition took a dreadful toll.

A hundred or so kilometres to the east stands the Marmolada, at 3,343 metres the highest mountain in the Dolomites. Overlooking a major pass, it has a large glacier spilling down its flanks and was a key strategic point. In spring 1916 the Austrians occupied several positions near the summit. Then the Italians stormed the massif's Serauta ridge, which overlooked the vital supply line across the glacier. For the Austrians, this was a big problem. Anyone taking provisions to the advance posts was a sitting duck.

One of the Empire's engineers, Leo Handl, had the idea of using the glacier's crevasses and caves as shelter; then he began to create connections between them. By autumn 1916, more than eight kilometres of tunnels had been dug into the glacier. As he explained: 'Unfortunately the valuable explosives ran out rather quickly but we made up for that by employing ice axes and boring tools so efficiently that in twenty-four hours of continuous work we could advance six to eight metres. It was all go in autumn 1916. Wooden huts were built in open crevasses at suitable points in the middle of the glacier, from where we tunnelled in two directions.'

In this Handl was a pioneer. Nobody understood ice, nor how glaciers moved and what the dangers might be. Nor had anyone ever put men into a glacier. 'Trenches intersected in all directions under the Marmolada glacier,' Gunther Langes wrote. 'Listening posts, observers and lookout posts were located to face the opponent, at the entrance of the tunnels. There was a front literally sunk into the ice, over which, as the only signs of human presence, ran the sparkling iron ropes of the cableways.'

Thus the Austrians were provisioned, protected and sheltered by ice. At its greatest extent, the *Eisstadt* – 'Ice City' – comprised around twelve kilometres of tunnels, at a maximum depth of fifty metres below the surface of the ice, all of which required constant maintenance and adaptation as the glacier shifted around and above them. From its lowest entrance, the *Eisstadt* rose more than a thousand vertical metres to 3,259 metres above sea level. Soldiers making the three-and-a-half-hour march to the top were directed through the labyrinth by signs, and the gangways, galleries and other features were given names – Kaiser Franz Josef Crevasse, for example, or Kärntner Straße, after Vienna's rival to Oxford Street or the Champs-Élysées – passing shelters, storage, latrines, dormitories, an infirmary, a telephone exchange, even a chapel. But woe betide the man who let his lantern blow out as he walked. Only part of the facility was lit with electric lights, powered by a steam engine in Canazei, and that only for a brief period of the war. Soldiers in the dark might easily walk off gangways or fall off ledges.

Many also became ill from the cold and the damp. Rheumatism, gout and joint pains were common and, despite ventilation systems and shafts to the surface, smoke from stoves made the air noxious. Worst of all, I think, must have been the knowledge that you were living in the bowels of a mysterious beast and that the very spaces that held you were at risk of shifting, deforming or being crushed out of existence without warning.

Still, it was better than being outside, where one might be shot at or enveloped by an avalanche at any moment. Inside the glacier the temperature hovered constantly around freezing, which was an improvement on the raging storms and thirty-below outside.

'We received special insights into the secrets of the glacier,' Langes wrote, 'its crevices, its various movements in winter when the ice is cold and brittle, and in summer when it is plastic. We discovered needs that no scholar, glaciologist or mountaineer had ever thought of . . . Under such conditions, almost everyone became a naturalist.'

The winter of 1915 had been severe, but that of 1916/17 was one of the harshest ever recorded. Snow began falling in September, and these high outposts received the brunt of it. On parts of the front it is estimated the mountainsides were smothered with eight to twelve metres of snow. The Austrians used Russian POWs to clear the valley roads that serviced the cableways, the lifelines of the troops above, but once it reached four metres, traffic was often forced to pass through snow tunnels. Almost all the horses died. On high, soldiers would spend most of the day digging themselves out of their barracks, only to go on patrol and return snowblind and with frostbite.

'Not even artillery fired another shot, for the shells mostly thudded into the snow as duds,' one soldier recorded in his diary. 'The personnel lay snowed in down below throughout the winter and killed time with sleeping and playing cards.'

On 13 December 1916, a quick thaw precipitated a huge avalanche above the Empire's Gran Poz barracks high on the Marmolada, killing about 270 Austrian and Bosnian men. The wooden barracks had been positioned safe from enemy fire but under a cornice; eight days previously, the Austrian captain

Robert Schmid, seeing the snow build up, had requested his men be allowed to relocate. The request had been refused. Only around forty of the bodies were recovered. Earlier in 1916 Schmid himself had decreed that no bodies should be buried in the glacier ice, to avoid contaminating drinking water, so one by one these fallen soldiers were carried down into the valley. That left the remains of more than 200 men scattered over a large area of dangerous and inaccessible terrain, destined for an icy grave.

On that same day, avalanches hit numerous other Italian and Austro-Hungarian positions, and contemporary reports suggest both armies shelled precarious snow formations in an attempt to bury the other side. Maybe around 2,000 soldiers died in avalanches on 'White Friday'[2] and in its aftermath. The European Centre for Medium-Range Weather Forecasts has called it 'one of the worst meteorological disasters in history'.

It is rarely remembered or commemorated, but to say that this little-known catastrophe was eclipsed by the war is to get things the wrong way around. Rather, the war on the Alpine Front was eclipsed by natural disaster. 'More men lost their lives to the extremes of cold, frostbite, illness and avalanches than to enemy action,' commented archaeologist Marco Balbi. 'Some estimates have calculated that two-thirds of overall mortalities were caused in this way.'

In early 1917, the Italian Private Giuseppe Ungaretti, a poet, wrote: 'Snow is truly a sign of mourning; I don't know why the westerners choose black; this is another thing where the Chinese are more intelligent. Black makes me feel mystery, fear, the absolute infinity, God, universal life; but white gives me the sense of things ending, the iciness of death.'

How desperate it must have been for anybody up there during those winters, surrounded by hostility and death, locked in a very obviously futile struggle. No wonder there are numerous reports of fraternisation, and of soldiers spontaneously stopping firing on the enemy. Being isolated together, cut off from civilised life

---

[2] One of the enduring myths of the White War was that this all happened on a Friday. But 13 December 1916 was a Wednesday.

kilometres below in a claustrophobic world without colour, must have bred a special kind of solidarity.

After Handl's success on the Marmolada, the Austrians used ice tunnels for attack as well as defence, notably on the Hohe Schneide, a 3,434-metre peak in the Ortler, which the Italians occupied in October 1916. The icy north face presented no opportunities for an advance, so, over the course of five months, the Austrians dug a tunnel two kilometres long, with picks, shovels and drills (explosives would have given the game away), displacing 4,000 tons of ice. They had no way of knowing exactly how close they were – on 17 March 1917, an Italian soldier broke through the ice and fell into the tunnel while the digging crew were on their lunch break, setting off the hostilities sooner than anybody, least of all that unlucky Italian, had expected.

As for the Italian Army, it was famed for its engineering prowess, having blasted gallery roads and supply tunnels of stunning complexity through the Dolomitic rock. So, once the Italians understood what this new game was, they began to play. One of their most impressive achievements was a grand tunnel through the Adamello glacier, 5.2 kilometres long and with twenty-five bridges over crevasses, which assured the passage of dog teams and donkeys pulling supply sleds to forward positions. And, not far from the Königspitze, twenty metres below the surface of the Zebrù glacier, they constructed a supply tunnel large enough for a narrow-gauge railway from their Capanna Milano HQ to strategic positions on the passes above.

That HQ, like many of the stone-built military buildings in the area, is now a mountain refuge, and it was there, one morning as the sun was coming up, that I began the trek up towards the Zebrù glacier with a friend, Tom Isitt, a historian of these high conflicts, to look at some of the sites. The complexities of the situation are hard enough to understand on a map, but as we walked the chaos of peaks, glaciers and scree gradually became intelligible and the torturous conditions of this tortuous line grew clearer. All around, over those few days labouring over passes in the snow, was the detritus of war – the barbed wire and cast-iron cable runs, and joists and planks abandoned when hostilities ceased – lying either where they had been left or where the glaciers, after chewing them up, had slowly disgorged them.

The high point of the hike – almost literally – was the 3,258-metre Eiskoffel (Cima Ghiacciata or 'Icy Peak'), where three cannon, weighing six tons each, were simply left by the Austrians. On our way up we negotiated barbed wire on the passes, found tin cans on the muddy slopes and picked iron hinges and planks out of glaciers, all relics of the century-old war. But the most affecting moment was, I think, slogging up the broad, steep expanse of the Zebrù glacier, at 3,000 metres or more, gasping for air and fearful of crevasses, thinking of the men who had lived and died above us – and, more frighteningly, below our feet, in the very ice we were standing on.

\*\*\*

The loss of South Tyrol to Italy at the end of the First World War created deep wounds in the Austrian psyche. And ice, an obvious symbol of purity, was embedded in the Nazi imaginary from its earliest days, at first quietly, insidiously, and then in an increasingly esoteric and occult fashion.

In 1921, Hitler became the leader of the National Socialist German Workers' Party, and from that moment on he began wrapping Nazism's abhorrent theories of Aryan racial superiority in an insular notion of the greater German people, or *Volk*. This *völkisch* thinking had a particular yearning for the natural, cultural and 'racial' purity of the mountains, and it was not limited to Germany's Alps, where Hitler made Obersalzberg both his strategic and personal HQ. The wider Alps represented simultaneously an actual homeland (Austria, Hitler's birthplace, which had mooted an *Anschluss* as early as 1919), a lost homeland (the German-speaking province of South Tyrol) and one that never was (Switzerland in the 1930s was more than two-thirds Germanophone; it spent the Second World War constantly fearing an invasion). This Alpine affinity was so marked that Wilfried Wilms, a cultural historian, has highlighted the centrality of the Alps to the Nazi concept of *Lebensraum* ('living space') – an imagined territorial unity that rightfully 'belonged' to Germany, integral to the national identity, which justified its expansionist ambitions.

Against this backdrop, mountain climbing became a symbol of national pride and Aryan strength, and ascents became propaganda tools. The purity of the glaciers beneath the climbers' feet was co-opted – white supremacy in every sense. In 1938, for example, a combined Austrian and German team made the first ascent of the legendary icebound north wall of the Eiger.[3] The four climbers had in fact started as two separate parties of different nationalities, but, in a richly symbolic turn of events, when the Austrians were caught from behind they all roped up together for the summit push, returning to a hero's welcome from Hitler.

The National Socialists also exported such displays of so-called superiority. In 1929, the first German expedition to the Himalaya since the Great War tackled Kanchenjunga, the world's third-highest mountain. 'Its goals were explicitly nationalistic, motivated by a desire to rebuild a faith in German manhood and to finally leave behind the defeat and humiliation experienced in World War,' the curator of a recent exhibition on the expedition wrote. 'Underpinning it all was a sense of German national destiny expressed in the language of racial theory and "struggle" (*Kampf*).'

Themes of struggle and redemption fit well into the climbing narrative, and both also work well in the movies. The popular 'mountain films' of the 1920s and 1930s showed pristine landscapes inhabited by exemplary Aryan people, and enjoyed great popular success as well as official approval. Perhaps the leading light of the movement was the writer and director Arnold Fanck; films he was involved in include *The White Hell of Pitz Palu*, *Storm Over*

---

[3] Notwithstanding many German failures on the Eigerwand in the preceding years. The near-vertical limestone of the Eiger's north face is covered by ice fields and verglas, which in summer used to melt and refreeze daily. It is so crumbly that only the snow and ice covering it and holding it together beneath the surface make the climb possible. Around 2003, the covering ice and most of the ice fields, including the infamous 'White Spider', almost completely disappeared, so it is now climbed mainly in autumn and spring.

*Mont Blanc, The White Ecstasy, Milak the Greenland Hunter* and polar expedition thriller *S.O.S. Eisberg.*

There were also several Weimar-era films that essentially replayed the First World War in the Dolomites at the expense of the Italians. *Berge in Flammen* (*The Doomed Battalion*) was director Luis Trenker's fictionalised account of his own experiences. Not only does Trenker, playing a young Austrian soldier, climb better than the Italians, he is also cleverer, alerting his brothers-in-arms to a plot to dynamite their position and winning the cinematic skirmish in the last reel. Thus was shameful history rewritten. In the years following *Berge*, a rash of books memorialising the conflict appeared, with titles such as *The Fortress in the Glacier* and Langes' *Front in Rock and Ice*, keeping alive the memory of the lost territories of the South Tyrol and the grievances about the White War.

While the National Socialist founding ideologies were rooted in the resonant idea of an icy, pure 'homeland', they also sought validation much further afield. The idea of a master civilisation somewhere in the far north – now lost under the ice – strongly appealed to a movement seeking evidence for its misguided racial theories, and above all to its leaders like Hitler, Heinrich Himmler and Rudolf Hess. Using a mishmash of verifiable observations (the climate in the Arctic was once far warmer than today), ancient sources (everything from Pytheas and the Ancient Greeks to the Egyptians and the Hindu Vedas) and cabbalistic and Theosophical interpretations of various myths and signs, they constructed a justification for the supremacy of a blond-haired, blue-eyed Aryan people. These people had lived in the sunny polar regions until a time of catastrophe around the last Ice Age, when they had descended to Scandinavia, central Asia or perhaps India, and from there spread into Europe.

Many leading Nazis also became enthusiastic proponents of World Ice Theory (*Welteislehre* or WEL). WEL had been known as 'Glacial Cosmogony' when it was first outlined in the 1890s by the Austrian Hanns Hörbiger, before being renamed to assume a veneer of Third Reich respectability. Hörbiger had received in a dream the revelation that much of the known universe had been created by the collision of an ice-filled star with a much larger one; the resulting explosion had caused frozen fragments to fly everywhere, creating solar systems, moons and meteorites made of ice. 'WEL attracted a number of Germans who, weaned on Ariosophy and other esoteric doctrines, sought an "Aryan" alternative to so-called Jewish physics, from relativity to quantum mechanics,' writes Eric Kurlander, an academic expert on Nazi hocus-pocus. 'I tend to support World Ice Theory,' Hitler said in 1942.

WEL was, of course, completely misguided, anti-scientific and wrong, and it took only a small mental leap to connect it to existing Hyperborean and Thulean myths: the disappearance of the Nordic/Aryan Atlantis could be explained by giant moons of ice hitting the earth and causing a great flood. For years, WEL was championed by Himmler's Ahnenerbe, the Institute for Ancestral Research. Himmler was one of the chief proponents of WEL in the Nazi movement, going as far as stating that these icy beginnings proved Aryans were descended not from apes but from gods. In 1938, he facilitated an expedition to Tibet to search for evidence of the lost master race.

Many good German scientists – and even pro-Nazi ones – opposed this charlatanism and inchoate thinking to the best of their abilities, but there was little they could do. Kurlander again: 'With its inane claims to constituting a grand, unified interdisciplinary theory of the universe, while simultaneously incorporating *völkisch* conceptions of race, space and Nordic mythology, World Ice Theory was the perfect exemplar of Nazi border science.'

I'm not going to dwell any more on these half-baked ideas, as they are frequently contradictory, offensive and, frankly, distasteful to write about. But it is a chilling reminder of how false and abhorrent ideas can take hold in a society unmoored from reason and fact. And that ice is a physical presence, but also one that, in its blankness, its very purity, can be talismanic, or put to ideological means.

\* \* \*

If the Nazis' attraction to ice was spiritual, the Allies' engagement was, well, more . . . concrete. Led by the British, it was, from start to finish, a strange affair. At one point in 1942, Lord Louis Mountbatten dropped a block of ice into Churchill's evening bath at Chequers, the prime minister's country residence. I like to imagine the corpulent prime minister in it. Just a few months later, Mountbatten, in a room crowded with Allied military top brass, shot at a block of ice, the bullet ricocheting off and whizzing past people's legs before lodging itself in the wall. Neither incident was out of the normal run of things for Geoffrey Pyke, the man behind the schemes.

Pyke, born in 1893, was by all accounts a singular and brilliant mind. Lancelot Law White, one of the inventors of the jet engine, once compared him to Einstein, adding: 'Pyke's genius was more intangible, perhaps because he produced not one but an endless sequence of ideas.' Another eminent scientist said he 'stood out among his fellows like the North Face of the Eiger in the foothills of the Alps'. He was known for approaching intractable problems and reframing them, finding some previously unimaginable angle that allowed progress. And also for impulsive, intuitive gambles that sometimes did not pay off.

In 1915, as a twenty-year-old Cambridge student, he had become the first Briton to smuggle himself into and then out of wartime Germany. Never mind that he spent months in solitary confinement under threat of execution for espionage, and then longer in the Ruhleben internment camp (which he was the first to successfully escape from) in between. That was a Pykean flourish and, anyway, it was all much more than MI6 had managed. At one point, before his investments bankrupted him, he controlled over one-third of the global supply of tin. He was a maverick but also a loose cannon, a communist sympathiser and strongly suspected of being a Russian spy.

Based on the above he might have seemed an unlikely recruit to the Combined Operations Headquarters wartime R&D unit that Mountbatten ran; then, again, pulling this off seems entirely in character.[4]

---

[4] Combined Operations integrated air, sea and ground offensive capabilities and ran the Special Operations Executive and Commandos. Mountbatten's task there was to harass the

Pyke gained Mountbatten's ear in 1942, after petitioning everybody he could for an entrée into the government war machine, and despite being scruffy, and a civilian, and possessing dubious political leanings, he became Mountbatten's confidant and friend. The particular problem he first applied himself to was the Nazi occupation of Norway, trying to think of a line of attack that might pierce their armour. As his most recent biographer, Henry Hemming, puts it: 'land, air or sea? . . . This appeared to be the next question, unless, of course, there was a fourth military element, one that did not yet exist, in the sense that it had not yet been thought of as a military element. This might sound pointless, like searching for a fourth primary colour. Nonetheless, Pyke paused to consider it.'

The fourth element Pyke found was frozen water – in his own words, 'a medium like the air and sea, which, if we can master it, can be made in a positive sense to serve the very ends of war'.

The Norway idea – Operation Plough, as it became known – involved a kind of screw-driven snowmobile that would give small British guerrilla units superior mobility over the country's frozen wastes, forcing Germany to commit greater resources to secure this vast territory that previously had demanded few. In some accounts of the plan, Plough had a base within the Jostedal glacier, and a secondary goal was to disrupt aluminium and even nuclear fuel production. Plough evolved into a cooperative project with the Americans and Canadians; Pyke was transferred to the Special Operations Executive and sent to the USA, where his style and manner rubbed many in the American military establishment up the wrong way. He complained of being sidelined and of having to fight to keep progressing, but, after a while, these setbacks mattered to him less and less: his attention was shifting elsewhere.

The Battle of the Atlantic was the longest military campaign of the Second World War. Britain required thousands of tons of vital materials delivered by sea every week to keep the war effort

---

Nazis in Europe and prepare the ground for D-Day. The organisation was unorthodox, with Evelyn Waugh, actor Douglas Fairbanks Jr and land speed record-holder Sir Malcolm Campbell on the payroll.

going, but from the outset Germany had choked the supply. Losses – mainly to U-boats – were almost catastrophic: in June 1942, the worst month so far, 652,487 tons of Allied shipping were sunk. The situation could only be improved with better air cover, but fighter planes had limited range and aircraft carriers were expensive, vulnerable and incredibly time-consuming to build – even if raw steel and aluminium could be found. And those were in very short supply.

During his time in the USA Pyke had become interested in the immense strength of icebergs; what if, somehow, ice could be used instead?

A 'bergship' made of ice and reinforced with steel or wood would be quick and cheap to construct, easy to maintain at sea and unsinkable – since ice naturally floats – and in case of damage more ice could always be manufactured to pack into the holes. A bergship might become a huge refuelling and provisioning platform for aircraft. Pyke imagined it as being 2,000 or even 3,000 feet long. Nothing like this had ever been made, and no innovation in wartime could be as useful, or as surprising to the enemy.[5] At least, that was his theory.

So Pyke began to investigate ice, in characteristic style. A meeting with an ice expert, Herman Mark, an Austrian Jewish émigré professor in New York, demonstrated to him water's peculiarly high specific heat capacity (its tendency, once frozen, to stay frozen) and how even a small amount of insulation could make a long-lasting iceberg last even longer. This was promising. However, ice in its pure form was unpredictably brittle, and natural icebergs or ice floes were too small or too vulnerable to waves.

But what about manufactured ice? And what if, as in a metal alloy, another material was added to give strength? Mark began experiments to test just these possibilities. Working with a wood mill in Canada, he had produced sheets of ice mixed with wood pulp that was incredibly strong. Ice, according to some

[5] There had in fact been some precedents, including preliminary experiments on an airport ice island in Lake Geneva by a German scientist, Dr A. Gerke, in 1930.

estimates at the time, needed for its manufacture only 1 per cent of the energy required for the equivalent weight of steel. Another benefit was that wood pulp significantly slowed the ice's thawing.

Pyke codenamed his project 'Habbakuk'[6] and sent it on to Mountbatten, the only way he might get the idea afloat, in a dense sheaf of papers entitled 'Mammoth Unsinkable Vessel with the Functions of a Floating Airfield'.[7] Mountbatten was captivated and in due course Churchill was too: 'The advantages of a floating island or islands, even if only used as refuelling depots for aircraft, are so dazzling that they do not at the moment need to be discussed,' the prime minister wrote in a memorandum.

Despite such enthusiasm from the highest quarters, Pyke and his extraordinary scheme had many detractors. However, given the life-or-death nature of the problem ('The only thing that ever really frightened me during the war was the U-boat peril,' Churchill later wrote), the project moved ahead quickly.

Pyke needed to do further tests, and for these he turned to Max Perutz. Perutz was an Austrian-Jewish scientist studying crystallography at Cambridge. Best known for his work on haemoglobin, he had also studied the process by which snow crystals become glacier ice. Pyke had been in touch with him previously, during Project Plough; the plan then had been to feign retreat from Norway but actually to hide the snowmobiles in tunnels bored into a glacier.[8] 'Despite my glacier research,

---

[6] This was a misspelling of the name of the Old Testament prophet who decreed, 'regard, and wonder marvellously: for I will work a work in your days, which ye will not believe, though it be told you.'

[7] 'Pyke did not attempt to solve all the problems of ice warfare, but he did suggest fairly explicitly the direction researchers should follow,' wrote Pyke's first biographer, David Lampe. Later sections of the 232-page memo (which Mountbatten probably never got round to reading entirely) expanded on the main idea, for example in the production of fake bergships, constructed out of real icebergs, with neon signs taunting the Luftwaffe with slogans like 'BOMB ME – I'M A DUMMY'. The conceptual play here between representation and reality seems more like postmodern installation art than warfare, but then that was Pyke's genius and also, as he acknowledged, his Achilles heel. In a footnote in the memorandum he implored Mountbatten: 'Do you think that the men who conceived and built the Trojan Horse were stiff and solemn men?'

[8] Pyke had read German sources on the tunnelling during the First World War according to his first biographer. Curiously, Leo Handl, the architect of the *Eisstadt*, moved to Norway

I was not exactly sure what the strength of ice was, and could find little about it in the literature,' Perutz wrote back, and so he set to work.

By the end of 1942, Pyke had given Perutz Herman Mark's report on reinforcing ice (as chance would have it, Perutz had been Mark's student in Vienna) and installed him in a frozen-meat locker five storeys underneath Smithfield meat market in London. There, at −18 °C, clad in an electrically heated suit, Perutz supervised a team of commandos and students testing ice composites. 'We built a big wind tunnel to freeze the mush of wet wood pulp, and sawed the reinforced ice into blocks. Our tests soon confirmed Mark [and his assistant]'s results. Blocks of ice containing as little as four per cent wood pulp were weight for weight as strong as concrete,' Perutz wrote. 'In honour of the originator of the project, we called this reinforced ice "pykrete".'

It was around this time that the Chequers bathtime demonstration took place. Mountbatten travelled there from Smithfield with some pykrete in a thermos of dry ice to demonstrate to Churchill its ability to survive in water, whether Atlantic or from the hot tap. Churchill, whether in the bath or not, was impressed.

Pykrete seemed at first to be a miracle material, 'stronger than ice but no heavier', according to Perutz. 'It can be machined like wood and cast into shapes like copper; immersed in warm water, it forms an insulating shell of soggy wood pulp on its surface, which protects the inside from further melting.' However, there was one grave snag: cold flow, also known as 'creep'. 'Though ice is hard to the blow of an axe, it is soft to the continuous pull of gravity,' Perutz reported. His team determined that, unless the pykrete was kept at −20 °C, an ice ship would slowly sag under its own weight, and to keep it that cold would require a refrigeration plant and an elaborate system of ducting.

Nevertheless, plans were forging ahead. Shipping was still being lost to U-boats at a disastrous rate and Churchill was

after the war and spent a year living in a glacier, studying its movement. He couldn't get enough.

increasingly impatient. By March 1943, Pyke was at Patricia Lake in the Canadian Rockies watching on as a team of conscientious objectors (who were not told exactly what they were constructing) built a scale model bergship. At sixty feet long and thirty feet wide, it was approximately one-fiftieth the size of the real thing.

From this high point the project's forward momentum began to ebb away. An engineering committee reported back with pessimistic evaluations of the vessel's seaworthiness, the schedule and the projected costs, but it was also losing steam because, as 1943 went on, the problems in the Atlantic were being solved. Among other factors, U-boats were being sunk faster than they could be built thanks to more numerous escort ships and better weaponry and tactics; and aeroplanes equipped with larger fuel tanks were able to spend more time over the Atlantic. Then a renewed treaty with Portugal gave the RAF a base in the Azores.

The strategic need for a giant ice ship was diminishing rapidly, yet Mountbatten and Churchill went ahead with presenting Habbakuk at the Quebec Conference in August (that the two men even travelled there on the *Queen Mary* is evidence of how the Atlantic was being tamed). This is where Mountbatten gathered Allied dignitaries together and shot at two blocks – one of pykrete, one of ice – to demonstrate the material's potential. The ice shattered; the pykrete held; the bullet ricocheted, narrowly missing an air chief marshal, or grazing an admiral's leg or even hitting Mountbatten himself, depending on which of the accounts you believe. Whether impressed, intimidated or simply glad to be alive, the assembled leaders agreed to continue investigating the viability of building a very large bergship, and also explore the idea of smaller ones, to be used offensively in Japan and Europe.

However, with international involvement came the familiar American antipathy to Pyke's iconoclasm (he had plenty of opponents in the British ranks too), and with the completion of the small-scale prototype – which in itself weighed a thousand tons – the implications of constructing a full-size bergship were becoming mindbendingly clear. With a runway of 600 × 60m., a freeboard of 15m. and an all-round wall thickness of 9m., it was found that the bergship would have to have a draft of 45m.

and a displacement of 2,200,000 tons,' Perutz wrote. 'To build a ship twenty-six times heavier than the *Queen Elizabeth*[9] from a material which had never been used before was a formidable proposition.'

Practical difficulties mounted. Initially the bergship was designed to be steered by its motors alone, but at some juncture a rudder was incorporated, of an unprecedented and unbuildable size. The first bergship would have to be built in a hundred days – a single winter – at a site in Newfoundland, but manufacturing 1.7 million tons of pykrete in such a remote location would have been an impossibility. Sir Charles Goodeve, the head of the Admiralty's R&D department, was one of the many naysayers who lined up against the bergships, later writing that each Habbakuk would involve '40,000 tons of cork insulation, some thousands of miles of steel tubing for brine [refrigerant] circulation and reinforcement, four power stations, and endless additional complications, especially in the building stage'. Clearly he was exaggerating to make a point, but not by much.

The tide had turned against Habbakuk. Mountbatten, eager to get back out to sea, left Combined Operations HQ in October 1943. By January 1944, all work on the project had ceased.

'Not only does ice melt, but it evaporates!' wrote Goodeve. 'And so did Habbakuk.'

Pyke hung on at Combined Operations, but with Mountbatten gone his days were numbered, and he left within the year. He had, in his own mind, been defeated by entrenched interests and inflexible and hidebound thinking, but in truth he had also been defeated by ice. Had cold flow not been such a problem – had ice not been so *weird* – then the spiralling complications of the build would have been reduced.

Was Pyke wrong to dream? It's possible he was, in the words of one of his fiercest opponents, the head of the USA's Office of Scientific Research and Development, 'short on physics, especially

---

[9] Along with the *Queen Mary*, one of the Cunard Line steamers that before the war had crossed the Atlantic from Southampton to the USA. It weighed some 86,000 tons and was at the time the largest passenger liner ever built.

short on engineering judgement', but his vision of ice as a new front in warfare swept along some of the greatest public figures of his age, and his innovative mind injected dynamism into the sclerotic practices of the military establishment. Ice was at once a testing ground and proof of his ingenuity, but it was just one of his theatres of operations. According to Pyke's biographer, Henry Hemming, some of the innovations most important to the Allies' D-Day success were concocted during his heyday at Combined Operations HQ. And was the development of a mega ice ship really that much more far-fetched than the idea of splitting the atom on an equally accelerated schedule?

While the bergships were a chimaera, the work on pykrete has proved of lasting scientific use. The M29 Weasel, the caterpillar-tracked vehicle that eventually emerged from Project Plough, despite compromises that Pyke deplored, did contribute to the Allied triumph in many arenas and had a respectable post-war career in the Canadian Arctic and in French Antarctic exploration. The mini Habbakuk in Patricia Lake took over a year to melt, and then its wooden skeleton was sunk.

\*\*\*

The US military might not have warmed to Pyke's style, but he did leave his imprint on its thinking. Most obviously there were his guerrillas on snowmobiles: First Special Service Force soldiers aboard M29 Weasels were the precursor of all later US and Canadian Special Forces units. There is also a kind of paranoid echo of Pyke's modus operandi in one of the most out-there, and certainly the coldest, episodes of the Cold War against the USSR. The First World War took fighting to the mountains of the Alps, the Second to the vast emptinesses of the North Atlantic; now, in a plan that mixed the fatal and the farcical, the Cold War would take it above the Arctic Circle.

The USA had benefited from a military presence in Greenland since a treaty signed in 1941. It began as a pragmatic arrangement, acknowledging that the Americans had strong strategic interests in being there – principally in keeping the North Atlantic lines of communication open – and that Denmark, which held sovereign power over the island nation, would not be able to defend it alone. (Denmark had in fact been occupied by the Nazis in 1940.) Recognising its lasting strategic value, the US government tried to buy Greenland from Denmark in 1946. When this land grab was turned down, the USA expanded its Greenlandic research programme, majoring on applied military science. It created the Snow, Ice and Permafrost Research Establishment (SIPRE)[10] in 1949. In 1951, the Danes, who had always been suspicious of US activities and were resentful of being strong-armed into the arrangement, renegotiated their access, limiting American activities to three 'defense areas' around three air bases – one in the south, one in the middle and the northern one at Thule.[11]

In 1959, about 150 miles from Thule, the Americans began work on Camp Century, a military scientific research base, which they proposed would exist almost entirely beneath the surface of the ice. According to a US Army technical report from 1965, the advantages of a 'subsurface' camp included ease of camouflage, lower initial construction costs, lower fuel costs, fewer imported building materials and less exposure to the harsh surface environment and drifting snow. Among the disadvantages were the maintenance costs, year-round power needs (for lighting) and the fact that it was 'psychologically undesirable'.[12]

There's a jolly declassified film freely available on the internet that documents the building of what can only be described as a secret ice base. Shot on 16 mm in cheerful mid-century tinges, it comes equipped with a breezy voiceover from Captain Tom Evans, project officer on its construction. He explains that the

---

[10] If this were James Bond it would definitely be called SnIPRE.
[11] It became a real settlement, named in 1910 after the mythical country. Now known as Qaanaaq, it was the closest supply base to Camp Century.
[12] In 1961, Walter Cronkite visited Camp Century for a CBS news report. In his autobiography he recalled staying overnight in the ice tunnel's accommodation. 'Not too uncomfortable, except that I suffered an attack of claustrophobia,' he wrote. 'I attribute it to the warning we received before we were left alone there. Under no circumstances were we to leave the tunnel.' This was because of the danger of getting caught in a whiteout: 'When the snows come and blot out the sun, the horizon disappears in a sea of white and human beings can suffer such total disorientation that they lose their sense of balance and cannot stand up.'

'city under the ice' is an 'ideal Arctic laboratory' which is there 'as part of man's efforts to master the secrets of survival in the Arctic . . . [and to] probe deeper into the secrets of the universe'. He continues:

> The basic concept was simple: a system of twenty-three trenches would be dug into the ice cap and covered with steel arches and snow. Branching off the main communication trench would be a series of lateral trenches housing complete research, laboratory and test facilities, modern living quarters and recreation areas, and a complex of support facilities.

This principal trench, which would become known as 'Main Street', was more than a thousand feet long, and there were two miles of tunnels in total, within which were erected prefabs housing the accommodation, laboratories, a barbershop, a chapel and even a theatre. At one end there was a giant steam hose with a special drilling nozzle, which was used to melt a circular hole 3.5 feet in diameter straight downwards, forming a pool of water over a hundred feet below. From that pool the Americans extracted up to 10,000 gallons of water daily, literally drinking, washing and cleaning the solid ice out from underneath themselves. At the other end of the complex was the sewage sump.

'Except for the fact that they have no windows, the men of Camp Century live exactly as do other soldiers,' Captain Tom trills over pictures of the 200 or so citizens of the city under the ice taking hot showers, relaxing, reading books and listening to records. All thousands of miles from home, in one of the most inhospitable environments on earth. And all in the name of 'science'. Everything, in other words, was completely and utterly normal.

You may be sensing there's a 'but' on the way; there is, and it's a big one. The informational film leaves the best news till last. 'Since transporting vast quantities of diesel over Arctic wastes was impractical, we would install a nuclear power plant,' Captain Tom explains. No reason to worry, though, because at only just over 400 tons it was a small one. Hardly even there, really. Sort of the 1950s equivalent of a USB powerbank.

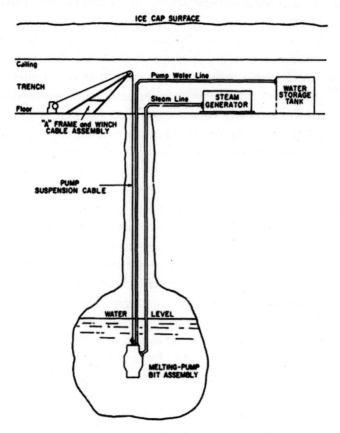

*Camp Century water supply.*

There follow blithe pictures of soldiers wrapped in cold-weather gear installing pipes to bring coolant water into the reactor's chamber. The reactor is then unloaded from a ship at Thule, transported by huge loaders on a reinforced sledge platform, then winched into place and assembled in an ice bunker to the necessary tolerances of an eighth of an inch. Then the forty-foot arched steel roof is placed over it and covered in snow and there is literally nothing to see.

Once the fuel elements are lowered into the reactor core by men in protective clothing (white T-shirts and hair nets), the reactor is slowly brought to critical status. This is achieved at 06.52 hours on a nameless day in October 1960, just as the sun is coming up, one of the last occasions it would do so before the long, dark polar winter.

'We took every precaution in the book, and some that weren't there, to make sure this would work right the first time,' intones Captain Jim Barnett, who oversaw the installation.

Call me a sceptic, but it seems like a lot of energy to expend purely in the name of science. Not that there wasn't important research going on. Some of the first ice-core samples ever taken from a glacier were by SIPRE scientists in 1957 and, in 1966, the first full ice core – stretching all the way down to the bedrock – was drilled at Camp Century. This 1,390-metre-long library of information allowed Danish scientist Willi Dansgaard – whom we met briefly all the way back in Chapter 2 – to document his groundbreaking theory that the relative levels of trace isotopes of oxygen and deuterium atoms trapped in glacier ice might be used to reconstruct past climates.

While this research has now been shown to be invaluable to our understanding of climate change, it seems very unlikely that it was the sole motivation behind the construction of Camp Century. The probable secret behind the ice base was not revealed until declassified documents in 1996 confirmed the existence of Project Iceworm.

Iceworm proposed nothing less than a shifting network of Russia-facing nuclear missile launch sites spread over an area three times larger than Denmark, all housed twenty-eight feet below the surface of the Greenland Ice Sheet. 'Iceman' mid-range ballistic missiles – more than 600 of them – would be deployed in thousands of miles of covered trenches similar to those at Camp Century. With a range of 3,500 miles, they would cover 80 per cent of all 'relevant Soviet targets'. Overseen by several control centres, they would all be mounted on a railway network under the ice, creating a system that was at once 'mobile and concealed'.

Documents currently in the public domain do not reveal the exact relationship between Iceworm and Camp Century – which was the chicken and which the egg. Iceworm was first tabled in 1960, before Camp Century was finished, and therefore well before any practical insight could be gleaned from it. However, it seems supremely unlikely that anyone would plan an extended network of tunnels containing nuclear missiles (and reactors) under the surface of an ice sheet without some kind of trial run. Nor that a project as elaborate and labour intensive as Camp Century would be undertaken without an ulterior motive. Certainly this was the feeling of the chairman of the Danish Atomic Energy Commission, who 'did not feel convinced that the purpose of this camp was not one which was not fully in the clear'. The triple negative in this assessment from 1959 is doing a lot of work. The Danish government would never have officially sanctioned any US offensive installations in Greenland, and it had a ban on nuclear weapons in its territories and airspace. Which is, I suppose, partly why the US planned to hide them in the ice.

There was a broadly positive Army review of the Century project in 1965, but if it was indeed a test of subsurface Arctic building techniques I don't think it could be said to have passed with flying colours. As for the reactor, that was potentially catastrophically dangerous.

As snow falls on the top of an ice sheet, it accumulates, compresses under the weight of new snow and slowly, with pressure and time, becomes ice. (Max Perutz could have explained exactly how.) At Century in the 1960s, snow was accumulating at the rate of around four feet per year, which meant the camp was, essentially, sinking at that speed. Its entrances and topside buildings were continually being dug out of drifts, and the mass of snow on its cut-and-cover metal roofs was constantly increasing. By 1962, the steel arch over the reactor had bowed dangerously low and had to be lifted five feet to avoid fatal contact. And although the US Army Corps of Engineers had chosen the flattest site they could find, an ice sheet is, like a glacier, like a bergship, in constant, if very slow, viscous flow. The bulging and deforming walls of the trenches had to be periodically reshaped and monitored in case of collapse.

The denizens of Camp Century were living with an intolerable weight above their heads, and walls that were creeping in on them. Sewage was spreading from the sump through the snow towards their living quarters, making some of the dorms stink, and there was an unstable (as in existing precariously) nuclear plant just along the ever-narrowing corridor. There are also rumours that some of the huge tracked supply vehicles, on which the camp was totally dependent, were being lost en route as crevasses opened in the ice beneath them. A more 'psychologically undesirable' situation is quite difficult to imagine.

The reactor was decommissioned and removed in 1963, and shipped back to the USA to undergo tests to see just how well it had stood up to life in an ice hole. That year was also the last during which Camp Century was occupied through the winter. In 1966, it was judged that science no longer justified keeping the entrances clear and the roofs from falling in. After that, Century was minimally decommissioned and abandoned.

Without maintenance, Camp Century sank. A return trip in 1969 revealed that many of the chambers had indeed collapsed. Now, whatever remains is around ninety metres below the ice sheet's surface. However, climate scientists foresee a point in the not too distant future when ablation at the site will exceed accumulation and the crushed steel arches, plus any debris, trash and nuclear materials or other fuels that were left, will again see the light of day. The almost immediately disastrous idea of placing a nuclear reactor within an ice sheet may have lasting repercussions.

\*\*\*

Like debris melting slowly back into the light of day, there are common elements to all these stories that return, and return, to echo across the years. The advancing technologies of warfare made fighting increasingly remote (even if the Italians and Austrians of the First World War ended up being remote together). This dragged conflicts into new arenas (the North Atlantic) and extreme and isolated environments (Greenland). Consequently, war's relationship with the natural environment changed.

But the vagaries of modern warfare, contrary to the forward march of technology, also produced a kind of awful and inhuman backwards pull, and condemned men to live and die in ice. To subsist in darkness and fight hand to hand in the mountains. Death

legitimised on an unprecedented scale. Cryo-atavism.[13] Geoffrey
Pyke and the Americans at Camp Century were defeated by the
same thing: creep. And the soldiers in the Dolomites were, like
the Americans, brought low by the awful impracticalities of living
in ice holes. Ice fought back.

---

[13] Even today there are Indian and Pakistani soldiers entrenched at over 4,000 metres on the
Siachen glacier in the Karakoram, a confrontation that has been going on for almost forty
years because of the carelessness and imprecision of the British when delineating post-
colonial borders. It is so remote and inaccessible that it is of no strategic importance: 'A
struggle of two bald men over a comb,' according to one US specialist on South Asia.
Since a ceasefire in 2003 neither side has suffered any fatalities in battle, but it is estimated
that 3,000 to 5,000 men have died, including 140 Pakistani personnel in a single avalanche
in 2012.

# The Meddlers

## *Ice in the Anthropocene*

*Science is magic that* works.
                    Kurt Vonnegut, *Cat's Cradle* (1963)

*The Anthropocene . . . an era in which humanity must recognise itself as an integral part of the Earth's natural history.*
        Michael Bravo, 'A Cryopolitics to Reclaim Our
                            Frozen States' (2017)

*Ice, of course, has no history that can be traced, only the history of melting and evaporation, leaving no sign that it existed.*
        Naomi Jacobs, *The Character of Truth: Historical
                Figures in Contemporary Fiction* (1990)

Although it has not yet formally been endorsed by the International Union of Geological Sciences (IUGS), the idea that humanity has inaugurated a new geological epoch has gained wide cultural acceptance. The coining of the term 'Anthropocene' is evidence of the widespread recognition that human activity has had a significant impact on the planet's ecosystems and climate. Some mark the Anthropocene's start at around 1850, when the Industrial Revolution was pumping soot into the atmosphere, ending Europe's Little Ice Age and forcing the glaciers of the

Alps into definitive and possibly terminal retreat;[1] others date it to 1945, when the first atomic detonations sprinkled a layer of unusual radioactive isotopes into the ice-core record. In 2019, the IUGS's Anthropocene Working Group voted to recommend a date in the mid-twentieth century, and the weight of opinion currently seem to favour the year 1952; but while the experts try to decide quite how and when we made our indelible mark in the record in the rocks, the planet's ice melts.

These causes and effects are proved beyond doubt. As for our relationship to ice in the Anthropocene, that is more complicated and equivocal. With the accelerating melt has come a greater awareness of icy environments and ecologies, of indigenous circumpolar and Third Pole communities and their right to environmental security – of cryopolitics, in other words. There has been an increased focus on ice at the ends of the earth and on the roof of the world.

But there has of course also been a gross dereliction of care towards our environment. We have become increasingly alienated from the natural world – and from its ice – in our daily lives. Since the post-war adoption across the developed world of fridge-freezers, central heating and air conditioning, it seems to me we no longer have the same fundamental bond with ice. We don't rely on the natural world to produce it and we do not need to work to store it; we do not need it to ease pain or preserve food; and nor do we get to delight so much in its presence. An ice cube now is something completely unremarkable, completely interchangeable with any one of the 5 billion others pumped out by the UK ice industry alone to be put in drinks every year.

In many previous chapters we have seen how ice has connected us to our past, but in this one the story is of disconnection, of losing touch with or even overriding natural phenomena. This final chapter, then, examines some ways that people in temperate

[1] It was long a puzzle to glaciologists and climatologists why European glaciers began retreating some fifty years before temperatures began to rise. Then a 2013 paper presented evidence of significant layers of soot in ice cores taken from glaciers in Switzerland and Italy starting around that time: the dark carbon particles would have absorbed more heat and accelerated melting.

parts of the world have interacted with ice once this natural connection has disappeared. Specifically it looks at some very particular – perhaps even odd – examples which demonstrate a disregard for natural processes and systems, and which show how hubristic and ethically fraught some of our forays into the cryosphere have become. Thanks to our interventions we taken control of ice and come close to perfecting the degenerate custom of turning the seasons upside down. The scale of this presumption has become quite astounding; but this mastery has come with a price.

*\*\**

Let's start with the story of two brothers, Kurt and Bernard Vonnegut. In 1963, the year the nuclear reactor was removed from Camp Century, Kurt published *Cat's Cradle*, a short novel with ice at its heart. Though he later became a literary superstar, Kurt was not at that time the more famous Vonnegut. That accolade fell to Bernard, some eight years older, a scientist who was deeply implicated in the genesis of *Cat's Cradle*. Together and apart, the two brothers explored cold and the limits of science: Kurt's contribution was a chilling tale of nuclear dread, Bernard's a fantastical attempt to control nature.

To take Bernard's story first, it begins with a pair of scientists, Irving Langmuir and Vincent Schaefer – a Nobel Prize-winner, by all accounts the stereotypical absent-minded boffin, and his young assistant – in a cloud atop Mount Washington in New Hampshire. The 1,917-metre peak served, for these two ski-mad men, as an open-air laboratory to investigate precipitation static (in short, why did planes flying through snowstorms become electrically charged and lose radio capabilities?) on behalf of the US government during the Second World War. But their focus soon turned to ice. The summit enjoyed strong winds and average winter temperatures of −4 °F (−20 °C), and was almost always wreathed in clouds, which, at these low temperatures, were made up of 'supercooled' liquid water – water suspended in the air that was well below its freezing point but which somehow refused either to freeze or to fall as precipitation.

However, there were occasions when it would spontaneously turn to ice. Any instruments they used, for example, would quickly end up covered in rime (ice that forms directly on solid surfaces from water droplets in the air).[2] It seemed that, when motionless and undisturbed, supercooled water would not freeze, but introducing another substance into it provoked a change. What the scientists were observing was that this 'seeding' somehow taught the water molecules how to arrange themselves, and gave the ice nuclei something to fix on to that helped them to grow.[3]

Supercooled water being coaxed into precipitating and freezing in this way had been observed well before Langmuir and Schaefer's time, but the processes behind it had not been properly understood. This lack of comprehension was dangerous for wartime aviation. It was imperative that aeroplanes fly over the North Atlantic in all types of weather, yet when aviators encountered clouds, rime could be catastrophic. According to a NASA history of ice research during the war, 'Ice formation on wings would cause loss of lift; on control surfaces, loss of control; on airspeed heads, loss of airspeed indications; on radio antennas, loss of communications; on wind-shields, loss of vision; and, in engine intakes and on propellers, loss of power.'

None of these outcomes was optimal.

While Kurt Vonnegut was fighting the war in Europe, Bernard, who had a PhD from MIT, was seconded to the US Army Air Force's Ice Research Base in Minneapolis. There he spent his

---

[2] Water droplets in clouds are simply too small to fall: only when they grow much bigger does the force of gravity overcome the pressure of the air buoying them up. And supercooled water exists because, as temperatures drop, water molecules do not spontaneously arrange themselves into the correct pattern to bond into ice. Incredibly small nuclei of ice-like clusters, tiny areas of order within the chaos of the liquid, will form, but the formations are random and may just as easily disperse again as they grow bigger. If the ice-like clusters are large enough, however, they will act as landing sites for other molecules. Eventually, a critical mass is reached and ice crystals appear.

[3] Any solid impurities in water can do this – dust and other particles work fine – but the more closely they resemble the structure of ice, the easier it happens. The best seed is snow or ice itself.

days above a trapdoor in a modified B-24 bomber measuring water droplets and ice formation while in flight. When he was released by the military in 1945, Bernard joined General Electric's most important research facility, the GE Research Lab, where Langmuir and Schaefer had progressed beyond thinking about aeroplane wings. Now they were interested in the clouds themselves.

The questions that excited Langmuir and Schaefer were, what were the mechanisms by which supercooled water turned into ice? And could these somehow be controlled?

In 1946, Schaefer modified a chest freezer, lining it with black velvet and installing a viewing light. By breathing into it, he could create tiny clouds of water vapour. No longer would they have to stand on top of a mountain. One day that summer the freezer was struggling in the heat to reach its usual temperature of −23 °C. Eager to cool it quickly, Schaefer fetched some dry ice from the lab and dropped it in, whereupon a million glistening ice crystals formed from the supercooled water vapour within and fell gently to the freezer bottom. This accident established that extreme cold could play a part in seeding. It must have seemed like magic.

When Schaefer showed his boss, Langmuir wrote in his GE notebook: 'Control of Weather'. It was around this point that Bernard Vonnegut was drafted into the team. Together, the men tried to harness the seeding process to change the weather and by artificial means to take control of nature itself.

On 13 November 1946, with pilot Curtis Talbot, they performed their first field test on an unsuspecting cloud above Mount Greylock, in the Berkshires in neighbouring Massachusetts. 'Curt flew into the cloud and I started the dispenser in operation,' Schaefer wrote in his lab notes of the first airborne test. 'I dropped about three pounds [of dry ice] and then swung around and headed south. About the time I looked toward the rear, I was thrilled to see long streamers of snow falling from the base of the cloud through which we had just passed.'

Where the cloud had been there was now a hole, the ragged edges in turmoil.

Schaefer's notes continued: 'We then swung west of the cloud and observed draperies of snow which seemed to hang for 2–3000 feet below us, and noted the cloud drying up rapidly, very similar to what we observe in the cold box in the laboratory . . . While still in the cloud as we saw the glinting crystals all over . . . I said "We did it!" '

'Scientist Creates Real Snowflakes', the *New York Times* announced the next morning. Yet the story was old news even as it hit the stands. That same day, 14 November, Bernard Vonnegut introduced a smoke of silver iodide into the chest freezer and produced a spectacular fallout of ice crystals. By using a substance structurally very similar to ice, he had created a longer-lasting and more considerable effect, and one that could nucleate ice crystals at temperatures as warm as −4 °C. It would require a lot of finessing to work well outside the lab, but the principle was now clear.

Following the announcement of the maiden cloud-seeding flight, GE was bombarded with correspondence from sources including a search-and-rescue team seeking help clearing fog to find a downed aircraft, a ski resort operator looking for better piste coverage and a Hollywood producer wanting 'tailor-made blizzards'. Undeniably, the technology had many exciting, powerful and, most importantly, benevolent real-world applications. Even before the Mount Greylock test, Schaefer had sent a memo speculating that 'it would seem possible with the right arrangements . . . to clear areas around airports, on flight paths, or possibly to precipitate snow in mountainous regions where it could be used for water storage and sport, and prevent it from being deposited in cities.' Later, GE reported that the results might 'have a profound influence on domestic and world economics'; elsewhere, the company wrote: 'all the air of the United States could be nucleated at one time with a few pounds of silver iodide.'

Although the GE Research Lab at Schenectady was the country's largest and most prestigious private sector industrial research facility, these implications were larger than even it could handle. To continue its research, it needed resources that could only be provided by one of its major partners: the government.[4] Unsurprisingly, Uncle Sam was enthusiastic about becoming involved.

*\*\**

After he returned from the horrors of the Second World War, twenty-two-year-old Kurt Vonnegut married his high-school sweetheart and enrolled in the University of Chicago, but dropped out when his master's thesis was rejected. Depressed, struggling and with a small baby to provide for, at Bernard's suggestion he applied for a job as an in-house journalist at GE.

By the time Kurt took up his post in the GE News Bureau in late 1947, tasked with generating stories for the corporation to send to the press, the military were running the cloud-seeding fieldwork and the original rainmakers were confined to their labs. Kurt's beat was not weather control, but he was now in his brother's orbit, and probably in the know about Bernard's project, albeit unofficially – working on Project Cirrus, as it was now known, required clearance.

The similarities between the plot of *Cat's Cradle* and Langmuir, Schaefer and Bernard's work are pronounced. Kurt's slim novella concerns ice-nine, the invention of a scientist called Felix Hoenikker who is also one of the fathers of the atomic bomb. As one of Hoenniker's colleagues explains:

> 'Now suppose,' chortled Dr. Breed, enjoying himself, 'that there were many possible ways in which water could crystallize, could freeze. Suppose that the sort of ice we skate upon and put into highballs – what we might call ice-one – is only one of several types of ice. Suppose water always froze as ice-one on Earth because it had never had a seed to teach it how to form ice-two, ice-three, ice-four? And suppose,' he rapped on his desk with his old hand again, 'that there were one form, which we will call ice-nine – a crystal as hard as this desk – with a melting point of, let us say, one-hundred degrees Fahrenheit.'

[4] GE later admitted it was also worried about being liable for potentially huge damages from cloud-seeding experiments and that the shareholders would not have tolerated it. The government was therefore a good foil.

This mutant ice has the ability to destroy the world: if unleashed, even a small chunk of ice-nine, a single seed, would teach all the water it touches a new way of crystallising and therefore, since it is a solid at room temperature, freeze everything. Unfortunately, a chunk of ice-nine falls into the hands of an aged dictator on a Caribbean island. It's not a plot spoiler to say that the novel does not end well.

*Cat's Cradle* was written during the coldest days of the Cold War around the Cuban missile crisis. The idea of ice being a substance that, casually misused, might end the world seems to be clear displacement activity covering anxiety over the all-pervasive nuclear threat – another example of humankind assuming godlike powers. What Kurt could not have known were the unwitting parallels with the Army captains at Camp Century: like them, he is disguising the palpable danger of nuclear oblivion under an icy covering.

Just as seeding was lifted from real science, the idea that ice can exist in multiple crystalline configurations, or 'phases', is also true. Normal ice is known as ice $I_h$ – 'h' for hexagon – and it has exactly the form we saw in Chapter 5: oxygen molecules and their satellite hydrogen molecules held by hydrogen bonding in a rigid tetrahedral lattice. It is pretty much the only type that exists naturally on earth;[5] but given the right conditions – crush the lattices somewhat – liquid water molecules will crystallise into a solid in several other ways. We currently know of twenty crystalline phases, with the newest, ice XIX, having been described and named by the University of Innsbruck in 2021. None except for ice I can exist at anything other than extremely high pressures (many times more pressure than is exerted at the base of Antarctica's thickest ice sheets) and mainly at very low temperatures. They do probably exist in quantity in outer space, in ice formed under high pressure in a meteorite collision, for example, so studying them is important to astrophysics;

[5] There is also ice $I_c$, which has a cubic rather than hexagonal packing arrangement, and can form from water vapour at temperatures around −80 °C. This is a metastable form of ice, which means that it reverts readily to ice $I_h$, so there's not much of it about.

but here on earth they can be summoned only in laboratory conditions and often only fleetingly, for fractions of a second only a computer can count. There are undoubtedly more phases of ice to come, but no reason to think they will be anything other than increasingly fugitive and extreme.[6] It's just one of the many examples of how ice, though so ubiquitous, still holds many secrets.

The real ice IX was discovered and described in 1968, five years after Kurt's made-up ice-nine. It is denser than normal ice, and melts well below zero degrees, so his cautionary tale, while based on solid conceptual underpinnings, is a flight of fancy.

Much of the news that came out of Project Cirrus in the immediate post-war years was positive. In 1948, Langmuir went to Honduras to study cloud seeding by the United Fruit Company, and Schaefer went to the Rockies to examine a plan to use cloud seeding to reduce forest fires. Promising tests took place that dumped millions of gallons of rain on to the high deserts of New Mexico. Langmuir was increasingly strident about weather control's potential. More and larger aircraft were being used, with specialised modifications, and Bernard Vonnegut was playing with fire to create his ice – using charcoal impregnated with silver iodide to seed precipitation via millions of sparks, treating 10,000 cubic miles of air in an hour. But there were also early signs that attempts to control the weather were potentially very dangerous.

In October 1947, the GE team dropped 180 pounds of dry ice on and around a hurricane to see if they could influence its course. After the seeding, the hurricane, which had been heading east out to sea from Florida, took an unexpected left turn and made landfall again in Georgia, causing damage running to millions of dollars. This could in all honesty not be squarely blamed on the actions of the GE men. Storms very often change course abruptly and the consensus is that hurricanes do not often

---

[6] There are also several forms of chaotically unstructured solid water known as amorphous ice, none of which normally occur on earth. A new kind of amorphous ice, with a similar density to water, was discovered in 2022 by vigorously shaking normal frozen water in a jar filled with small steel balls at a temperature of −200 °C. It's pretty certain that there is more than one type of liquid water, too. But that's a whole other book.

contain large quantities of supercooled water, so the seeding probably had little effect. But it was, obviously, a PR disaster. The southerners affected by the about-turn threatened to sue or imprison the meddling Yankees who had, they believed, created havoc across their lands.

Another very murky case was a 1950 plan hatched with the New York City water commissioner to supply NYC's growing needs by manipulating local rainclouds. This was, in the most straightforward sense, successful, adding billions of gallons to the city's reservoirs. But it also became mired in expensive legal problems. The mayor of Albany, upstate, threatened to sue, claiming that clouds containing his city's water were being intercepted, and a country-club owner in the Catskills filed an injunction against the rainmakers complaining that non-stop gloomy weather would harm his business.

Though the application for an injunction was thrown out by the state's Supreme Court, this case, and the hurricane debacle, highlighted the complex ethical and legal questions that cloud seeding threw up. There was no doubt that, properly applied, cloud seeding could nucleate ice crystals which, in turn, could cause precipitation. But it was incredibly difficult to determine cause and effect in a system as large and infinitely varied as the weather, or to safeguard against unintended consequences. These were potentially enormous and completely unpredictable, adding to the ethical jeopardy of messing with the weather. It is a question that has popped up time and again: just because we can do something, should we?[7]

Kurt Vonnegut was famously a prisoner of war and, as a captive in Dresden, he had spent days carrying bodies out of underground shelters after the city had been firebombed by the Allies, so he knew something about technocracy and moral responsibility. In

---

[7] For Kurt, this line was definitively crossed in Operation Popeye during the Vietnam War, when cloud seeding was used to weaken roads, cause landslides and stop Viet Cong supplies getting through. Bernard was, said Kurt, 'deeply chagrined to find out that the Air Force had been spewing silver iodide all over Vietnam in an effort to bring those people to their knees . . . it sickened him to hear that they had hoped that his invention would have some destructive use.'

a later interview he drew clear parallels between his experiences in the war and the path GE was taking. 'During the Depression we really believed that scientists and engineers should be put in charge and that a technological utopia was possible,' he said. 'For me it was terrible, after having believed so much in technology . . . to see the actual use of this technology in destroying a city and killing 135,000 people . . . I was sickened by this use of the technology that I had had such great hopes for. And so I came to fear it.' He was also personally critical of Langmuir, who he said was 'more or less the model for Felix Hoenikker. Langmuir was absolutely indifferent to the uses that might be made of the truths he dug out of the rock and handed out to whomever was around. But any truth he found was beautiful in its own right, and he didn't give a damn who got it next.'

GE's pursuit of weather control was, for Kurt, one of megalomania, hubris and a lack of understanding of, or respect for, nature. He was not the only one. Many meteorologists had voiced concerns about lab-trained scientists claiming mastery of forces and systems they did not truly understand. Take these few telling lines written by one such Norwegian, Sverre Petterssen, who had been among the many doubters of GE's plans:

> Langmuir did not appreciate the complexity of meteorology as a science. In the atmosphere, processes of vastly different spatial scales and life spans exist together and interact; impulses and energy are shuttled through the whole spectrum of phenomena – all the way from molecular processes to global circulations and changes in the atmosphere as a whole. No chemist, physicist, or mathematician who has not lived with and learned to understand the peculiar nature of meteorology can pass valid judgment on how the atmosphere will react if one interferes with the details of the natural processes.

With regard to the intervening sixty years or so of environmental history, these do not feel like lessons we have yet learned.

***

Let's move from controlling the actual environment to creating an ersatz one. To wit, the snow machine, an invention that was, on a smaller scale, far more successful at stealing nature's thunder, but which also has had far-reaching consequences.

It was born on a Burbank back lot in 1934 during the filming of *As the Earth Turns*, a pastoral drama that deserves a place in the history books for this and little else. The brainchild of Warner Bros' technical director Louis Geib, the first snow machine consisted of three rotating blades that shaved their way through a 400-pound block of ice, plus a fan to blow the resulting crystals into the air. Hollywood's 'snowmen' had previously faked the white stuff using, among other things, dustings of soapflakes, gypsum, salt or bleached cornflakes, and pyrocel (similar to the material dentists use for taking dental impressions) to create footprints in the snow. Punched paper holes from a hole punch also did a decent job of substituting for drifting flakes.

The shaved ice was a useful trick since it fell like real snow; but it also melted like real snow under the arc lights and the Californian sun, so it wasn't any good for set dressing. The quintessentially Christmassy *It's a Wonderful Life* (1946) deployed 300,000 tons of shaved ice, 300 tons each of gypsum and plaster, plus 6,000 gallons of chemicals to make foamite (the chemical mix used in fire extinguishers), which was combined with soap and water and could deputise for everything from soft and fluffy drifts to a wild and raging blizzard. So much time and effort to create something that would just disappear! In 1939's *The Wizard of Oz*, meanwhile, asbestos crystals deputised for frozen water. This was also true for many, many other films: according to one book about cinematic special effects, asbestos used to be 'delivered to studios and spread across every surface. It was even arranged on actors' hair and clothing, and shovelled into wind machines to create picturesque but toxic blizzards.'

Outside Hollywood, Geib's invention was quickly taken up by the winter sports industry. In the winter of 1934, facing a shortage of natural snow for an event it was hosting, the Toronto Ski Club borrowed an ice planer from a local ice rink. In the years following, the ice-shaving technique produced snow in the Boston

Garden arena during a winter sports exhibition, in Madison Square Garden in New York and even in LA where, according to *Smithsonian Magazine*, 'On a 63-degree [17 °C] day in March 1938, the studio snowmen ground 350 tons of ice to create four- and five-foot drifts on a towering ski jump in the middle of the Memorial Coliseum. Twenty-thousand people gathered for the competition, as skiers hurled themselves more than a hundred feet into the air.'

A less labour-intensive and more scientific way of making artificial snow was discovered by accident in 1944 while a Canadian low-temperature lab was investigating – bizarre coincidence – the formation of rime on jet engines. When lead scientist Dr Ray Ringer and his colleagues sprayed water droplets towards an engine housing in a below-freezing wind tunnel, they found that instead of producing a coating of rime, as they had anticipated, the cooled water froze in mid-air, passed through the jet and sprayed snow from the back end.

Dr Ringer did not patent his accidental snow-production system; perhaps it seemed more of an annoyance than an opportunity. That was left to a man called Wayne M. Pierce Junior, who ran a ski-manufacturing company in Connecticut with two friends, Art Hunt and Dave Richey; during the winter of 1949, he confected a snowmaking machine using a paint-spray compressor, a nozzle and a garden hose, turning the water into tiny ice crystals by blowing it through freezing air.

The patent was filed in 1950 – almost year zero of the Anthropocene – and granted a few years later. Pierce's system had actually been in use at one Connecticut ski resort, Mohawk Mountain, as early as the winter of 1949, but it seems it was not a commercial success. Pierce sold the patent on after a couple of years, and eventually it was overturned – because Ringer had done it first.

The snow cannon we know today use Pierce's principles in an updated design. They combine a large fan with several nozzles that spray a fine mist of cold water, plus another set of nozzles that spray water and compressed air. As the pressurised air expands, it cools, turning small amounts of water into ice crystals, which then act as seeds for the rest of the water. All of this is propelled by the powerful fan up to fifty metres into the air and, as it falls, the magic happens and the ice crystals band together into snow. A separate nucleating agent is usually added (modern machines often use a bacteria-produced protein supplied in freeze-dried pellets), sprayed by adjoining nozzles to maximise the amount of ice crystals produced and make the machine effective over a range of temperatures and atmospheric conditions.

However. One of the problems with machine-made snow is that you might say it is not *really* snow. Trying to sew up all the angles in his patent application, Wayne Pierce quoted a US Weather Bureau glossary of meteorological terms: '*Snow* – Precipitation in the form of small ice crystals falling either separately or in loosely coherent clusters (snowflakes).' And artificial snow does indeed fit the dictionary definition. But because it does not form at a great height like natural snow, the small ice crystals do not hang in the air long enough to accumulate more mass and the delicate and beautiful dendrite arms of natural snowflakes do not have time to form. Instead, artificial snow (the industry does not like the 'A' word) is more likely to fall as tiny, hollow crystalline ice spheres that are up to five times more dense than natural snow. They are more durable, and easier to groom on pistes, but they do not have the dry, fluffy quality that skiers love. And when you faceplant they can really smart.

Another problem is the amount of resources snow cannons use. A Swedish study from 2011 estimated that creating a cubic metre of snow with a mobile snow cannon took 3.5 to 4.3 kWh of electricity – enough to drive a Tesla around twenty kilometres – though in some cases consumption might be over three times that.[8] To make a cubic metre of decent artificial snow can require around

---

[8] Clearly there are a lot of variables involved in this, not least the type of cannon, and the report's authors say that modern cannon can consume more like 1.1 kWh. The ski industry is undoubtedly improving its efficiency, and not only for environmental reasons. A 2001 study of US ski resorts estimated that 73 per cent of their electricity went to snowmaking pumps and fans – enormous costs that are an incentive to change in themselves. These are also fairly old studies, so efficiency is bound to have improved. But the fact remains that almost all ski areas are increasingly dependent on these environmentally problematic technologies.

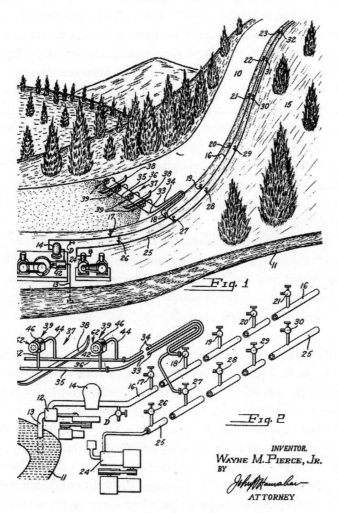

W. M. PIERCE, JR

METHOD FOR MAKING AND DISTRIBUTING SNOW

*Fig. 1*

*Fig. 2*

INVENTOR.

WAYNE M. PIERCE, JR.

BY

*Jeffry M Hanrahan*

ATTORNEY

*Patent drawing from 1954 for the first commercial
artificial snowmakers.*

400 litres of water, and a high-powered modern snow cannon can make 120 cubic metres of snow an hour. Another study from 2011 estimated that it takes 3 or 4 *million* litres of water to cover a hectare of ski slope. I'm not going to do the sums on that, but it could take you a long way in an electric car. Nearly all ski resorts

use artificial snow. The 2022 Beijing Olympic Winter Games intended to rely completely upon artificial snow – using 25 *billion* litres of water by some counts – though in the event some competitions, including the Giant Slalom, were disrupted when natural snow fell. Officials, in fact, had to clear natural snow from the cross-country skiing course with leaf blowers.

My point here is not the utter absurdity and waste of removing inconvenient snow from a ski course with leaf blowers, although of course it is utterly absurd and wasteful. Rather it is the scale of these interventions in the natural world. The cryosphere – that part of our world made up of frozen water – used to be the domain solely of natural ice and snow. But, starting with the use of saltpetre, via the work of natural philosophers like Cornelis Drebbel, it has been colonised by artificial cold. And around 1950 this colonisation underwent a great acceleration. The rise in cooling technologies and chilled spaces – air conditioning,[9] home refrigeration, the cold chain, data centres – has expanded the cryosphere and changed it beyond recognition. A new country, a new continent, the coldscape.

Snow machines are just an infinitesimally tiny part of the coldscape, and, since they produce actual ice crystals and not just the artificial absence of heat, they're very much a minority component. But they are a microcosm of the costly paradox of all our efforts to create artificial cold. Snow machines consume power that has been generated elsewhere and throw off heat as they produce snow. Every time we create cold somewhere, we heat up the world somewhere else. The more unnatural cool we make, the more natural cool we destroy and the scarcer it becomes. This is why the ice melts. Why do we need snow machines? Because there is not enough snow. What do snow machines do? Add

---

[9] Early air conditioning in the USA – notably in theatres – often involved ice. When the twentieth American president, James A. Garfield, was shot in July 1881, his sickroom in the White House was kept cool and dehumidified in the Washington summer heat by a primitive air conditioner that circulated air over large amounts of ice. 'Two tons per day would have to be melted by a current of warm air; allowing for waste, it might be estimated that three or four tons of ice per day must be melted by the air itself,' stated the engineer's report. The air was found to be 'cool, dry and ample in supply', but the president nevertheless died that September.

carbon to the atmosphere. What does that do? Causes less snow. And so the snake eats its own tail.

Or as Michael Bravo, who if you remember coined the term 'cryopolitics', put it: 'The more our economies grow, the more cooling we need to keep our environments temperate, and the more heat, greenhouse gases and carbon we produce as externalities or unintended by-products. The consequence . . . is that we consume ever-increasing supplies of our frozen reserves from the vaults of our poles and mountain regions.'

\*\*\*

Next we come to one of the most bizarre twists in the logic of late-stage capitalism: recurrent plans to tow icebergs long distances to mitigate drought in parched countries – a spectacular blurring of science and science fiction, as if we as a species no longer recognise where the boundaries are.

The idea of towing icebergs has been floating around for at least 200 years. There is a cryptic reference in a literary compendium of 1825 to 'the old project of towing icebergs into the southern ocean, for the purpose of equalising the temperature of the Earth', which is, perhaps, satire, but it shows that this crazy scheme was present at least in the collective imaginary.[10] And it is recorded that during the nineteenth century small icebergs (often equipped with sails) were indeed towed to Valparaíso, Chile, and Callao, Peru, where they were used in breweries during the brewing process, and generally to cool drinks and food. In the 1860s, there were at least two schemes to tow icebergs to India – clearly influenced by, though never challenging, Frederic Tudor's unlikely success shipping ice.

The idea was revived after the Second World War (again, right around the Anthropocene year zero) by a maverick

---

[10] *A Journey in Other Worlds*, a novel from 1894 by the millionaire hotelier J. J. Astor, has a similar conceit: it is the year 2000 and the Terrestrial Axis Straightening Society is proposing to do away with the seasons by, you've guessed it, straightening the axis of the earth. This will be achieved by shifting water around in the Arctic and the Southern Oceans. For this meddling, ice had its revenge: Astor was perhaps the most famous victim of the sinking of the *Titanic*.

oceanographer, John D. Isaacs, of the Scripps Oceanography Institute in California. He 'sought to relieve California's water shortage by towing icebergs from Alaska or Antarctica' but the plan, which he promoted on and off for the next several decades, divided opinion at the Institute. Isaacs determined that Antarctic tabular (long, flat and low) bergs would travel best, and he believed Chile and Peru the best destinations, for their proximity to Antarctica and also the strong cold ocean currents that sweep from the south past their coasts. Despite the projected cost of towing an iceberg containing 100 million dollars' worth of water being only 1 per cent of that amount, his efforts never came to anything.[11]

From the 1960s on, oil companies began to lasso and divert icebergs that were threatening their rigs, and there were recurrent schemes to tow icebergs as water resources much larger distances. Perhaps the biggest and most elaborate was presented by the Rand Corporation, the US government-backed think tank, in 1973. Rand proposed towing 'trains' of icebergs, each 300- to 600-metres wide and with an optimal total length of twenty kilometres or more, to thirsty cities. Modelling a transport from Antarctica's Ross Sea to California, it claimed the water would cost around $30 per acre-foot (water an acre in area and a foot deep), compared with up to $100 for a similar quantity of drinkable water produced by desalination. Plastic quilting would cover the forward edge of each iceberg, to trap a layer of cold meltwater and minimise ablation.

The Rand document is thick with formulae calculating water resistance and maps of shipping routes that would get the icebergs to the California coast in a year or less, where they would be moored and gently heated (probably by the surrounding seawater) to release their freshwater cargo. The Rand iceberg train would have needed a not inconsiderable amount of energy: the authors recommended attaching a floating nuclear plant to provide the convoy's power.

---

[11] Dealing with the ice once *in situ* and distributing the water are two lacunae in many iceberg-towing plans. The towing is the sexy bit, the rest admin.

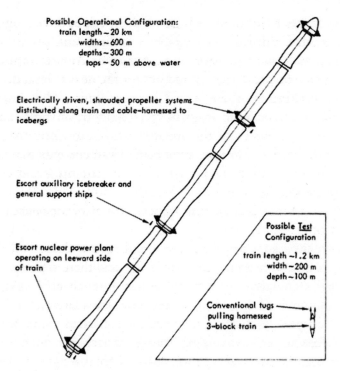

Possible Operational Configuration:
train length ~ 20 km
widths ~ 600 m
depths ~ 300 m
tops ~ 50 m above water

Electrically driven, shrouded propeller systems
distributed along train and cable-harnessed to
icebergs

Escort auxiliary icebreaker and
general support ships

Escort nuclear power plant
operating on leeward side
of train

Possible Test
Configuration

train length ~1.2 km
width ~200 m
depth ~100 m

Conventional tugs
pulling harnessed
3-block train

*A Rand Corporation diagram depicting an iceberg*
*train in transit.*

Rand's proposal did not take off. But it did not die. In 1977, the First International Conference and Workshops on Iceberg Utilization for Freshwater Production, Weather Modification and Other Applications were held at Iowa State University in the landlocked American Midwest, about as far from iceberg danger as could possibly be. It was sponsored by Prince Mohammed al Faisal, a nephew of Saudi Arabia's King Khalid – the ruler of a desert country that clearly had an interest in plentiful cheap, pure water.

The conference produced a quantity of papers, calculations and discussion that highlighted the many, many obstacles that faced the serious iceberg tower. Topics ranged from selecting an iceberg of the right shape, purity and strength (studies showed that vibrations from towing at even half a knot could cause an iceberg to break up) to hydrodynamics, soil composition at potential landing sites, myriad environmental worries and questions of international law: the Antarctic Treaty, which was ratified in 1961, bans any resource extraction south of 60° latitude. The iceberg melting en route was a huge problem. Not everyone thought that you could insulate your way out of this situation. 'Once you get north of the equator, you'll have nothing but a rope at the end of your tow,' commented Wilford Weeks, an Iowa delegate representing the US Army Cold Regions Research and Engineering Laboratory.

The truth was that towing icebergs for water is such a large undertaking that it was not going to get off the ground without governmental support. After the Rand report, Prince Al Faisal had quit his job heading the Saudi state desalination programme, founded a company, Iceberg Transport International, and sunk large amounts of his own money into the idea. But those in power eventually chose to invest Saudi resources in desalination technology instead, leaving Al Faisal's efforts dead in the water.

Barring a minor intervention from NASA in 1979, there was little discussion in the public sphere of towing icebergs until the 2010s. By then, computer modelling, among other things, had improved greatly, making some of the giant logistical problems of towing easier to plan for. More importantly, the need for water had only grown. In the last few years, both the Emiratis and the South Africans have announced serious plans, either state sponsored or seeking state sanction, to bring the Antarctic to their water-stressed territories.

I searched high and low for anything similar in ambition to these iceberg schemes, and came up only with Geoffrey Pyke and his bergships. However, even the imperative of surviving a world war was insufficient to make his self-propelled icebergs viable, and it remains to be seen whether slowly mounting water shortages provide enough of an incentive to move an ice mountain halfway across the world.

The only other comparable interventions took place in the art world, though these were on a much smaller scale. In 2019, Olafur Eliasson placed large chunks of Greenlandic glaciers that he'd removed from the North Atlantic outside Tate Modern and the London office of Bloomberg (a sponsor), bringing the physical effects of the climate crisis tangibly to London. I visited and saw this ancient ice from far away melt silently into the tarmac in between the art gallery's glass façade and the choppy brown Thames. An artist called Katie Paterson, meanwhile, has taken sound recordings from three glaciers in Iceland, which were pressed into three records, then cast using the meltwater from each glacier and refrozen. The discs of ice were then played simultaneously on three turntables until they melted completely.

Why the comparison with artists? Eliasson and Paterson's work was concerned with raising awareness of natural vulnerability and climate plight; the Emirati iceberg-towing scheme, which is the most advanced, also claims to have green credentials, mainly in reducing the pollution spewing from the country's 120 desalination plants. By its own figures these water factories flush nearly twenty-four tons of chlorine, sixty-five tons of chemical descaling agents and 300 kilograms of copper into the Arabian Gulf every day. Second on the project's official list of environmental benefits is that by recuperating icebergs for drinking water and irrigation, the scheme will reduce sea-level rises due to ice melting.

That last claim I was planning to place on the page and leave without comment. Like leaf-blowing excess snow, it seemed self-evidently ridiculous, but actually it deserves a bit of delving into. Since icebergs are already floating, and therefore displacing an equal weight of seawater, their contribution to upping sea levels has *mostly* already happened. But since they are freshwater, which is less dense than salt water, the water they release when they melt takes up a slightly larger volume than the equivalent weight of seawater. So sea levels rise; maybe only infinitesimally, but they do. It may be 99.9 per cent sophistry, but that Emirati claim is right.

The real logical fallacy, I think, lies in the idea of fighting the problem of overconsumption with yet more consumption, to shore up an unsustainable situation. Towing an iceberg into the Persian Gulf (average minimum winter water temperature 22 °C) is inherently and obviously unsustainable. Moreover, it is an intervention that enacts the larger global processes of ice-cap depletion in miniature – it actually doubles down on climate-related ice melt – in a performance that makes these processes the star of the show.

For this reason, iceberg towing seems, to my boggling mind at least, like something approaching conceptual art. Except that, in the end, artists like Eliasson and Paterson are, in their own ways, concerned with mitigating the effects of a growing population on a warming world and the iceberg towers quite the reverse: with mitigating the effects of a warming world on a growing population.

It is a huge moral mess. Perhaps it is indeed better to recover the freshwater while it can be put to good use instead of letting it dilute the oceans. There are strong humanitarian reasons for exploring every possible way of supplying water to global populations in need.

If iceberg towing appears dystopian, that is perhaps because it is a rational response to an increasingly dystopian world.

*\*\**

One final thing about water. These days there are scores of bottled-water companies that sell 'glacial' water drawn from streams flowing in glacial regions; but there are also a very few that sell meltwater from actual icebergs. Water that started life as snowflakes falling from the sky in the clear cold air of pre-industrial times, snowflakes that were lucky enough to fall on to a glacier surrounded by billions of their kind, which were then compacted into close union with their neighbours and purified as they were compressed and compressed as they sank – now in the cold and harmonious array of the glacier ice – into the middle of the slow-moving frozen river, before processing over the course of many centuries to the sea's edge, where, eventually, the tongue became unstable and calved and our now-ancient snowflakes began a whole new life as an iceberg. There on the ocean waves it attracted the eye of – according to various marketing materials – 'experienced gatherers' of 'carefully selected' icebergs, men practised and capable, shrewd operatives searching only for product of 'superior virginality'. And so our iceberg was recuperated from the sea, taken into captivity and lugged to a processing hangar on some gloomy rock. Here our snowflakes were forcibly released from their hydrogen bonds and returned to a liquid state and bottled (in flint glass if they were lucky, or, bizarrely, for all the claims these waters make to luxury and environmental conscience, PET plastic). Then our berg, or a very small fraction of it now, was shipped or flown around the world, perhaps to be drunk, or perhaps to be frozen again before consumption: 'Iceberg waters have a great story and are perfect for making ice cubes for special cocktails.'

Rainmakers, snow machines, icebergs, bottled water: undoubtedly strange final contributions to this history of humans and ice. I could have picked others, but they seemed somehow appropriate to this very complicated moment, dramatising as they do the ethical predicament we are facing. For centuries or even millennia people worked to gain mastery over ice, which is another way of saying mastery over nature. Pliny feared turning the seasons upside down; Drebbel boasted of turning summer into winter; Thomas Mort dreamed that climate and seasons would shake hands. Langmuir believed he could control the weather itself. The earth, its temperatures and its systems eventually became malleable in our hands.

Perhaps too malleable. In 1981, a respected, if controversial, scientist called Fred Hoyle published *Ice: The Ultimate Human Catastrophe*, in which he suggested that we were teetering on the brink of another ice age, one that would destroy life as we know it. Only forty-something years on, that view seems naive: scientists now believe that anthropogenic carbon emissions have delayed the next ice age by over 50,000 years. The truth is that we are accelerating away from ice faster than ever before. Our cities and modern ways of being have long left the natural world behind. Cold is proliferating but ice is a diminishing resource, a vanquished enemy, a vanished friend. We no longer have an appreciable connection to it. Ice has added so much to our societies, to our art and literature, our physical health and wellbeing, our food and drink, given us life and helped us over the boundary of death.

It has been something we have wondered over, that has inspired us, has sent us on fantastic adventures and caused us to dream. We have coveted it, used it and misunderstood it, grasping for its shining solidity it even as it has slipped through our fingers and melted to nothing. Like William Windham staring at the Mer de Glace, we are still not sure how to account for it properly. There are still many aspects of it we do not understand. Ice has taken us to so many places over the course of our relationship. But with these strange, involuted codas to this history, we might just be saying goodbye.

# Sky glow snatched from heaven
## (an afterword)

It may seem like I went about it the wrong way around, but just after I finished writing this book I went to Antarctica. I hadn't intended it that way. In fact, I hadn't intended it at all: I won the trip in an Instagram competition, and I found out the good news on the day I accepted a book offer from Bloomsbury – this book – a serendipity I still can scarcely believe.[1] But that was in the first lockdown of 2020 and it felt like the worst ever moment in history, barring world wars, to win a cruise. Quickly it was postponed a year. Then, a year later, Omicron put paid to the second sailing just a week before we were meant to embark. When the cancellation email came through, I put the piles of thermals and woolly socks back in their drawers, and the suitcase back in the loft, convinced that it was never going to happen. But then, finally, after years of thinking about ice, years in libraries poring over books and journals, years nosing around art galleries and ice houses and clambering in the Alps, I made it to Patagonia. Some time after that, in Ushuaia port, we boarded a ship, the MS *Seaventure*, and, improbably, unbelievably, we were off.

A very long time ago, Antarctica was at the heart of Gondwana, the ancient supercontinent. It was, in fact, the only piece of the jigsaw puzzle that adjoined all the other major constituent parts, which would go on to become Africa, South America, India and Australasia – central, you might say. But then, as Gondwana

---

[1] Yes really.

broke up around 180 Ma, Antarctica spun down towards the South Pole, and when it separated from South America a great rift opened up. Surrounded by oceans and isolated at the bottom of the world, Antarctica became encircled by the Antarctic Circumpolar Current. It was like shutting a freezer door: around 45 Ma Antarctica started icing up, and much of it has not seen the sunlight since.

That rift with South America is now called the Drake Passage (after Sir Francis) and is legendarily one of the roughest seas in the world. Waking up on the other side, after two tempest-tossed days and nights was like emerging into an enchanted frozen world. I could tell you about the humpback whales and the orcas, the Weddell seals and the chinstrap and gentoo penguins, but really the ice was most remarkable. Something like 90 per cent of the world's ice is down there, in shapes, colours and sheer quantity that are almost unimaginable. 'Blue caverns shone with sky glow snatched from heaven itself,' is how Ernest Shackleton described the first iceberg he saw as his ship entered the seas around South Georgia, just a few days before he died in 1922.

Sky glow snatched from heaven. A phrase that one might discount as hyperbole, but which, having experienced it, only imperfectly describes the wonder.

If I'd made it to Antarctica beforehand, funnily enough, I don't think I would have written the book differently. An important point of departure for this project was that Antarctica, the North Pole, the Himalaya, even the glaciers in the high Alps, are very distant from and outside of our everyday experience, and I wanted to concentrate on how ice has affected our lives in *our* world – how it has been something we've used and benefited from routinely, without a second thought.

Had I been to Antarctica or Greenland first, it would also not have helped me tackle the big conundrum I have been puzzling my way through – the one that I posed in the introduction with a little help from Michael Bravo. In case your memories need refreshing: 'What hasn't yet been adequately explained are the politics of frozen ecologies, and why they matter for the majority of the citizens of the globe living in cities with no special interest in the polar regions.'

To put it another way, why care? I hope that in its own way this book responds to that question.

I don't think it would matter if I'd never gone to Antarctica – or if you don't go either. Because we are all realising now how connected Antarctica is to everything on earth, how our fates are so intimately bound together. Ice, as we've seen, collapses time and space and creates illusions and truths, and so, in all those little pieces of ice I've picked out – in kitchens and hospitals and freezers, on mountains and in novels, paintings and museums – maybe Antarctica has been in these pages all along.

Ice has fascinated me, and this book has been full of stories of ice obsessives over the centuries, people who have been enchanted by ice and who have tried to master it and use it to their own ends, but who all too often have found that the prize they have reached for has simply melted through their fingers. That said, I have steered clear of the over-familiar stories of polar heroics, those remote and solitary tales we've all heard before. What I have tried to find instead is a sense of the extraordinary in the ordinary. Something to connect the magnificence of those faraway poles to things we can touch and taste. But if you'll permit, just in closing, let's venture out into those great white spaces with William Scoresby, one last bona fide fanatic and one of the great students and teachers of ice.

Scoresby was a Whitby whaler in the early nineteenth century who, the son of a famous and wealthy whaler himself, studied meteorology and natural history and became a ship's captain at an early age. His feeling for both the physical and fairy-tale qualities of ice ran deep, which was lucky, since he spent large portions of his life almost completely surrounded by it, sailing on the seas of Greenland. Scoresby did much to advance the common understanding of icebergs and sea ice and how to sail in the Arctic. But life on the high seas wasn't all work and no play. To amuse his shipmates he would often take a piece of clear, hard freshwater ice from a passing berg, chop and shape it with an axe then scrape it with his knife to fashion a rudimentary lens, and polish it with his hand until it was:

> capable of concentrating the rays of the sun, so as to produce a considerable intensity of heat. With a lump of ice, of by no means regular convexity, I have frequently burnt wood, fired gunpowder, melted lead, and lit the sailors' pipes, to their great astonishment; all of whom, who could procure the needful articles, eagerly flocked around me for the satisfaction of smoking a pipe ignited by such extraordinary means.

Ice, which surrounded their ship in fantastic quantities, which they thought they knew, could still make the sailors cry out in delight and come running. Something to both chill your drink and light your pipe. The extraordinary in the ordinary. Fire from ice.

# General bibliography, notes and further reading

I consulted far too many books, journals, newspaper articles and web sources when absorbing the information to write this book for it be useful to most readers to include them all. So I've listed some general further reading here, then some selected reading (mostly very accessible), under each chapter heading below, after the sources for the specific references and quotes in the text.

To start off, Hisami Nakamura and Julyan H. E. Cartwright's articles in the Royal Meteorological Society's journal *Weather* present a good cross-cultural look at the history of ice and snow in science and literature. Mariana Gosnell's 2005 work *Ice: The Nature, the History, and the Uses of an Astonishing Substance*, never published in the UK, was invaluable for its broad span of information about ice, from lakes to sea ice to ice-road trucking to outer space. Another very important foundation for this book was the collection *Cryopolitics: Frozen Life in a Melting World* (ed. Joanna Radin and Emma Kowal), for its overview of the political and other issues surrounding cold. Similarly, the anthology *History of Artificial Cold, Scientific, Technological and Cultural Issues* (ed. Kostas Gavroglu). There is also a whole issue of *Interdisciplinary Science Reviews* (vol. 29, no. 4, 2004) devoted to ice. All the above are worth consulting in their entirety, not just the specific essays referenced and quoted in this book. Eric G. Wilson's *The Spiritual History of Ice* is brilliant on ice and the Romantics, and the more esoteric reaches of ice in the eighteenth and nineteenth centuries. And Andri Snaer Magnason's *On Time and Water* is a beautiful meditation on ice, geological time and human time. Tété Michel Kpomassie's *An African in Greenland* is a fascinating anthropological account of Inuit life in Greenland in the 1960s and 1970s, written by a Togolese traveller who became obsessed with ice as a teenager. Nancy Campbell's *The Library of Ice*, meanwhile, covers some of the same topics but focuses on a personal and lyrical description of life in Greenland.

Finally, to move fully on to areas I purposefully did not cover – Francis Spufford's *I May Be Some Time: Ice and the English Imagination* (later retitled *I May Be Some Time: The Story Behind the Antarctic Tragedy of Captain Scott*) masterfully tells the story of Scott and the wider context of his doomed charge for the South Pole. Steven J. Pyne's *The Ice* is a comprehensive natural and social history of Antarctica. And Barry Lopez's beautifully written *Arctic Dreams* is a sensitive and nuanced account of Arctic fauna and our presence in the Arctic north.

Campbell, Nancy, *The Library of Ice: Readings from a Cold Climate* (London: Scribner, 2018).

Cartwright, J. H. E., and H. Nakamura, '*De nive sexangula* – a history of ice and snow – part 1', *Weather*, vol. 71, no. 11 (November 2016), pp. 291–4.

— — 'Icy hell – a history of ice and snow – part 2': *Weather*, vol. 72, no. 4 (April 2017), pp. 102–6.

— — 'Hot ice and wondrous strange snow – a history of ice and snow – part 3': *Weather*, vol. 72, no. 9 (September 2017), pp. 306–9.

— — 'Why Eastern snowflakes are six-sided while Western snowflakes are unique – a history of ice and snow – part 4', *Weather*, vol. 72, no. 10 (October 2017), pp. 272–5.

Gavroglu, Kostas (ed.), *History of Artificial Cold, Scientific, Technological and Cultural Issues* (Dordrecht: Springer, 2014).

Gosnell, Maria, *Ice: The Nature, the History, and the Uses of an Astonishing Substance* (New York: Knopf, 2005).

Kpomassie, Tété-Michel, *An African in Greenland*, trans. James Kirkup (New York: New York Review Books, 2001).

Lopez, Barry, *Arctic Dreams* (London: The Harvill Press, 1986).

Pyne, Stephen J., *The Ice* (London: Weidenfeld & Nicolson, 2003).

Radin, Joanna and Kowal, Emma (eds), *Cryopolitics: Frozen Life in a Melting World* (Cambridge, MA, and London: MIT Press, 2017).

Snaer Magnason, Andri, *On Time and Water* (London: Serpent's Tail, 2020).

Spufford, Francis, *I May Be Some Time: Ice and the English Imagination* (London: Faber & Faber, 1996).

Wilson, Eric G., *The Spiritual History of Ice* (Basingstoke: Palgrave Macmillan, 2003).

## ON LEARNING HOW TO SEE (AN INTRODUCTION)

x **'I own to you, I am extremely at a loss'**: William Windham, *An Account of the Glacières or Ice Alps in Savoy, in two letters, one from an English gentleman to his friends at Geneva; the other from Peter Martel, Engineer, to the said English gentleman* (London, 1744), p. xx.

xii **'Not a Sea'**: John Tyndall, *The Glaciers of the Alps*, new edn (London: Longmans, Green, 1896), p. viii.

xiv **'From whose womb comes the ice?'**: Job 38:29, New King James Version.

xiv **'world's principal cultural artefacts'**: Alison Flood, 'Unesco lists Exeter Book among "world's principal cultural artefacts"', *Guardian* (22 June 2016), accessed online, theguardian.com/books/2016/jun/22/unesco-lists-exeter-book-among-worlds-principal-cultural-artefacts

xiv **'The wave, over the wave'**: anon., in Michael J. Alexander (ed.), *The Earliest English Poems: A Bilingual Edition*, 3rd rev. edn (London: Penguin Classics, 1991), p. 140.

xvi **'What hasn't yet been adequately explained'**: Michael Bravo, 'A Cryopolitics to Reclaim Our Frozen Material States', in Radin and Kowal (eds), *Cryopolitics*, p. 29.

## I: THE CAVE PAINTERS

3 **'aesthetics of darkness'**: Colm Tóibín, 'Alone in Venice', *London Review of Books*, vol. 42, no. 22 (19 November 2020), accessed online, lrb.co.uk/the-paper/v42/n22/colm-toibin/diary

5 **'pulses'**: Ludovic Slimak et al., 'Modern Human Incursion into Neanderthal Territories 54,000 Years Ago at Mandrin, France',

*Science Advances*, vol. 8, no. 6 (February 2022), accessed online, science.org/doi/10.1126/sciadv.abj9496

8 **'metabolic demands'**: Anna Bellisari, 'Evolutionary Origins of Obesity', *Obesity Reviews*, vol. 9 (2008), pp. 165–80, quoted in Jesse Bering, 'The Fattest Ape: An Evolutionary Tale of Human Obesity', *Scientific American* (2 November 2010), accessed online, blogs.scientificamerican.com/bering-in-mind/the-fattest-ape-an-evolutionary-tale-of-human-obesity

9 **'Mankind, under the influence'**: Sigmund Freud, *A Phylogenetic Fantasy: Overview of the Transference Neuroses*, ed. Ilse Grubrich-Simitis, trans. Axel Hoffer and Peter T. Hoffer (Cambridge, MA, and London: The Belknap Press of Harvard University Press, 1987), pp. 13–14.

11 **'the activity of a complex super brain'**: Jill Cook, *Ice Age Art: The Arrival of the Modern Mind* (London: British Museum Press, 2013), p. 30.

13 **'The invention of material forms'**: Randall White, 'Beyond Art: Toward an Understanding of the Origins of Material Representation in Europe', *Annual Review of Anthropology*, vol. 21 (1992), pp. 537–64 at p. 537.

13 **'Art would have played'**: C. Michael Barton, G. A. Clark and Allison E. Cohen, 'Art as information: Explaining Upper Palaeolithic art in western Europe', *World Archaeology*, vol. 26, no. 2 (1994), pp. 185–207 at p. 192.

14 **'calendar of rutting'**: Paul Pettit, professor of palaeolithic archaeology, University of Durham, speaking on *In Our Time*, first broadcast on BBC Radio 4, 24 September 2020 and accessible online, bbc.co.uk/programmes/m000mqn7

14 **'proto-writing'**: Bennett Bacon et al., 'An Upper Palaeolithic Proto-writing System and Phenological Calendar', published online by Cambridge University Press (5 January 2023), doi.org/10.1017/S0959774322000415

*Further reading*

Clottes, Jean, *Pourquoi l'Art Préhistorique?* (Paris: Éditions Gallimard/Folio, 2011).

Hewitt, Godfrey, 'The genetic legacy of the Quaternary ice ages', *Nature*, vol. 405 (22 June 2000).

Hoffecker, John F., *Modern Humans: Their African Origin and Global Dispersal* (New York: Columbia University Press, 2017).

Mithin, Steven, *The Prehistory of the Mind* (London: Thames & Hudson, 1996).

Stewart, J. R., and C. B. Stringer, 'Human Evolution Out of Africa', *Science*, vol. 335 (16 March 2012), pp. 1317–21.

Rutherford, Adam, *The Book of Humans* (London: Weidenfeld & Nicolson, 2018).

Vince, Gaia, *Transcendence: How Humans Evolved through Fire, Language, Beauty and Time* (London: Penguin, 2019).

Woodward, Jamie, *The Ice Age: A Very Short Introduction* (Oxford: Oxford University Press, 2014).

Wragg-Sykes, Rebecca, *Kindred: Neanderthal Life, Love, Death and Art* (London: Bloomsbury Sigma, 2020).

## 2: THE REVENANTS

18 '**the Eskimos**': Konrad Spindler, *The Man in the Ice* (London: Weidenfeld & Nicolson, 1994), p. 3.

18 '**A first-year archaeology student . . . Tutenkhamen**': *ibid.*, p. 6.

20 '**a theory was advanced that he had died in the valley**': A. Vanzetti et al., 'The iceman as a burial', *Antiquity*, vol. 84 (2010), pp. 681–92.

19 '**cryopolitical subject whose emergence**': David Turnbull, 'Out of the Glacier into the Freezer: Ötzi the Iceman's Disruptive Timings, Spacings, and Mobilities', in Radin and Kowal (eds), *Cryopolitics*, p. 160.

20 '**studies on glaciers close by**': Pascal Bohleber et al., 'New glacier evidence for ice-free summits during the life of the Tyrolean Iceman', *Nature* (17 December 2020), accessed online, doi.org/10.1038/s41598-020-77518-9

20 '**gastro-intestinal chronotopograph**': *ibid.*, p. 164.

21 '**The time during which glaciers**': Ralph Lugon quoted in Xavier Lambiel, 'En Valais, les glaciers recrachent leurs trésors', *Le Temps* (26 January 2016), accessed online, letemps.ch/suisse/valais-glaciers-recrachent-leurs-tresors. My translation.

22 '**This is Balmat's hand**': Stephen D'Arve, *Histoire du Mont Blanc et de la Vallée de Chamonix* (Paris: Ch. Delagrave, 1878), p. 74; my translation.

23 'the end of everything': Natalia Polosmak, 'A Mummy Unearthed from the Pastures of Heaven', *National Geographic* (October 1994), p. 87.

23 'plausibly explaining the striking uniformity': Marina Unterlander et al., 'Ancestry and demography and descendants of Iron Age nomads of the Eurasian Steppe', *Nature Communications* (published online, 3 May 2017), p. 1, doi.org/10.1038/ncomms14615

24 'The Scythian custom': *ibid.*, book IV, chapter 64.

24 'The whole region I have been describing': Herodotus, *The Histories*, book IV, chapter 28.

25 'It is only by digging': Alfred Brehm, *From North Pole to Equator*, in Margaret Swainson Anderson (ed.), *Splendour of Earth: An Anthology of Travel* (London: G. Philip, 1954), p. 244.

25 'Even modern iron spades rebound': Natalia Polosmak, 'Twenty Years After', *Science First Hand*, vol. 37, no. 1 (14 April 2014), accessed online, scfh.ru/en/papers/twenty-years-after/

26 'The main practical effect': from the translator's preface to Sergei Rudenko, *Frozen Tombs of Siberia: The Pazyryk Burials of Iron Age Horsemen*, trans. M. W. Thompson (London: Dent, 1970), p. xxiii.

27 'wondering what the Pazyryk people had really been like': Polosmak, 'A Mummy Unearthed from the Pastures of Heaven', p. 95.

27 'When you spend day after day in the ice vault': *ibid.*

28 'hemp seed . . . howled aloud': Herodotus, *The Histories*, book IV, chapter 75.

29 'To measure an alien culture': quoted in Polosmak, 'Twenty Years After'.

30 'arangas': S. Duchesne et al., 'Frozen Graves of Yakutia, A Chronological Sequence', *Vestnik Archeologii, Antropologii i Etnografii*, vol. 51, no. 4 (2020), accessed online, doi. org/10.20874/2071-0437-2020-51-4-11

30 'kept in rooms cold as freezers': reports collected in Vanzetti et al., 'The iceman as a burial', p. 688.

30 'nearly the whole skeleton': James D. Forbes, *Travels through the Alps of Savoy and Other Parts of the Pennine Chain with Observations on the Phenomena of Glaciers* (Edinburgh and London, 1843), p. 281.

31 'Connemara picnic surprised by a snowstorm': quoted in Mike Parsons and Mary B. Rose, *Invisible on Everest* (Philadelphia: Northern Liberties Press, 2003), p. 2.

*Further reading*

Barry, Roger and Thian Yew Gan, *The Global Cryosphere: Past, Present and Future* (Cambridge: Cambridge University Press 2011).

Ceruti, Maria Costanza, 'Frozen Mummies from Andean Mountaintop Shrines: Bioarchaeology and Ethnohistory of Inca Human Sacrifice', *BioMed Research International* (2015).

Chatwin, Bruce, 'The Nomadic Alternative', in *'Animal Style' Art from East to West* (New York: Asia House Gallery, 1970).

Dixon, E. James et al., 'The Emergence of Glacial Archaeology', *Journal of Glacial Archaeology*, vol. 1, no. 1 (2014), pp. 1–9.

Lynnerup, Niels, 'The Thule Inuit Mummies from Greenland', *Anatomical Record*, vol. 298, issue 6 (June 2015), pp. 1001–6.

Mair, Victor H., and Jane Hickman, *Reconfiguring the Silk Road: New Research on East–West Exchange in Antiquity* (Philadelphia: University of Pennsylvania Museum of Archaeology and Anthropology, 2014).

Reinhard, Johan, *The Ice Maiden: Inca Mummies, Mountain Gods, and Sacred Sites in the Andes* (Washington, DC: National Geographic Society, 2005).

## 3: THE REVELLERS

34 **'I first in my life, it being a great frost'**: Samuel Pepys's diary, accessed online, pepysdiary.com/diary/1662/12/01/

34 **'Having seene the strange, and wonderfull dexterity'**: John Evelyn, *The Diary of John Evelyn*, ed. William Bray (London: Frederick Warne, 1882), pp. 290–1.

34 **'General Crisis'**: for more on the general crisis see Geoffrey Parker, *Global Crisis: War, Climate Change & Catastrophe in the Seventeenth Century* (New Haven and London: Yale University Press, 2013), pp. xix–xx.

34 **'Another cultural historian has argued'**: see Philipp Blom, *Nature's Mutiny: How the Little Ice Age Transformed the West and Shaped the Present* (London: Picador, 2019).

35 **'A strange and wondrous succession'**: Parker, *Global Crisis*, p. 3.

35 'With rivers icing up more frequently': see *ibid.*, pp. 3–5.

36 'the population decline in the Americas': Alexander Koch et al., 'Earth system impacts of the European arrival and Great Dying in the Americas after 1492', *Quaternary Science Reviews*, vol. 207 (2019), pp. 13–36, accessed online, doi.org/10.1016/j.quascirev.2018.12.004

37 'Compared to the changes in the proper ice ages': Mike Lockwood et al., 'Frost fairs, sunspots and the Little Ice Age', *Astronomy and Geophysics*, vol. 58, no. 2 (April 2017), p. 2.18. There are others even more sceptical, for example, Morgan Kelly and Cormac Ó Gráda, 'The Waning of the Little Ice Age: Climate Change in Early Modern Europe', *Journal of Interdisciplinary History*, vol. 44, no. 3 (2013), pp. 301–25.

37 'weakened populations have little resistance': on this point about disease, see Byron Breedlove, 'An Icy Vista from a Golden Age', *Emerging Infectious Diseases*, vol. 24, no. 12 (December 2018), pp. 2389–90.

37 'The times are so miserable', and to the end of the paragraph: Parker, *Global Crisis*, pp. 3–5.

38 'When the great marsh': Professor H. E. Butler, 'Norman London: An Essay, with a Translation of William Fitz Stephen's Description', *Historical Society leaflet 93* (London: G. A. Bell and Sons, 1934), p. 31.

39 'one study in 2008 named Finland': Federico Formenti and Alberto E. Minetti, 'The first humans travelling on ice: an energy-saving strategy?', *Biological Journal of the Linnean Society*, vol. 93, no. 1 (January 2008), pp. 1–7.

39 'A 2007 study estimated that ancient bones': Federico Formenti and Alberto E. Minetti, 'Human locomotion on ice: the evolution of ice-skating energetics through history', *Journal of Experimental Biology*, vol. 210, no. 10 (2007), pp. 1825–33.

39 'The oily external surface of the animal bones': 'Bone Ice Skates Invented by Ancient Finns, Study Says', *National Geographic News* (28 October 2010), accessed online, web.archive.org/web/20140301140724/http://news.nationalgeographic.com/news/2008/01/080104-first-skates_2.html

40 'a very thin layer of molecules at the ice's surface': Federico Formenti, 'A Review of the Physics of Ice Surface Friction and the Development of Ice Skating', *Research in Sports Medicine*, vol. 22,

no. 3 (2014), p. 3. See also 'Why your feet slip and slide on ice', *Nature*, vol. 557 (2018), pp. 470–1, accessed online, doi.org/10.1038/d41586-018-05225-7

40 **'ice frolicking'**: 'Get your skates on!', *Global Times* (16 February 2012), accessed online, globaltimes.cn/content/696143.shtml

40 **'Skaters moved on ice like shooting stars'**: quoted in *Sports & Games in Ancient China* (Beijing: New World Press, 1986), p. 51.

40 **'The surface, lately a very good hard one'**: Extracts from Captain Robert Falcon Scott's polar diary posted online in 'Scott's Last Expedition' by the Scott Polar Research Institute (Cambridge), https://www.spri.cam.ac.uk/museum/diaries/scottslastexpedition/page/2/

42 **'shedding the vestiges'**: Wolfgang Stechow, *Dutch Landscape Painting of the Seventeenth Century* (London: Phaidon, 1966), p. 83.

44 **'After four hundred years'**: Adriaan M. J. de Kraker, introductory essay to *Hendrick Avercamp: Master of the Ice Scene* (Amsterdam: Rijksmuseum, 2009), p. 7.

45 **'the risk of falling into sin'**: on this see Albert Blankert's essay 'Hendrick Avercamp' in *Avercamp – Frozen Silence* (Amsterdam: Waterman Gallery, 1982).

45 **'scratching into the wet paint on the canvas'**: Arie Wallert and Ige Verslype, 'Ice and Sky, Sky and Ice', in *Hendrick Avercamp: Master of the Ice Scene*, p. 135

46 **'ice fever'**: De Kraker, introductory essay in *Hendrick Avercamp: Master of the Ice Scene*, p. 54.

46 **'Of iron shoes in winter time in Holland goes this talk'**: lines by Hugo Grotius, a lawyer; de-Latined by Stechow, *Dutch Landscape Painting of the Seventeenth Century*, p. 89.

46 **'Steven J. H. van Hengel, advances'**: for this and details in the paragraph that follows, see Steven J. H. van Hengel, *Early Golf* (Vaduz, Liechtenstein: Frank P. Van Eck, 1985).

49 **'*A Dictionary of Chronology*'**: Thomas Tegg, *A Dictionary of Chronology, or the Historian's Companion; being an Authentic Register of Events, from the Earliest Period to the Present Time, Comprehending an Epitome of Universal History, with a Copious List of the most Eminent Men in all Ages of the World*, 3rd edn (London, 1824), all citations from p. 144.

49 'frozen ale and wine were sawn into chunks': William Andrews, *Famous Frosts and Frost Fairs in Great Britain: Chronicled from the Earliest to the Present Time* (London: George Redway, 1887), p. 5.

49 'The Mediterranean was frozen over': Tegg, *A Dictionary of Chronology*, p. 24.

49 'The ploughman's hands': Anon., 'The Great Frost: Cold doings in London, except it be at the Lottery' (1608?), collected in Edward Arber (ed.), *An English Garner: Ingatherings from Our History and Literature*, vol. 1 (London: E. Arber, 1877), pp. 77–99 at p. 80.

49 'unique climatic anomaly': Parker, *Global Crisis*, p.3.

50 'frozen vacation . . . cold doings': *ibid.*

50 'slippery world', *ibid.*, p. 86.

50 'The frost hath made a floor on it': *ibid.*, p. 81.

50 'pavement of glass', *ibid.*, p. 82.

50 'tumultuous possession': Robert Bell, 'Frosts on the Thames', *Once a Week Magazine*, series 1, vol. iv (1860–1), accessed online, en.wikisource.org/wiki/Once_a_Week_(magazine)/Series_1/Volume_4/Frosts_on_the_Thames

50 'Above Westminster the Thames is quite frozen': John Chamberlain, *The Letters of John Chamberlain*, ed. Norman Egbert McClure (Philadelphia: The American Philosophical Society, 1939), p. 253.

50 'It is a place of mastery': Anon., 'The Great Frost', pp. 84–5.

51 'freeze coat': *ibid.*, p. 83.

51 'bull-baiting, horse and coach races': Evelyn, *The Diary*, p. 454.

52 'Folk do tipple, without fear to sink': quoted in Andrews, *Famous Frosts and Frost Fairs in Great Britain*, p. 33.

52 'heterogeneous and shifting space': Joseph Monteyne, *The Printed Image in Early Modern London: Urban Space, Visual Representation, and Social Exchange* (Aldershot: Ashgate, 2007), p. 215.

52 'a boy in the service': *Frostiana: or a History of the River Thames in a Frozen State* (London: G. Davis, 1814), p. 115.

52 'Where gentle Thames': Jonathan Swift, *Saint Patrick's Purgatory, Or Dr S---T's Expostulation with his Distressed Friends in the TOWER and Elsewhere, Shewing the True Reasons Why He Withdrew Himself to Ireland Upon a Certain Occasion; and Discovering All That Happened to Him Thereupon. With a Poetical Description of the Frozen Thames* (London: R. Burleigh, 1716).

54 'They are accosted by two ice-skating men': this anonymous pamphlet from 1683 referenced by Monteyne, *The Printed Image in Early Modern London*, p. 223.

54 'flying man': James P. Bowen, 'A Provincial Frost Fair: Urban Space, Sociability and Spectacle in Shrewsbury during the Great Frost of 1739', *Midland History*, vol. 43, no. 1 (2018), pp. 43–61 at p. 51.

54 'The cracking crystal yields': John Gay(?), collected in Andrews, *Famous Frosts and Frost Fairs in Great Britain*, p. 49.

55 'To Madame Tabitha Thaw': Anon., reproduced by Ian Currie, *Frosts, Freezes and Fairs: Chronicles of the Frozen Thames and Harsh Winters in Britain since 1000 AD* (Coulsden: Frosted Earth, 1996), p. 65.

*Further reading*

Fagan, Brian, *The Little Ice Age: How Climate Made History 1300–1850* (New York: Basic Books, 2002).

Ferris, Toby, *Short Life in a Strange World: Birth to Death in 42 Panels* (London: 4th Estate, 2020).

Mann, Michael E., 'Little Ice Age', in Michael C. MacCracken and John S. Perry (eds), *The Earth System: Physical and Chemical Dimensions of Global Environmental Change*, vol. 1 of Ted Munn (ed.), *Encyclopedia of Global Environmental Change* (New York: Wiley, 2002), pp. 504–9.

Reed, Nicholas, *Frost Fairs on the Frozen Thames* (London: Lilburne Press, 2002).

Stechow, Wolfgang, 'The Winter Landscape in the History of Art', *Criticism*, vol. 2, no. 2 (Spring 1960), pp. 175–89.

## 4: THE BUCCANEERS

57 'we made a staffe to plaie at colfe': Gerrit de Veer, *The three voyages of William Barents to the Arctic regions*, 2nd edn (London: Hakluyt Society, 1876), p. 168.

60 'curdled . . . sea lungs': for this, see L. P. Kirwan, *A History of Polar Exploration* (London: Penguin, 1962), p. 16.

60 'all that was known of the farthest north': Fridtjof Nansen, *In Northern Mists: Arctic Exploration in Early Times*, trans. A. G. Chater (London: William Heinemann, 1911), p. 43.

60 'newes were brought that Don Christopher Columbus': as reported by Baptista Rasmusius, collected in Richard Hakluyt, *Principal Navigations, Voyages and Discoveries of the English Nation*, vol. 3 (London, 1812), p. 28; spellings somewhat modernised.

61 'monstrous heapes of ice': Peter Martyr, 'Another testimony of the voyage of Sebastian Cabot to the West and Northwest', collected *ibid.*, p. 29.

62 'The answer to your query': Anon., *The King's Mirror*, trans. Laurence Marcellus Larson (Norway *c.* 1240, translation 2020), accessed online, gutenberg.org/files/61264/61264-h/61264-h.htm

66 'frostie zone': Richard Willes, Gentleman, 'Certaine other reasons, or arguments to prooue a passage by the Northwest', collected in Hakluyt, *Principal Navigations, Voyages and Discoveries of the English Nation*, vol. 3, p. 48.

66 'A joint-stock company was a chartered organisation': for more on this, see Britannica (online: britannica.com/topic/joint-stock-company and britannica.com/topic/chartered-company); also Samuel Eliot Morison, *The European Discovery of America: The Northern Voyages* (Oxford: Oxford University Press, 1971), p. 483.

67 'Two frozen-up vessels full of stiffened corpses': Dr Joseph Hamel, *England and Russia; Comprising the Voyages of John Tradescant the Elder, Sir Hugh Willoughby, Richard Chancellor, Nelson, and Others to the White Sea, etc.*, trans. John Studdy Leigh (London: Richard Bentley, 1854), p. 87.

68 'an arrangement between bankers and dreamers': Barry Lopez, *Arctic Dreams* (London: The Harvill Press, 1986), p. 335.

69 'England's First Empire Builder': William Gilbert Gosling, *The Life of Sir Humphrey Gilbert, England's First Empire Builder* (London: Constable, 1911).

69 'Elizabeth's Racketeer': Donald Barr Chidsey, *Sir Humphrey Gilbert, Elizabeth's Racketeer* (New York: Harper & Bros., 1932).

69 'a flatterer, a lyer, and a naughtie man': Leslie Stephen (ed.), *Dictionary of National Biography* (London: Smith, Elder, 1890), vol. 21, p. 328.

69 'dry-land sailor': David Beers Quinn (ed.), *The Voyages and Colonising Enterprises of Sir Humphrey Gilbert* (London: Hakluyt Society, 1940), introduction, p. 29.

69 'armchair sailor': Chidsey, *Sir Humphrey Gilbert*, p. 34.

69 'in the loytering vacation between military stratagemes': Gascoine's words are from his 1576 introduction to Humphrey Gilbert, *A New Passage to Cataia*, collected in Quinn (ed.), *The Voyages and Colonising Enterprises of Sir Humphrey Gilbert*, p. 131.

70 'the pearcing colde of the grose thick ayre': Gilbert, *A New Passage to Cataia*, p. 151.

71 'great iland[s] of yce': Christopher Hall, 'The first Voyage of Mr. Martine Frobisher, to the Northwest, for the search of the straight or passage to China', collected in Hakluyt, *Principal Navigations, Voyages and Discoveries of the English Nation*, vol. 3, p. 54.

72 'many mountains and great Islands of yce': Master Dionise Settle, 'The second voyage of Master Martin Frobisher: made to the west and north-west regions, in the year 1577', collected in Hakluyt, *Principal Navigations, Voyages and Discoveries of the English Nation*, vol. 3, p. 59.

72 'any hope of a passage through temperate latitudes': Quinn (ed.), *The Voyages and Colonising Enterprises of Sir Humphrey Gilbert*, introduction, p. 68.

76 'There is more to twenty-first century Arctic politics': Michael Bravo and Gareth Rees, 'Cryo-politics: Environmental Security and the Future of Arctic Navigation', *Brown Journal of World Affairs*, vol. 13, no. 1 (2006), p. 206.

77 'illegitimate': Leyland Cecco, 'Mike Pompeo rejects Canada's claims to Northwest Passage as "illegitimate"', *Guardian* (7 May 2019), accessed online, theguardian.com/us-news/2019/may/07/mike-pompeo-canada-northwest-passage-illegitimate

77 'There will be ships with Chinese flags': Nash Jenkins, 'China Could Be Preparing to Challenge Canada's Sovereignty Over the Northwest Passage', *Time* (21 April 2016), accessed online, time.com/4302882/china-arctic-shipping-northwest-passage/

77 'This isn't the fifteenth century': Ryan C. Maness and Brandon Valeriano, *Russia's Coercive Diplomacy: Energy, Cyber, and Maritime Policy as New Sources of Power* (Basingstoke: Palgrave Macmillan, 2015), p. 173.

*Further Reading*

Barber, Peter, and Tom Harper, *Magnificent Maps: Power, Propaganda and Art* (London: The British Library, 2010).

Evans, James, *Merchant Adventurers: The Voyage of Discovery That Transformed Tudor England* (London: Weidenfeld & Nicolson, 2013).

Fleming, Fergus, *Barrow's Boys: A Stirring Story of Daring, Fortitude and Outright Lunacy* (London: Granta Books, 1998).

Kurlansky, Mark, *Cod: A Biography of the Fish That Changed the World* (London: Vintage, 1999).

Stefansson, Vilhjalmur, *Ultima Thule: Further Mysteries of the Arctic* (New York: Macmillan, 1940).

Thomson, George Malcolm, *The North-West Passage* (London: Secker & Warburg, 1975).

White, Sam, *A Cold Welcome: The Little Ice Age and Europe's Encounter with North America* (Cambridge, MA: Harvard University Press, 2017).

## 5: THE SCIENTISTS AND GOURMETS

81 'The polar regions of physics': see Dirk Van Delft, 'The Cryogenic Laboratory of Heike Kamerlingh Onnes: An Early Case of Big Science', in Kostas Gavroglu (ed.), *History of Artificial Cold: Scientific, Technological and Cultural Issues* (Dordrecht: Springer, 2014), pp. 65–81 at p. 65.

82 'These were little plates of ice': quoted in and translated by F. C. Frank, 'Descartes' Observations on the Amsterdam Snowfalls of 4, 5, 6 and 9 February 1634', *Journal of Glaciology*, vol. 13 (1974), p. 535.

82 'The phenomenon of freezing': Christiana Christopoulou, 'Early Modern History of Cold: Robert Boyle and the Emergence of a New Experimental Field in Seventeenth Century Experimental Philosophy', in Gavroglu (ed.), *History of Artificial Cold*, pp. 21–51 at p. 34.

84 'subtle . . . spirituous': Robert Boyle quoted *ibid.*, p. 31.

84 'Accademia del Cimento': as reported in Anon., *Essayes of Natural Experiments Made in the Academie Del Cimento Under the Protection of the Most Serene Prince Leopold of Tuscany Englished by Richard Waller* (London, 1684), p. 77, accessed online, quod.lib.umich.edu/e/ eebo/A24159.0001.001

84 'A piece of ice that to the eye': Robert Boyle, *New Experiments and Observations Touching Cold or, An Experimental History of Cold, Begun*, collected in Michael Hunter and Edward B. Davis (eds), *The Works of Robert Boyle*, vol. 4: *Colours and Cold, 1664–5* (London: Pickering & Chatto, 1999), p. 309.

88 'The use of snow was very common in Greece': quoted in Sylvia P. Beamon and Susan Roaf, *The Ice Houses of Britain* (Abingdon: Routledge, 1990), p. 8.

88 'degenerate custom of turning the seasons upside down': Elizabeth David, *Harvest of the Cold Months* (London: Michael Joseph, 1994), p. 1.

89 'ice-encrusted fruit and peeled peaches in wine': *ibid.*, p. 58.

89 'in *Italy* and some other Regions': Boyle, *New Experiments and Observations Touching Cold*, p. 266

90 'Yonder the harvest of cold months laid up': Ellen Leslie, 'The Ice House Uncovered', *Country Life* (4 October 2010), accessed online, countrylife.co.uk/comment-opinion/the-ice-house-uncovered-20789

90 'ice houses became fashionable almost overnight': Beamon and Roaf, *The Ice Houses of Britain*, p. 19.

91 'in the English public imagination the Greenland Seas were only vaguely known': David, *Harvest of the Cold Months*, p. 328.

92 'product . . . manufacture': Anon., 'The confectioners have been able to lay in a store of ice to freeze their creams in summer!', *The Times* (21 January 1822), p. 3, quoted in Helen Watkins, 'Fridge Space: Journeys of the Domestic Refrigerator' (unpublished PhD thesis, University of British Columbia, 2008), p. 42, accessed online, open.library.ubc.ca/media/stream/pdf/24/1.0066461/1

92 'his cold cargo would turn to water': quoted in Beamon and Roaf, *The Ice Houses of Britain*, p. 46.

92 'not before seen . . . between May and November': quoted in Beamon and Roaf, *The Ice Houses of Britain*, p. 46.

93 'Ice six inches thick': *Morning Post* (31 March 1826), quoted in Sarah Murden, 'William Leftwich and the Ice Well', *All Things Georgian* (17 January 2019), online, georgianera.wordpress.com/2019/01/17/william-leftwich-and-the-ice-well/

93 'A very large number of the street ice-sellers are Calabrians': J. Thomson and Adolphe Smith, 'Halfpenny Ices', *Street Life in London* (1877), accessed online, victorianlondon.org/publications/thomson-19.htm

94 'absolute snare and delusion ... wholesome and delicious': *ibid.*

96 'acres of land for ice fields': David G. Dickason, 'The Nineteenth-Century Indo-American Ice Trade: An Hyperborean Epic', *Modern Asian Studies*, vol. 25, no. 1 (February 1991), pp. 53–89 at p. 67.

96 'Ice must be considered as out-doing most other luxuries': *ibid.*, p. 61.

96 'No JOKE': quoted in Philip Chadwick Foster Smith, *Crystal Blocks of Yankee Coldness: The Development of the Massachusetts Ice Trade from Frederic Tudor to Wenham Lake 1806–1886* (The Essex Institute Historical Collections, 1961), accessed online, iceharvestingusa.com/crystalblocks1.html

96 'sending ice to Calcutta was cheaper': *ibid.*, p. 64.

97 'ANXIETY, ANXIETY, ANXIETY': see Dickason, 'The Nineteenth-Century Indo-American Ice Trade', p. 60.

98 'How many Calcutta tables glittered': quoted *ibid.*, p. 71.

99 'Michael Faraday proclaimed': see Chadwick Foster Smith, *Crystal Blocks of Yankee Coldness.*

99 'unroofs the house of fishes': Henry David Thoreau, *Walden* (Cologne: Könemann, 1996), p. 257.

99 'an obelisk designed to pierce the clouds': *ibid.*, p. 258.

99 'pure Walden water': *ibid.*, p. 261.

100 'Every mutiny, every danger': John Ruskin, *The Pleasures of England*, quoted in Daryl Ogden, 'The Architecture of Empire: "Oriental" Gothic and the Problem of British Identity in Ruskin's Venice', *Victorian Literature and Culture*, vol. 25, no. 1 (1997), pp. 109–20 at p. 118.

100 'Tudor is widely held as being America's first millionaire': on this see Dickason, 'The Nineteenth-Century Indo-American Ice Trade', p. 55.

*Further reading*

Brown, Jared, 'The surprising history of the cocktail', *Telegraph* (13 December 2012).

Masters, Thomas, *The Ice book: Being a Compendious & Concise History of Everything Connected with Ice from Its First Introduction Into*

*Europe as an Article of Luxury to the Present Time: with an Account of the Artificial Manner of Producing Pure & Solid Ice, and a Valuable Collection of the Most Approved Recipes for Making Superior Water Ices and Ice Creams at a Few Minutes' Notice* (London: Simpkin, Marshall, 1844).

Paterson, Stanley, and Carl Seaberg, *The Ice King: Frederic Tudor and his Circle*, ed. Alan Seaburg (Boston, MA: Massachusetts Historical Society, c. 2003).

## 6: THE SHEEP SHIFTERS

104 'one writer has suggested could plausibly': Sylvia P. Beamon, in Beamon and Roaf, *The Ice Houses of Britain*, notes to p. 3.

104 'ice cellars': Kelsey E. Nyland et al., 'Traditional Iñupiat Ice Cellars (SIGLUAQ) in Barrow, Alaska: Characteristics, Temperature Monitoring and Distribution', *Geographical Review*, vol. 107, no. 1 (2017), pp. 143–58.

104 'snow preserveth fish': David, *Harvest of the Cold Months*, p. 232.

104 'Later, during the Tang Dynasty': K. C. Chang, *Food in Chinese Culture: Anthropological and Historical Perspectives* (New Haven and London: Yale University Press, 1977), pp. 62, 116.

105 'alighted out of the Coach': John Aubrey, *Brief Lives* (London: Penguin Classics, 2000), p. 30.

105 'insipid . . . dispirited, like phlegm': Boyle, *New Experiments and Observations Touching Cold*, p. 297.

106 'large sturgeon and some other fresh fish . . . This method': John Bell, *Travels from St. Petersburgh in Russia to Various Parts of Asia*, vol. 2 (Glasgow, 1763), p. 56.

106 'Elizabeth David reports that in France a monk': David, *Harvest of the Cold Months*, p. 233.

107 'Spying a good wheeze, he fired off a letter': George Dempster, letter to Sir John Sinclair, *The Correspondence of the Right Honourable Sir John Sinclair* (London, Edinburgh [printed], 1831), p. 360

107 'made the experiment rather in consequence of Mr Dempster's earnest manner': quoted in Ian Aitken Robertson, 'The Tay Salmon Fisheries in the Nineteenth Century' (unpublished PhD thesis, Stirling University, 1989), p. 96, accessed online, hdl.handle.net/1893/12153

108 'subversive of every principle of commerce': quoted *ibid.*, p. 80.

110 'the ice house forms an excellent larder': the sources are *Rural Residences* and *The Encyclopedia of Cottage, Farm and Villa Architecture*, quoted in Christina Hardyment, *Home Comfort: A History of Domestic Arrangements* (London: Viking, 1992), pp. 105–6.

110 'many persons are deterred from forming an ice house': quoted in Beamon and Roaf, *The Ice Houses of Britain*, p. 130.

110 'Every housekeeper . . . may have one in his cellar': quoted in Oscar E. Anderson, *Refrigeration in America: A History of a New Technology and its Impact* (Princeton: Princeton University for the University of Cincinnati, 1953), p. 9.

110 'Ice is an American institution': *De Bow's Review*, quoted *ibid.*, p. 3.

112 'that amazing iron net': a quote from the memoirs of the famous actor Fanny Kemble, who had been one of the first travellers on the Liverpool-to-Manchester railway in 1830; collected in Matthew D. Esposito, *A World History of Railway Cultures, 1830–1930*, vol. 1 (Abingdon: Routledge, 2020), p. 217.

112 'Elizabeth David . . . any ice destined for fisheries came in tax free': David, *Harvest of the Cold Months*, p. 336.

113 'the locomotive and the steamboat, like enormous shuttles': Ralph Waldo Emerson, 'The Young Americans', first part quoted in Rebecca Solnit, *River of Shadows: Eadward Muybridge and the Technological Wild West* (London: Penguin, 2003), p.11; the last sentence continuation accessed online, archive.vcu.edu/english/engweb/transcendentalism/authors/emerson/essays/youngam.htm

115 '2,683 tons . . . 70,000 tons . . . 20 per cent': figures from *Railway Review* (29 January 1887), p. 62, via Wikipedia, en.wikipedia.org/wiki/Gustavus_Franklin_Swift

115 'the whole country into a garden for our great cities': *American Railroad Journal*, 1842, quoted in John H. White, *The American Railroad Freight Car: From the Wood-Car Era to the Coming of Steel* (Baltimore and London: Johns Hopkins University Press, c. 1993), p. 272.

115 '880 lb (400 kg) of ice and 660 lb (300 kg) of salt': figures from Marco D'Eramo, *The Pig and the Skyscraper: Chicago: A History of Our Future* (London: Verso, 2003), p. 37.

116 'disassembly line': a turn of phrase used by many, e.g. Richard Perren, *The Meat Trade in Britain, 1840–1914* (Abingdon: Routledge, 1978), and Dominic A. Pacyga, *Slaughterhouse: Chicago's Union Stock Yard and the World It Made* (Chicago: University of Chicago Press, 2015).

117 'The Producing of Cold is a thing very worthy the Inquisition': Francis Bacon, *Sylva Sylvarum* (1624), quoted in Jonathan Rees, *Refrigeration Nation* (Baltimore: Johns Hopkins University Press, 2013), p. 1.

117 'artificial cold may be made very cheap': Richard Trevithick, letter to Davies Gilbert (29 June 1828), quoted in David, *Harvest of the Cold Months*, p. 337.

119 'cool wines!': Minna Scherlinder Morse, 'Chilly Reception', *Smithsonian Magazine* (July 2002), accessed online, smithsonianmag. com/history/chilly-reception-66099329/

120 'crank . . . God Almighty': quoted in Margaret Visser, *Much Depends on Dinner* (London: Penguin, 1989), p. 295.

120 'Moral causes . . . have been brought into play': V. M. Sherlock, *The Fever Man: A Biography of Dr. John Gorrie* (Tallahassee, FL: Medallion Press, 1982), p. 118.

120 'This discovery must be *of immense value*': *ibid.*, p. 116.

121 'The winter has thus far proceeded': *Berwick Examiner* (14 February 1846), accessed online, mouthofthetweed.co.uk/046%20 Ice.pdf

122 'to see what the polar regions might look like . . . innocent steam machinery': Mark Twain, *Life on the Mississippi* (Boston: James R. Osgood, 1883), pp. 409–10.

123 '1,760,865 people and 47,824,299 sheep': figures from Rees, *Refrigeration Nation*, p. 255.

124 'I now feel that the time is not far distant': J. T. Critchell and J. Raymond, *A History of the Frozen Meat Trade* (London: Constable, 1912), p. 20.

124 'by 1882 the UK was importing 654,000 tons of livestock from Europe and the US': see Ian Arthur, 'Shipboard Refrigeration and the Beginning of the Frozen Meat Trade', *Journal of the Royal Australian Historical Society*, vol. 92, no. 1 (June 2006), pp. 63–4.

125 'the beef and the pigeon they'd just eaten had been killed more than a year previously': see Marea Donnelly, 'Thomas Mort's picnic train to Lithgow was first step in frozen food trade', *Daily Telegraph* (Australia, 9 September 2017), accessed online, dailytelegraph.com.

au/news/thomas-morts-picnic-train-to-lithgow-was-first-step-in-frozen-food-trade/news-story/75ba5dca24646a4faf1db374bfc
d5d79

126 'alimentary truculence': Rebecca J. H. Woods, 'From Colonial Animal to Imperial Edible: Building an Empire of Sheep in New Zealand, ca. 1880–1900', *Comparative Studies of South Asia, Africa and the Middle East*, vol. 35, no. 1 (2015), p. 127.

126 'The ability to control, produce and claim ownership over cold': Rebecca J. H. Woods, 'Nature and the Refrigerating Machine', in Radin and Kowal (eds), *Cryopolitics*, pp. 89–116 at p. 90.

126 'imperial transit': Jennifer A. Hamilton, 'Reindeer and Woolly Mammoths: The Imperial Transit of Frozen Meat from the North American Arctic', in Sushmita Chatterjee and Banu Subramaniam (eds), *Meat! A Transnational Analysis* (Durham, NC: Duke University Press, 2021), pp. 61–95.

127 'natives catching fish in fifty below zero weather': Birdseye's words appeared in the *Beaver* magazine, quoted *ibid.*, p. 84.

128 'coldscape … a constellation of social and technical systems': Nicola Twilley coined the term 'coldscape' in 'The Coldscape', *Cabinet*, 47 (Fall 2012), pp. 78–84. The longer definition comes in Joanna Radin and Emma Kowal, 'Introduction: The Politics of Low Temperature', in Radin and Kowal (eds), *Cryopolitics*, pp. 3–26 at p. 5.

*Further Reading*

Kurlansky, Mark, *Birdseye: The Adventures of a Curious Man* (New York: Doubleday, 2012).

Roberts, Brian, *Thomas Sutcliffe Mort, Pioneer in Food Refrigeration* (CIBSE Heritage Group, undated), accessed online, hevac-heritage. org/built_environment/pioneers_revisited/surnames_m-w/mort.pdf

Woolrich, W. R., *The Men Who Created Cold: A History of Refrigeration* (New York: Exposition Press, 1967).

## 7: THE TOURISTS

130 'unmelted hail accumulating through the summer': David Bressan, 'The Discovery of the Ruins of Ice: The Birth of Glacier Research', *Scientific American* guest blog (3 January

2011), blogs.scientificamerican.com/guest-blog/the-discovery-of-the-ruins-of-ice-the-birth-of-glacier-research/

130 'a substance which assumes a concrete form from excessive congelation': Pliny, *The Natural History*, book 37, chapter 9.

131 'As regards the stony kinds of naturally occurring substances': Avicenna, 'De Congelatione et Conglutinatione Lapidum', in Stanton J. Linden (ed.), *The Alchemy Reader* (Cambridge: Cambridge University Press, 2003), p. 96.

131 'the high mountains make the ice so hard . . . juice thickened by cold': Albertus Magnus (*ex illo sicco coagulat glaciem in crystallum*) and Agricola (*succus frigore densatus*), quoted in Alfred E. H. Tutton, 'Rock Crystal: Its Structure and Uses', *Journal of the Royal Society of Arts*, vol. 59, no. 3072 (6 October 1911), p. 1049.

131 'the common Opinion hath been, and still remaineth': Thomas Browne, *Pseudodoxia Epidemica* (1646), Book 2, Chapter 1, available online, gutenberg.org/files/39960/39960-h/39960-h.htm

131 'all of ice and crystal': Claire Elaine Engel, *Mountaineering in the Alps*, new edn (London: George Allen & Unwin, 1971), p. 23.

131 'Here, Madame, I see five mountains': letter from René le Pays (16 May 1669) quoted in Walter Woodburn Hyde, 'The Ascent of Mont Blanc', *National Geographic*, vol. 14, no. 8 (August 1913), p. 669.

132 'As in all countries of ignorance': Windham, *An Account of the Glacières or Ice Alps in Savoy*, p. 20.

132 'Whenever the bishop would make his visits': Andrew Toland, 'The Exorcism of the Glaciers', *Scapegoat*, vol. 8 (undated), p. 43, accessed online, scapegoatjournal.org/docs/08/TOLAND_5.pdf

132 'musket shot': Emmanuel Le Roy Ladurie, *Times of Feast, Times of Famine: A History of Climate Since the Year 1000*, trans. Barbara Bray (New York: Doubleday, 1971), p. 170.

132 'They saw it as the gradual extinction of the World': Beda Weber (1798–1859) quoted in Hubert Steiner and Rupert Geitl, 'Glacial Archaeology in South Tyrol', *Journal of Glacial Archaeology*, vol. 4 (2020), accessed online, journal.equinoxpub.com/JGA/article/view/18727

133 'the most severe sanction or punishment': Toland, 'The Exorcism of the Glaciers', p. 43.

133 'They make moral judgements': Julie Cruickshank, *Do Glaciers Listen? Local Knowledge, Colonial Encounters and Social Imagination* (Toronto: UBC Press, 2005), p. 3.

133 'According to John Tyndall': Tyndall, *The Glaciers of the Alps*, p. 21.

135 'I try in vain to be persuaded . . . habitable globe': Mary Shelley, *Frankenstein; or the Modern Prometheus* (London: Penguin Classics, 1992), p. 15.

135 'often sat up in conversation': Mary Wollstonecraft Shelley, *The Journals of Mary Shelley 1814–1844*, ed. Paula R. Feldman and Diana Scott-Kilvert (Baltimore and London: Johns Hopkins University Press, 1995), p. 108.

136 'This is the most desolate place . . . opened up to our view': *ibid.*, p. 119.

136 'I suddenly beheld the figure of a man': *ibid.*, p. 101.

136 'The abrupt sides of vast mountains': Shelley, *Frankenstein*, p. 99.

137 'We walked some distance . . . changed into a mass of frost': Percy Bysshe Shelley, *The Letters of Percy Bysshe Shelley*, ed. Frederick L. Jones (Oxford: Oxford University Press, 1964), p. 500.

138 'nuclear winter': Robert Macfarlane, *The Mountains of the Mind* (London: Granta Books, 2008), p. 128.

139 'Of all the landscapes in nature': Eric G. Wilson, quoted in Cian Duffy, *The Landscapes of the Sublime, 1700–1830: Classic Ground* (London: Palgrave Macmillan, 2013), p. 102.

140 'more than doubling the total number': Hyde, 'The Ascent of Mont Blanc', p. 875.

140 'Only one of those [Alpine] travellers... without the smallest danger or fatigue': Charles Dickens, 'Mountain Thoroughfares: Charles Dickens and the Alps', *Dickens Quarterly*, vol. 29, no. 2 (June 2012), pp. 151–61, accessed online, jstor.org/stable/45292380

140 'carried on to a glacier to eat': Fergus Fleming, *Killing Dragons: The Conquest of the Alps* (London: Granta Books, 2001), p. 94.

142 'Pouring a little of its candied contents': John Ruskin, *The Works of John Ruskin*, ed. E. T. Cook and Alexander Wedderburn, vol. 26: *Deucalion and Other Studies in Rocks and Stones* (London: George Allen, 1906), p. 162.

143 'People who visit a glacier and return': James D. Forbes quoted in Bruce Hevly, 'The Heroic Science of Glacier Motion', *Osiris*, vol. 11 (2006), pp. 66–86 at p. 70.

143 'You cannot contract a closer relationship': John Tyndall quoted in Matthew Shipton, 'John Tyndall: Our Changing Relationships with Mountains', *UK Climbing* (10 December 2018), online, ukclimbing. com/articles/features/john_tyndall_-_our_changing_relationships_with_mountains-11486

145 'between 1854 and 1880, English climbers': from R. D. Eaton, 'In the "World of Death and Beauty": Risk, Control, and John Tyndall as Alpinist', *Victorian Literature and Culture*, vol. 41, no. 1 (2013), pp. 55–73 at p. 58.

145 'a desire to exert oneself': Lopez, *Arctic Dreams*, p. 358.

145 'soaped poles in a bear-garden': John Ruskin quoted in Hevly, 'The Heroic Science of Glacier Motion', p. 74.

146 'increasingly regulated and safe Victorian Britain created a frustrated, macho desire for danger': see Macfarlane, *The Mountains of the Mind*, Chapter 3: 'The Pursuit of Fear'.

146 'in a fast-changing society, with rapidly evolving structures': see the introduction to Elaine Freedgood, *Victorian Writing about Risk* (Cambridge: Cambridge University Press, 2000).

146 'On the heights to our right, loose ice crags': Tyndall, *The Glaciers of the Alps*, p. 75.

148 'there really exist three distinct Switzerlands': Charles Dickens, 'Foreign Climbs', *All the Year Round*, vol. 14 (2 September 1865), p. 135. For more on this, see Michael S. Reidy, 'Mountaineering, Masculinity, and the Male Body in Mid-Victorian Britain', *Osiris*, vol. 30 (2015), pp. 158–81 at p. 159: 'Dickens's use of a spatial metaphor of "distinct" zones should come as no surprise. He had a knack for feeling the pulse of his age. His move through the vertical – from civilization to wilderness, from common sense to hubris, and from the feminine to the masculine – mimicked the spatial perspective that had taken hold in the sciences by midcentury. Vertical zonation had become a steady guide to research in the geological, botanical, and zoological sciences. It was a guiding organizational force behind biogeography and early oceanography, atmospheric studies of light and heat, and the Humboldtian sciences of terrestrial magnetism, meteorology, and radiation physics.'

149 'Travellers, like plants': Leslie Stephen, *The Playground of Europe* (Oxford: Blackwell's Mountaineering Library, 1936), p. 291.

150 'struck away the snow': Ann C. Colley, *Victorians in the Mountains: Sinking the Sublime* (Farnham: Ashgate, 2010), p. 101.

151 'Suddenly you sink in much deeper': Frederica Plunket, *Here and There Among the Alps* (London; Longmans, Green, 1875), p. 37.

151 'It was a keen, frosty morning': Margaret Jackson, 'A Winter Quartette', *Alpine Journal*, vol. 14, no. 103 (February 1889), pp. 200–10 at p. 202.

151 'Icicles of all shapes and sizes': *ibid.*, p. 209.

152 'No glacier can baffle': quoted in Jenny Hall, 'Women Mountaineers: A Study of Affect, Sensoria and Emotion' (unpublished PhD thesis, York St John University, 2018), accessed online, ray.yorksj.ac.uk/id/eprint/3793/

152 'There was nothing for it': Mrs A. Le Blond, 'Then and now', *Ladies' Alpine Club Yearbook, 1932*, p. 6.

152 'I owe a supreme debt of gratitude to the mountains': Elizabeth Alice Frances Le Blond, *Day In, Day Out* (London: John Lane, 1928), p. 90.

*Further reading*

De Beer, Sir Gavin, *Early Travellers in the Alps* (London: Sidgwick & Jackson, 1966).

Carlen, Martin W., *The Rhone-Glacier and its Ice Grotto*, trans. Dr Michael Hunt (Belvedere: Touristische Betriebe am Rhonegletscher, 2005).

Clarke, Garry K. C., 'A Short History of Scientific Investigations on Glaciers', *Journal of Glaciology*, vol. 33, no. S1 (1987), pp. 4–24.

Fournier, André, *Mer de Glace* (Montmélian: La Fontaine de Siloé, 2005).

Hodgson, Francis et al., 'The Shrouds on the Glacier du Rhône', *Granta* (6 April 2020), online, granta.com/the-shrouds-on-the-glacier-du-rhone/

McNee, Alan, 'The Haptic Sublime and the "cold stony reality" of Mountaineering', *Interdisciplinary Studies in the Long Nineteenth Century*, vol. 19 (2014), pp. 1–20.

Nicolson, Marjorie Hope, *Mountain Gloom and Mountain Glory: The Development of the Aesthetics of the Infinite* (Ithaca, NY: Cornell University Press, 1959).

Robbins, David, 'Sport, Hegemony and the Middle Class: The Victorian Mountaineers', *Theory, Culture & Society*, vol. 4, no. 4 (1987), pp. 579–601.

Roche, Clare, 'Women Climbers 1850–1900: A Challenge to Male Hegemony?', *Sport in History*, vol. 33 (2013), pp. 233–59.

Smith, Albert, *The Story of Mont Blanc* (Reading: Alpine Facsimile Library, 1974).

Tutton, A. E. H., *The High Alps: A Natural History of Ice and Snow* (London: Kegan Paul, Trent, Trubner, 1927).

Unsworth, Walt, *Savage Snows: The Story of Mont Blanc* (London: Hodder & Stoughton, 1986).

Whymper, Edward, *Scrambles Amongst the Alps in the Years 1860–1869* (Washington, DC: National Geographic Classics, 2002).

## 8: THE PACHYDERM

156 'the summer being colder': Mikhail Adams, 'Some Account of a Journey to the Frozen Sea, and of the Discovery of the Remains of a Mammoth. Translated from the French', *Philosophical Magazine*, vol. 29, no.114 (1807), pp. 141–53 at p. 147.

156 'clear . . . but of a nauseous taste': *ibid.*, p. 149.

158 'According to several writers, the term "Mammoth"': Wilhelm Tilesius von Tillenau, *On the Mammoth or Fossil Elephant Found in the Ice at the Mouth of the River Lena, in Siberia* (London: W. M. Phillips, 1819), p. 5.

158 'In the regions of the north, where ice is piled up': quoted in John J. McKay, *Discovering the Mammoth: A Tale of Giants, Unicorns, Ivory, and the Birth of a New Science* (New York: Pegasus, 2017), p. 46.

159 'According to one source, about 16.3 tons': I. P. Tolmachoff, 'The Carcasses of the Mammoth and Rhinoceros Found in the Frozen Ground of Siberia', *Transactions of the American Philosophical Society*, New Series, vol. 23, no. 1 (1929), pp. i–x and 11–74 at p. 12.

162 'it appears incontestable to me': Adams, 'Some Account of a Journey to the Frozen Sea', p. 153.

165 'If the analogy of the facts . . . unstratified gravel is found': *Proceedings of the Geological Society of London, November 1838 to June 1842*, vol. 3, p. 331.

165 'I have accumulated so much proof': quoted in Diarmid A. Finnegan, 'The Work of Ice: Glacial Theory and Scientific Culture in Early Victorian Edinburgh', *British Journal for the History of Science*, vol. 37, no. 1 (March 2004), pp. 29–52 at p. 32; my translation.

166 'The idea of what they are pleased to call a 'Great Ice Sheet': Reverend H. N. Hutchinson, *Prehistoric Man and Beast* (London: Smith, Elder, 1896), p. 86.

166 'I have had the sincerest pleasure in avowing that I was wrong': Roderick Murchison in Elizabeth Cary Agassiz (ed.), *Louis Agassiz: His Life and Correspondence*, vol. 1 (Boston: Houghton, Mifflin, 1887), p. 341.

167 'The situation in which these weapons were found': John Frere, 1797, quoted at hoxnehistory.org.uk/Frere.php

169 'I have just got scent of some fossil bones of a Mammoth': Charles Darwin, *The Beagle Record: Selections from the Original Pictorial Records and Written Accounts of the Voyage of HMS Beagle*, ed. Richard Darwin Keynes (Cambridge: Cambridge University Press, 1979), p. 227.

170 'Lyell's book brought the case for the "men among the mammoths"': A. Bowdoin Van Riper, *Men Among the Mammoths: Victorian Science and the Discovery of Human Prehistory* (Chicago: University of Chicago Press, 1993), p. 9.

171 'What was the use of this great engine': Louis Agassiz, 'Ice Period in America, *Atlantic Monthly*, vol. 14, no. 8 (1846), accessed online, en.wikisource.org/wiki/The_Atlantic_Monthly/Volume_14/Number_81/Ice-Period_in_America

172 'glacier ghosts': letter of 15 May 1873 in John Muir, *Letters to a Friend* (Good Press, Kindle edn, 2020).

172 'Though the storm-beaten ground': John Muir, *Travels in Alaska* (1915), quoted in Paul J. Willis, 'He Hath Builded the Mountains', *Christianity & Literature*, vol. 65, no. 3 (2016), pp. 298–309 at p. 305.

173 'one long gigantic blunder': Charles Darwin, quoted in Jamie Woodward, *The Ice Age*, p. 4.

173 'To him his work had but one meaning': Cary Agassiz (ed.), *Louis Agassiz*, p. 335.

173 'When we try to pick out anything by itself': John Muir, *My First Summer in the Sierra* (Createspace Independent Publishing Platform, Kindle edn, 2015).

*Further reading*

Davies, Gordon L., 'Early Discoverers XXVI: Another Forgotten Pioneer of the Glacial Theory: James Hutton (1726–97)', *Journal of Glaciology*, vol. 7, no. 49 (1968), pp. 115–16.

Digby, George Bassett, *The Mammoth and Mammoth-Hunting in North-East Siberia* (London: H. F. & G. Witherby, 1926).


## 9: DR SAWBONES

175 'bestowing animation upon lifeless matter': Shelley, *Frankenstein*, p. 53.

177 'quinsy, "trembling of the heart" and other complaints': see, for example, Mark Kurlansky, *Milk* (London: Bloomsbury, 2019), p. 119, or David, *Harvest of the Cold Months*, pp. 5, 136, 161–4, 220–1, for the many pros and cons of taking ice.

178 'Some have heated together sulphur': Joseph Needham, *Science and Civilisation in China*, Part 7 (Cambridge: Cambridge University Press, 1986), p. 112.

179 'you cannot drink it but by sucking and drawing in of your breath': Giambattista della Porta, quoted in David, *Harvest of the Cold Months*, p. 71. Other details in this paragraph also from this chapter of David's.

179 'China snow': 'Potassium Nitrate in Arabic and Latin Sources', *History of Science and Technology in Islam* online, history-science-technology.com/articles/articles%203.html

179 'It was recorded in use in the *History of Medicine*': see J. R. Partington, *A History of Greek Fire and Gunpowder* (Cambridge: W. Heffer & Sons, 1960), p. 311.

179 'which in gunpowder produces explosive heat': Anon., *The Institutions of Akbar*, quoted in David, *Harvest of the Cold Months*, p. 246.

180 'Russians were using gunpowder to lob cannonballs': Partington, *A History of Greek Fire and Gunpowder*, p. 211.

181 'In applying cold . . . I have taken care to avoid reaction': Dr James Arnott, 'On Cold as a Means of Producing Local Insensibility', *Lancet* (22 July 1848), quoted in H. Marcus Bird, 'A Pioneer in Refrigeration Analgesia', *Anesthesiology*, vol. 10, no. 366 (May 1949), p. 11.

182 'in dissolving, reduce the temperature to below zero': James Arnott, *On the Treatment of Cancer by the Regulated Application of an Anaesthetic Temperature* (London: J. Churchill, 1851), p. 6.

182 'The skin does not cut as crisp': a certain Paget quoted in Bird, 'A Pioneer in Refrigeration Analgesia', p. 14.

182 'Some were the size of a fig': T. W. Nunn, a surgeon, again quoted *ibid.*, p. 12.

183 'These methods are still insufficient': Albert C. Eyclesheimer and Daniel Schoemaker, *A Cross-Section Anatomy* (New York and London: D. Appleton, 1911), p. x.

184 'Nobody before me, as far as I know': Nikolaï Pirogov, quoted *ibid.*, p. x.

184 'The "Ice Age" of anatomy and obstetrics': Salim Al-Gailani, 'The "Ice Age" of Anatomy and Obstetrics: Hand and Eye in the Promotion of Frozen Sections around 1900', *Bulletin of the History of Medicine*, vol. 90, no. 4 (Winter 2016), pp. 611–42 at p. 613.

184 'they are the size of nature': Wilhelm Braune, *An Atlas of Topographical Anatomy: After Plane Sections of Frozen Bodies*, trans. Edward Bellamy (London: J. & A. Churchill, 1877), p. vii.

185 'Though it was the month of March when the body was brought': Wilhelm Braune, *The Position of the Uterus and Foetus at the End of Pregnancy: Illustrated by Sections through Frozen Bodies* (New York: L. Schmidt, 1872), first text page.

186 'The parts into which the foetus': *ibid.*

187 'I place special emphasis upon careful details': Braune, quoted in Eyclesheimer & Schoemaker, *A Cross-Section Anatomy*, p. xi.

187 'Doctors described what for centuries . . . the surface of the gaze': Michel Foucault, *The Birth of the Clinic*, trans. A. M. Sheridan Smith (New York: Vintage, 1994), pp. xxi.

188 'He who neglects anatomy': quoted in 'Anatomy: A History of Anatomy: The Post-Vesalian Era', *Journal of the American Medical Association*, vol. 279, no. 10 (1998), p. 804.

188 'He must mangle the living': Sir Astley Cooper, quoted in Mary Roach, *Stiff: The Curious Lives of Human Cadavers* (London: Penguin, 2004), p. 45.

189 'Since being dissected rendered a body unrecognisable': for more on this paragraph, see Sanjib Khumar Ghosh, 'Human Cadaveric Dissection: A Historical Account from Ancient Greece to the Modern Era', *Anatomy and Cell Biology*, vol. 48, no. 3 (2015), pp. 153–69.

189 'turning their professors into shills for the corpses': see Elizabeth T. Hurren, *Dying for Victorian Medicine: English Anatomy and its*

*Trade in the Dead Poor, c.1834–1929* (London: Palgrave Macmillan, 2016), pp. 186–8.

189 **'dead train'**: *ibid.*, pp. 189, 197.

189 **' "ice service" of ninety-four staff'**: Thomas Schachtman, *Absolute Zero and the Conquest of Cold* (Boston: Houghton Mifflin, 1999), p. 17.

190 **'Believing as I do'**: Thomas Dwight, *Frozen Sections of a Child* (New York: W. Wood, 1881), pp. iv–v.

193 **'We used rigidly frozen cadavers'**: Wilhelm Braune and Otto Fischer, *On the Centre of Gravity of the Human Body as Related to the Equipment of the German Infantry Soldier*, trans. P. G. J. Maquet and R. Furlong (Berlin and New York: Springer, 1985), p. 11.

193 **'Although they date from the end of the last century'**: *ibid.*, back cover copy.

193 **'the freezing eye'**: Rebecca Solnit, *River of Shadows*, p. 19.

## Further Reading

Kemp, Martin: 'Style and non-style in anatomical illustration: From Renaissance Humanism to Henry Gray', *Journal of Anatomy*, vol. 216, no. 2 (February 2010), pp. 192–208.

Silver, K. and J., 'The place of James Arnott (1797–1883) in the development of local anaesthesia in dentistry', *British Dental Journal*, vol. 220, no. 5 (March 2016), pp. 249–52.

### 10: THE FIGHTERS

197 **'Last Sunday a boy was saved'**: taken from a Bayern Radio online feature, Google translated, br.de/radio/bayern2/wenn-adi-hitler-1894-ertrunken-waere-berlinger104.html

200 **'most colossal, murderous, mismanaged butchery'**: Ernest Hemingway (ed.), *Men at War: The Best War Stories of All Time* (New York: Crown, 1942), p. xiii.

200 **'front among rocks and ice'**: Gunther Langes, *Die Front in Fels und Eis* (Bozen: Athesia AG, Kindle edn, 2015).

202 **'Unfortunately the valuable explosives ran out'**: quoted in Michael Wachtler, *The First World War in the Alps*, trans. Tom O'Toole (Bozen: Athesia Spectrum, 2006), p. 165.

202 'Listening posts, observers and lookout posts': Aldino Bondesan et al., 'Leo Handl and the Ice City (Marmolada Glacier, Italy)', *Rendiconti Online Societa Geologica Italiana* (September 2015), p. 34.

203 'special insights into the secrets of the glacier': Langes, *Die Front in Fels und Eis*, p. 211, Kindle translated.

203 'Not even artillery fired another shot': quoted in Wachtler, *The First World War in the Alps*, p. 133.

204 'one of the worst meteorological disasters in history': Yuri Brugnara et al., 'Reanalysis Sheds Light on 1916 Avalanche Disaster', *Newsletter*, no. 151 (Spring 2017), online, ecmwf.int/en/newsletter/151/meteorology/reanalysis-sheds-light-1916-avalanche-disaster

204 'More men lost their lives to the extremes of cold': Marco Balbi, 'Great War Archaeology on the Glaciers of the Alps', in Nicholas J. Saunders and Paul Cornish (eds), *Contested Objects: Material Memories of the Great War* (Abingdon: Routledge, 2014), accessed online.

204 'Snow is truly a sign of mourning': Giuseppe Ungaretti quoted in Mark Thompson, *The White War: Life and Death on the Italian Front 1915–1919* (London: Faber & Faber, 2008), p. 193.

206 '*Lebensraum* . . .': Wilfried Wilms, 'The Alps as *Lebensraum* – Cinematic Representations of the Alpine War and the South Tyrol Question in 1930s Germany', *German Studies Review*, vol. 40, no. 1 (February 2017), pp. 61–77.

207 'Underpinning it all was a sense of German national destiny': Jonathan Westaway, accompanying text to *Mountain of Destiny: Kanchenjunga 1929*, an exhibition of photos and ephemera from the German expedition to the Himalaya that year, which he curated (Heaton-Cooper Gallery, Grasmere, 15 November–31 December 2018), accessed online, heatoncooper.co.uk/blogs/blog/mountain-of-destiny

209 'WEL attracted a number of Germans . . . I tend to support World Ice Theory': Eric Kurlander, *Hitler's Monsters: A Supernatural History of the Third Reich* (New Haven and London: Yale University Press, 2017), p. 150.

209 'With its inane claims': *ibid.*, p. 151.

210 'Pyke's genius was more intangible . . . in the foothills of the Alps': both quoted in Henry Hemming, *Churchill's Iceman: The True Story of Geoffrey Pyke: Genius, Fugitive, Spy* (London: Arrow, 2015), p. 6.

211 'land, air or sea?': *ibid.*, p. 237.

211 'a medium like the air and sea': *ibid.*, pp. 243–4

213 'The advantages of a floating island': Max Perutz, 'Enemy Alien', collected in Max Perutz, *I Wish I'd Made You Angry Earlier: Essays on Science, Scientists and Humanity* (Oxford: Oxford University Press, 1998), p. 88.

213 'The only thing that ever really frightened me': handwritten note on the galleys for Winston S. Churchill, *The Second World War*, vol. 2: *Their Finest Hour* (London: 1949), Churchill Archive, accessed online, churchillarchive.com/explore/page?id=CHUR%20 4%2F176#image=5

213 'Despite my glacier research': Perutz, *I Wish I'd Made You Angry Earlier*, p. 83.

213 'Pyke did not attempt . . . stiff and solemn men': David Lampe, *Pyke: The Unknown Genius* (London: Evans Brothers, 1959), pp. 135–6.

214 'We built a big wind tunnel': Perutz, *I Wish I'd Made You Angry Earlier*, p. 83.

214 'stronger than ice . . . the continuous pull of gravity': *ibid.*, p. 89.

215 'With a runway of 600 × 60m.': Max Perutz, 'Description of the Iceberg Aircraft Carrier and the Bearing of the Mechanical Properties of Frozen Wood Pulp upon Some Problems of Glacier Flow', *Journal of Glaciology* (March 1948), pp. 95–104, accessed online.

216 '40,000 tons of cork insulation': Sir Charles Goodeve, 'The Ice Ship Fiasco', *Evening Standard* (19 April 1951), accessed online, chem.ucl. ac.uk/resources/history/people/goodeve_cf/habakkuk.html

216 'Not only does ice melt, but it evaporates!': *ibid.*

216 'short on physics': Hemming, *Churchill's Iceman*, p. 313.

218 'According to a US Army technical report . . . "psychologically undesirable"': Lt Col. Elmer F. Clark, *Camp Century – Evolution of Concept and History of Design, Construction, and Performance* (Hanover, NH: US Army Materiel Command, Cold Regions Research & Engineering Laboratory, October 1965), p. 6.

218 'There's a jolly declassified film': *The City in the Ice* (US War Office, R&D Progress Report #6, 1963), watched online; all commentary transcribed from youtube.com/watch?v=1Ujx_pND9wg

218 'In 1961 Walter Cronkite': film and subsequent quotes from Cathy Feldman, 'Cronkite Visits "City under the

Ice"', *CBS News* online (31 January 2016), cbsnews.com/news/60-minutes-overtime-cronkite-visits-city-under-the-ice/

221 **'mobile and concealed'**: Nikolaj Petersen, 'The Politics of US Military Research in Greenland in the Early Cold War', *Centaurus*, vol. 55 (2013), pp. 294–318 at p. 308.

222 **'did not feel convinced that the purpose of this camp'**: Nikolaj Petersen, 'The Iceman That Never Came: "Project Iceworm", the Search for a NATO Deterrent, and Denmark, 1960–1962', *Scandinavian Journal of History*, vol. 33, no. 1 (2008), pp. 75–98 at p. 78.

224 **'A struggle of two bald men over a comb'**: Barry Bearak, 'The Coldest War: Frozen in Fury on the Roof of the World', *New York Times* (23 May 1999), accessed online, nytimes.com/1999/05/23/world/the-coldest-war-frozen-in-fury-on-the-roof-of-the-world.html

*Further reading*

Godwin, Joscelyn, *Arktos: The Polar Myth in Science, Symbolism and Nazi Survival* (London: Thames & Hudson, 1993).

Gold, Lorne W., 'Building Ships from Ice – Habbakuk and After', *Interdisciplinary Science Reviews*, vol. 29, no. 4 (2004), pp. 373–84.

Gravino, M., 'A Century Later, Relics Emerge from a War Frozen in Time', *National Geographic* (18 October 2018).

Ring, Jim, *Storming the Eagles' Nest* (London: Faber & Faber, 2013).


11: THE MEDDLERS


226 **'5 billion others'**: George Reynolds, 'Super Cubes: Inside the (Surprisingly) Big Business of Packaged Ice', *Guardian* online (10 December 2020), theguardian.com/news/2020/dec/10/super-cubes-inside-the-surprisingly-big-business-of-packaged-ice

226 **'a 2013 paper presented evidence of significant layers of soot'**: see Quirin Schiermeier, 'How soot killed the Little Ice Age', *Nature* (2 September 2013), accessed online, nature.com/articles/nature.2013.13650

228 **'Ice formation on wings would cause loss of lift'**: Edwin P. Hartman, *Adventures in Research: A History of the Ames Research Center, 1940–1965*, Nasa Center History Series (Washington,

DC: Scientific and Technical Information Division, Office of Technology Utilization, NASA, 1970), p. 69.

229 'Control of Weather': Ginger Strand, *The Brothers Vonnegut: Science and Fiction in the House of Magic* (New York: Farrar, Straus & Giroux, 2015), p. 54.

229 'Curt flew into the cloud . . . I said, "We did it!"': Duncan C. Blanchard, 'Science, Success and Serendipity', *Weatherwise*, vol. 32, no. 6 (1979), pp. 236–41 at p. 236.

230 'Scientist Creates Real Snowflakes': *New York Times* (14 November 1946), accessed online, timesmachine.nytimes.com/times machine/1946/11/14/93177725.pdf

230 'tailor-made blizzards': James Rodger Fleming, *Fixing the Sky: The Checkered History of Weather and Climate Control* (New York: Columbia University Press, 2012), p. 147.

230 'clear areas around airports': quoted *ibid.*, p. 144.

230 'a profound influence on domestic and world economics': Tomas Kellner, 'Cool Science: How Kurt Vonnegut's Brother Tried to Break Up Hurricanes', news blog on GE.com (8 July 2020), ge.com/news/reports/cool-science-vonnegut-ge-research

230 'all the air of the United States': *ibid.*

231 '"Now suppose," chortled Dr. Breed': Kurt Vonnegut, *Cat's Cradle* (London: Penguin Modern Classics, 2008), p. 33.

234 'the Air Force had been spewing silver iodide': *ibid.*, p. 129.

235 'During the Depression we really believed': Robert K. Musil, 'There Must be More to Love than Death: A Conversation with Kurt Vonnegut', *Nation* (2–9 August 1980), pp. 128–130.

235 'Langmuir did not appreciate the complexity of meteorology': Fleming, *Fixing the Sky*, p. 156.

236 'delivered to studios': Kristi McKim, *Cinema as Weather: Stylistic Screens and Atmospheric Change* (New York and London: Routledge, 2013), p. 139.

237 'the studio snowmen ground 350 tons': Amy White, 'How Artificial Snow Was Invented', *Smithsonian Magazine* (November 2019), accessed online, smithsonianmag.com/arts-culture/how-artificial-snow-was-invented-180973334/

238 '*Snow* – Precipitation in the form of small ice crystals': Wayne Pierce, Patent 2,676,471 at the United States Patent Office (applied 14 December 1950, patented 27 April 1954), first text page.

238 'a cubic metre of snow takes 3.5 to 4.3kWh . . . three times that': Jörgen Rogstam and Mattias Dahlberg, *Energy Usage for Snowmaking: A Review of the Energy Use of Mobile Snowmaking at Swedish Ski Resorts* (Älvsjö: Energi & Kylanalys AB, 1 April 2011), p. 2.

238 'enough to drive a Tesla around twenty kilometres': Tesla's European Union Energy Label states that a Model S60 consumes 18.1kWh per 100 kilometres, therefore 20 kilometres is 3.62kWh: tesla.com/en_EU/support/european-union-energy-label

238 'A 2001 study of US ski resorts': Gary Epstein et al., 'Energy Efficiency Opportunities for Ski Industry Snowmaking Processes', American Council for an Energy Efficient Economy (2001), accessed online, aceee.org/files/proceedings/2001/data/papers/SS01_Panel1_Paper27.pdf

239 'To make a cubic metre . . . an hour': for the first part, see the figures in Table 2 in C. M. Pickering and R. C. Buckley, 'Climate Response by the Ski Industry: The Shortcomings of Snowmaking for Australian Resorts', *Ambio*, vol. 39, nos. 5–6 (July–September 2010), pp. 430–8. Meanwhile, snow-machine manufacturer Demaclenko boasts that its Titan 4.0, 'the most powerful fan gun on the market', can produce this amount: demaclenko.com/snow-guns/fan-guns/titan-4-0/

239 'Another study from 2011': André Evette et al., 'Environmental Risks and Impacts of Mountain Reservoirs for Artificial Snow Production in a Context of Climate Change', *Journal of Alpine Research/Revue de Géographie Alpine*, vol. 99, no. 4 (2011), pp. 1–13 at p. 8.

240 'The 2022 Beijing Olympic Winter Games': 'Winter Olympics in Beijing Disrupted as Real Snow Falls on China's Capital', *Sky News* online (13 February 2022), news.sky.com/story/winter-olympics-in-beijing-disrupted-as-real-snow-falls-on-chinas-capital-12541143

240 'Two tons per day': Simon Newcomb, 'Reports of Officers of the Navy on Ventilating and Cooling the Executive Mansion During the Illness of President Garfield', *Executive Documents of the House of Representatives for the First Session of the Forty-Seventh Congress 1881–82*, vol. 8 (Washington, DC: Government Printing Office, 1882), p. 824.

241 'The more our economies grow': Bravo, 'A Cryopolitics to Reclaim Our Frozen Material States', p. 29.

242 'sought to relieve California's water shortage': Beau Riffenburgh (ed.), *Encyclopedia of the Antarctic*, vol. 1 (Abingdon: Routledge, 2006), p. 525.

244 'nothing but a rope': 'Science: Towing Icebergs', *Time* (17 October 1977), accessed online, content.time.com/time/subscriber/article/0,33009,915637-1,00.html

245 'By its own figures': from icebergs.world/benefits.html

247 'Iceberg waters have a great story': from finewaters.com/bottled-water-sources/iceberg-water

247 'delayed the next ice age by over 50,000 years': see, for example, 'Carbon emissions "postpone ice age"', Jonathan Amos, *BBC News* online (13 January 2016), bbc.co.uk/news/science-environment-35307800

*Further reading*

Barton, Victoria, 'Faking It: The Science of Artificial Snow', *ChemViews Magazine* (1 March 2016).

Dorrian, Mark, 'Utopia on Ice', *Cabinet*, 47 (Fall 2012), pp. 25–32.

Hobbs, Peter V., *Ice Physics* (Oxford: Oxford University Press, 2010).

Hoyle, Sir Fred, *Ice: A Chilling Scientific Forecast of a New Ice Age* (London: Hutchinson, 1981).

Madrigal, Alexis C., 'The Many Failures and Few Successes of Zany Iceberg Towing Schemes', *Atlantic* (August 2011), online.

Pretor Pinney, Gavin, *The Cloudspotter's Guide* (London: Hodder & Stoughton, 2006).


SKY GLOW SNATCHED FROM HEAVEN (AN AFTERWORD)

250 'Blue caverns shone': Ernest Shackleton, 2 January 1922, posted online in 'Ernest Shackleton's diary of the Quest Expedition, 1921–22' by the Scott Polar Research Institute (Cambridge), spri.cam.ac.uk/archives/shackleton/articles/1537,3,9.html

250 'What hasn't yet been adequately explained': Bravo, 'A Cryopolitics to Reclaim Our Frozen Material States', p. 27.

252 'capable of concentrating the rays of the sun': William Scoresby, 'On the Greenland or Polar Ice', *Memoirs of the Wernerian Natural History Society*, vol. 2 (Edinburgh and London, 1815), pp. 261–328 at p. 270.

# Acknowledgements

This book involved a massive amount of research, lots of it undertaken under difficult conditions during the Covid lockdowns of 2020 and 2021. So, first of all, a huge thank you to all the staff at the British Library, who served me books most of the way through. Also to the Wellcome Collection for help with some gruesome anatomy texts. Thank you to Marcus Bicknell (even though the Merveilles didn't make the final cut!), Jill Cook, Alistair Pike and Christian Wolmar for answering questions on their respective specialities; Caitlin Graf at the *Nation* for supplying the Robert Musil/Kurt Vonnegut article; Jess Fagin for online help and Luke Turner for library chats; Eleanor Brown for the residency at the Nose, and Steve Jones and James Simpson for putting me up at various points in my writing odyssey; Anna Hart and Rob Penn for good advice early on; James Fairbank for the Ötzi hike, and Tom Isitt for guiding me on a magical few days in the snow above Santa Caterina. Tom also read an early chapter, as did Ross Hallard. And thanks to Polar Latitudes and Shackleton for the once-in-a-lifetime Antarctica competition win!

Thanks especially to Jasmine Horsey, who has brilliantly edited this book and steered it into its final shape, and to Peter James, for a hugely appreciated copyedit, as well as Francisco Vilhena and everyone at Bloomsbury who has worked on it, or will do from the time of writing onwards. Big thanks also to my agent Carrie Plitt, for helping me through, but most of all to Jenny Lord, for her encouragement, patience, support and love.

# Index

# Image Credits

# A Note on the Author

Max Leonard writes about mountains, cycling and travel; his previous books include *Higher Calling, Bunker Research and Lanterne Rouge*. He lives in London, where he is also publisher and creative director at Isola Press.